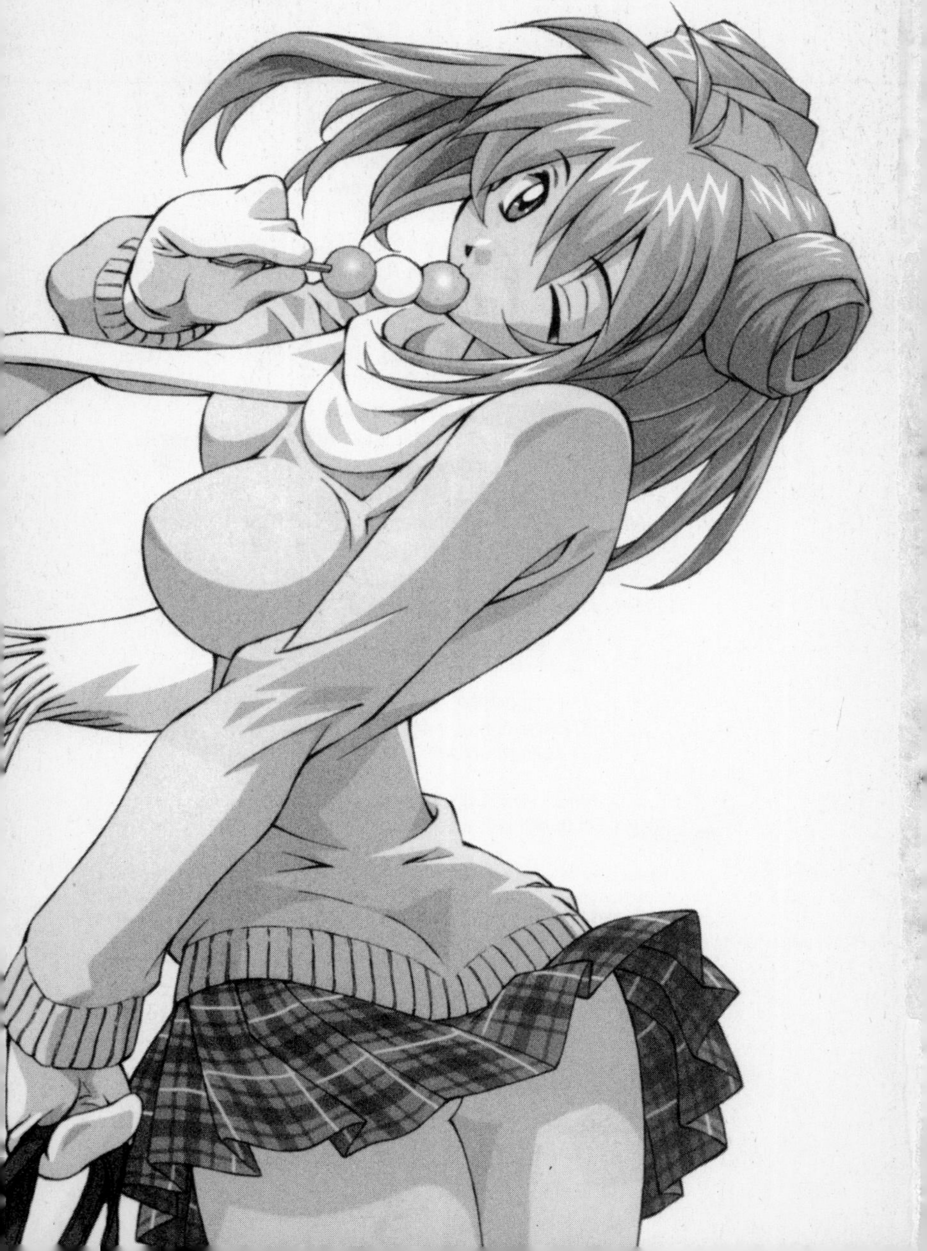

Battle Vixens Vol. 6
Created by Yuji Shiozaki

Translation - Louie Kawamoto
English Adaptation - Keith Giffen
Associate Editor - Troy Lewter
Copy Editor - Aaron Sparrow
Retouch and Lettering - William Suh
Production Artist - Bowen Park
Cover Design - Patrick Hook

Editor - Rob Tokar
Digital Imaging Manager - Chris Buford
Pre-Press Manager - Antonio DePietro
Production Managers - Jennifer Miller and Mutsumi Miyazaki
Art Director - Matt Alford
Managing Editor - Jill Freshney
VP of Production - Ron Klamert
Editor-in-Chief - Mike Kiley
President and C.O.O. - John Parker
Publisher and C.E.O. - Stuart Levy

A  Manga

TOKYOPOP Inc.
5900 Wilshire Blvd. Suite 2000
Los Angeles, CA 90036

E-mail: info@TOKYOPOP.com
Come visit us online at www.TOKYOPOP.com

ISBN: 1-59182-948-8

First TOKYOPOP printing: February 2005
10 9 8 7 6 5 4 3 2 1
Printed in the USA

BATTLE VIXENS™

Vol. 6

by
Yuji Shiozaki

TOKYOPOP®

HAMBURG // LONDON // LOS ANGELES // TOKYO

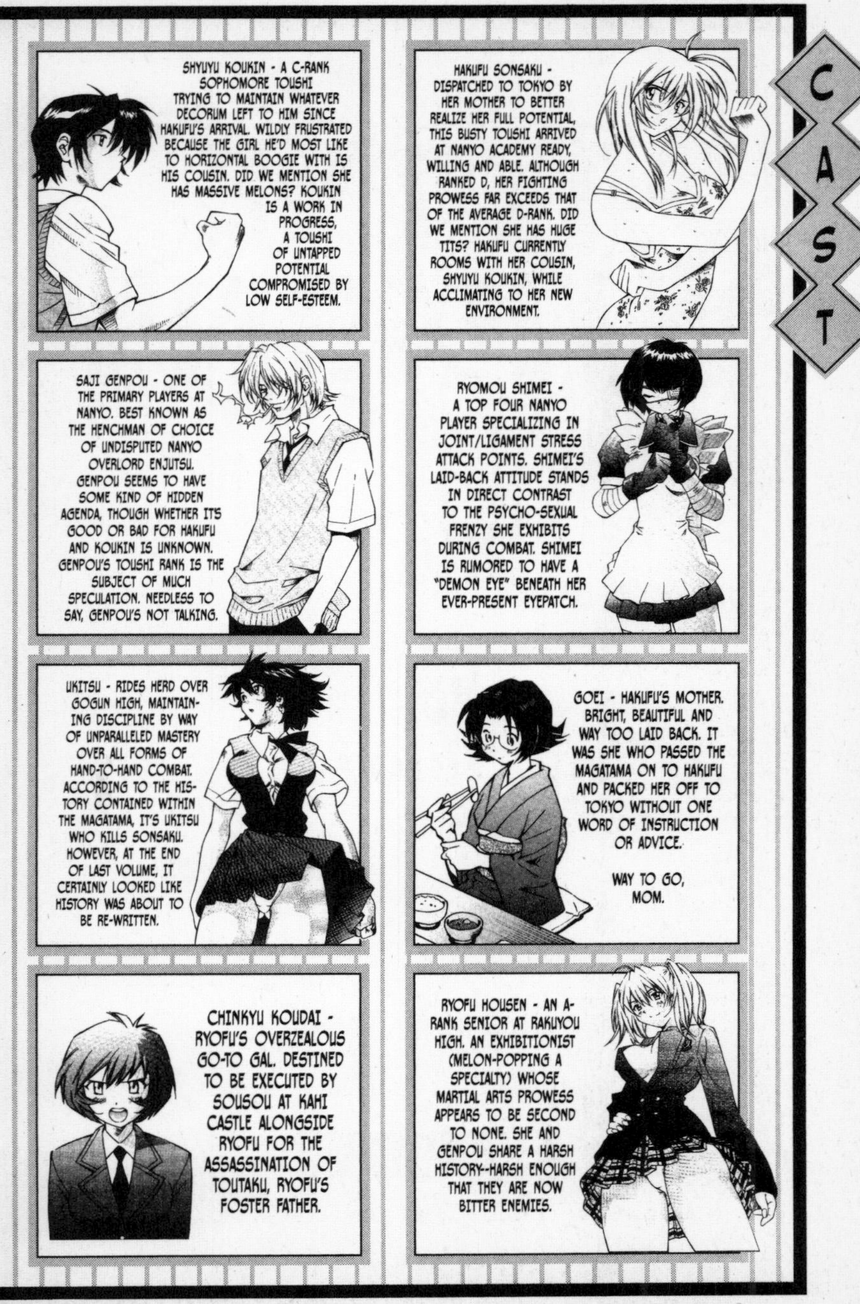
CAST
HAKUFU SONSAKU - DISPATCHED TO TOKYO BY HER MOTHER TO BETTER REALIZE HER FULL POTENTIAL, THIS BUSTY TOUSHI ARRIVED AT NANYO ACADEMY READY, WILLING AND ABLE. ALTHOUGH RANKED D, HER FIGHTING PROWESS FAR EXCEEDS THAT OF THE AVERAGE D-RANK. DID WE MENTION SHE HAS HUGE TITS? HAKUFU CURRENTLY ROOMS WITH HER COUSIN, SHYUYU KOUKIN, WHILE ACCLIMATING TO HER NEW ENVIRONMENT.
SHYUYU KOUKIN - A C-RANK SOPHOMORE TOUSHI TRYING TO MAINTAIN WHATEVER DECORUM LEFT TO HIM SINCE HAKUFU'S ARRIVAL. WILDLY FRUSTRATED BECAUSE THE GIRL HE'D MOST LIKE TO HORIZONTAL BOOGIE WITH IS HIS COUSIN. DID WE MENTION SHE HAS MASSIVE MELONS? KOUKIN IS A WORK IN PROGRESS, A TOUSHI OF UNTAPPED POTENTIAL COMPROMISED BY LOW SELF-ESTEEM.
RYOMOU SHIMEI - A TOP FOUR NANYO PLAYER SPECIALIZING IN JOINT/LIGAMENT STRESS ATTACK POINTS. SHIMEI'S LAID-BACK ATTITUDE STANDS IN DIRECT CONTRAST TO THE PSYCHO-SEXUAL FRENZY SHE EXHIBITS DURING COMBAT. SHIMEI IS RUMORED TO HAVE A "DEMON EYE" BENEATH HER EVER-PRESENT EYEPATCH.
SAJI GENPOU - ONE OF THE PRIMARY PLAYERS AT NANYO. BEST KNOWN AS THE HENCHMAN OF CHOICE OF UNDISPUTED NANYO OVERLORD ENJUTSU. GENPOU SEEMS TO HAVE SOME KIND OF HIDDEN AGENDA, THOUGH WHETHER IT'S GOOD OR BAD FOR HAKUFU AND KOUKIN IS UNKNOWN. GENPOU'S TOUSHI RANK IS THE SUBJECT OF MUCH SPECULATION. NEEDLESS TO SAY, GENPOU'S NOT TALKING.
GOEI - HAKUFU'S MOTHER. BRIGHT, BEAUTIFUL AND WAY TOO LAID BACK. IT WAS SHE WHO PASSED THE MAGATAMA ON TO HAKUFU AND PACKED HER OFF TO TOKYO WITHOUT ONE WORD OF INSTRUCTION OR ADVICE.
WAY TO GO, MOM.
UKITSU - RIDES HERD OVER GOGUN HIGH, MAINTAINING DISCIPLINE BY WAY OF UNPARALLELED MASTERY OVER ALL FORMS OF HAND-TO-HAND COMBAT. ACCORDING TO THE HISTORY CONTAINED WITHIN THE MAGATAMA, IT'S UKITSU WHO KILLS SONSAKU. HOWEVER, AT THE END OF LAST VOLUME, IT CERTAINLY LOOKED LIKE HISTORY WAS ABOUT TO BE RE-WRITTEN.
RYOFU HOUSEN - AN A-RANK SENIOR AT RAKUYOU HIGH. AN EXHIBITIONIST (MELON-POPPING A SPECIALTY) WHOSE MARTIAL ARTS PROWESS APPEARS TO BE SECOND TO NONE. SHE AND GENPOU SHARE A HARSH HISTORY--HARSH ENOUGH THAT THEY ARE NOW BITTER ENEMIES.
CHINKYU KOUDAI - RYOFU'S OVERZEALOUS GO-TO GAL. DESTINED TO BE EXECUTED BY SOUSOU AT KAHI CASTLE ALONGSIDE RYOFU FOR THE ASSASSINATION OF TOUTAKU, RYOFU'S FOSTER FATHER.

KAKOUTON (TON-CHAN) GENJOU - A D-RANK SOPHOMORE AT THE SCHOOL OF CIVIL ENGINEERING (KYOSHO HIGH) TON-CHAN IS A STREET-FIGHTING PURIST WHOSE STRICT ADHERENCE TO TRADITION TENDS TO CONFUSE RATHER THAN ENLIGHTEN. AN OKAY GUY, ALL THINGS CONSIDERED.

SOUSOU MOUTOKU - A KYOSHO HIGH B-RANK TOUSHI PRONE TO LENGTHY BOUTS OF DAYDREAMING. THE DAYDREAMS, FOR THE MOST PART, ARE ABOUT CONQUEST, CARNAGE, AND, IN KEEPING WITH THE SPIRIT OF THE SERIES, CAMEL-TOES AND EXPLODING SHIRTS.

OUR STORY SO FAR

MAGATAMAS ARE GEMS CONTAINING THE SPIRITS OF SANGOKU-ERA HEROES WHO FELL WHILE STRIVING TO UNITE CHINA. THE STORY OF HOW THE GEMS FOUND THEIR WAY TO JAPAN AND AND GOT DISSEMINATED IS, THANK-FULLY, TOO LONG A STORY TO TELL HERE. SUFFICE TO SAY, THEY'RE OUT THERE--EACH A CONDUIT/AMPLIFIER FOR ITS WEARER'S AGGRESSIONS. THOSE WHO WEAR MAGATAMA ARE CALLED TOUSHI. FUELED BY MAGATAMA-AMPLIFIED AGGRESSION, TOUSHI FIGHT (MOSTLY ONE ANOTHER) TO DETERMINE WHO'S THE STRONGEST TOUSHI OF ALL.

UP TO HER NECK IN ALL OF THIS IS HAKUFU SONSAKU, WHOSE TOUSHI AWAKENING WAS DELAYED BY HER WELL-MEANING MOTHER...DELAYED, BUT NOT AVERTED. HAKUFU FIGHTS. HAKUFU ATTENDS NANYO ACADEMY, A TOUSHI SCHOOL/TRAINING GROUND AND FIGHTS. SHE LIVES WITH HER TOUSHI COUSIN, BREAST-OBSESSED KOUKIN SHYUYU, AND FIGHTS. HAKUFU AND KOUKIN FIGHT. AS DO RYOFU AND SHIMEI RYOMOU AND SAJI GENPOU AND...EVERYBODY FIGHTS, OKAY? ESPECIALLY DURING THE BIG TOUSHI TOURNAMENT, WHICH HAKUFU MISSED DUE TO HER COM-PLETE LACK OF ANYTHING EVEN REMOTELY RESEMBLING A SENSE OF DIRECTION.

AFTER HAKUFU PASSED THE CHALLENGE OF MASTER CHOUSHOU (WHO TURNED OUT TO BE THE WORLD'S OLD-EST LITTLE KID) HAKUFU AND KOUKIN WENT TO GOGUN HIGH TO CONFRONT UKITSU, WHO--ACCORDING TO THE MAGATAMA HISTORY--IS DESTINED TO KILL HAKUFU. THEY FOUGHT, THE GROUND WAS COVERED IN CRACKS, THEIR BARELY COVERED CRACKS HIT THE GROUND, AND BRAS (AND THE REST OF THEIR CLOTHES) WENT UP LIKE A-BOMBS.

WHEN HAKUFU WENT ALL DEMONY AGAIN AND WAS ABOUT TO KILL UKITSU, AN ENCHANTED-SWORD-WIELDING KOUKIN STEPPED IN AT THE LAST MINUTE AND TRIED TO STOP HER...WHICH BRINGS US TO THE HAZZARD COUNTY FREEZE FRAME AT THE END OF THE LAST VOLUME.

KAKU BUNWA - A RAKUYOU HIGH TOUSHI PLEDGED TO SERVE TOUTAKU. WITH TOUTAKUS SUICIDE, KAKU NEEDED A NEW MAN AND A NEW PLAN, WHICH LED HER TO FORM AN ALLIANCE WITH SOUSOU. SHE ALSO ENGINEERED THE BRUTAL RAPE AND BEATING OF RYOFU HOUSENS GOOD FRIEND CHINKYU. NOW *THAT'S* MEAN!

KAKOUEN MYOUSAI - AN A-RANK TOUSHI OUT OF KISSHO HIGH. A MASTER ASSASSIN; COLD, EMOTIONLESS, ZERO FASHION SENSE. MYOUSAI OWES SOUSOU A DEBT OF HONOR BECAUSE SOUSOU ONCE SAVED HER LIFE.

UNCHOU KANU - AN A-RANK PRIME (SENIOR) OUT OF SEITO HIGH. LETHAL EYE CANDY, BOASTING KI SO POWERFUL IT PHYSICALLY OVERWHELMS HER OPPONENTS. UNCHOU WIELDS THE DRAGON SWORD REIENKYO AND IS MOST PRONE TO USE IT ON THOSE WHOSE RESPONSE TO HER FIRST NAME IS "GESUNDHEIT".

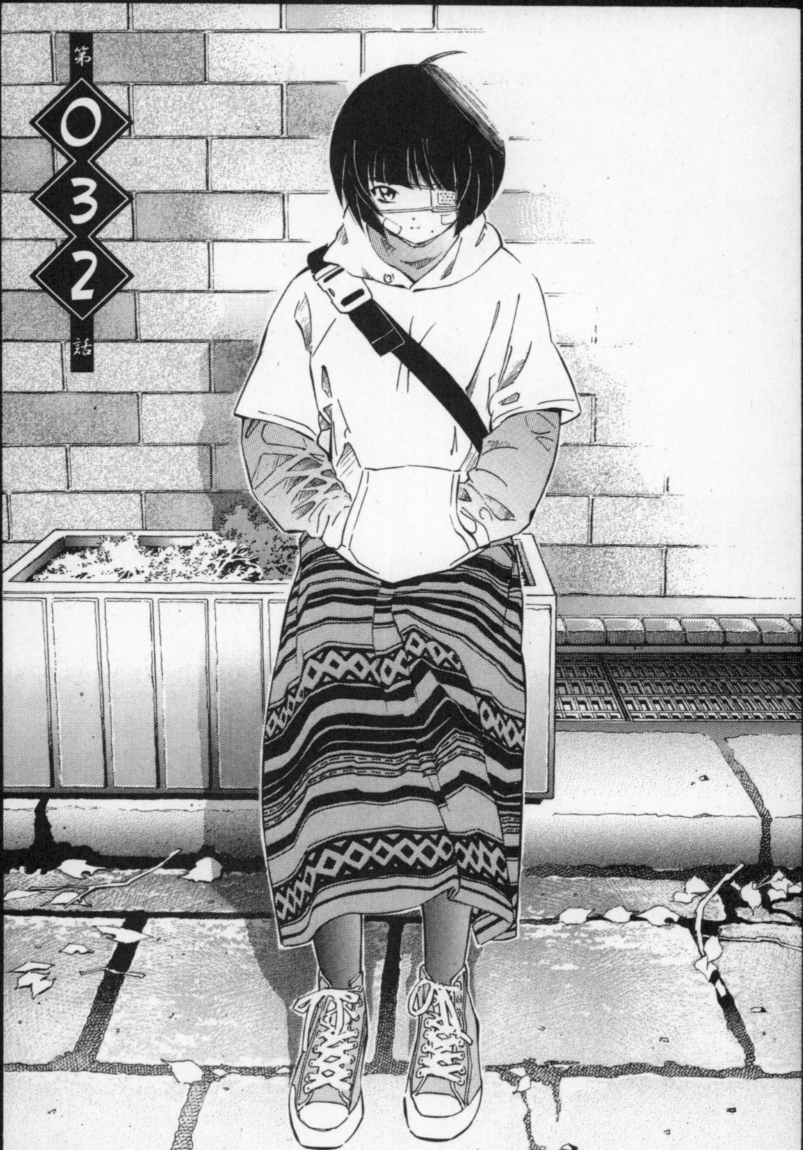
第032話

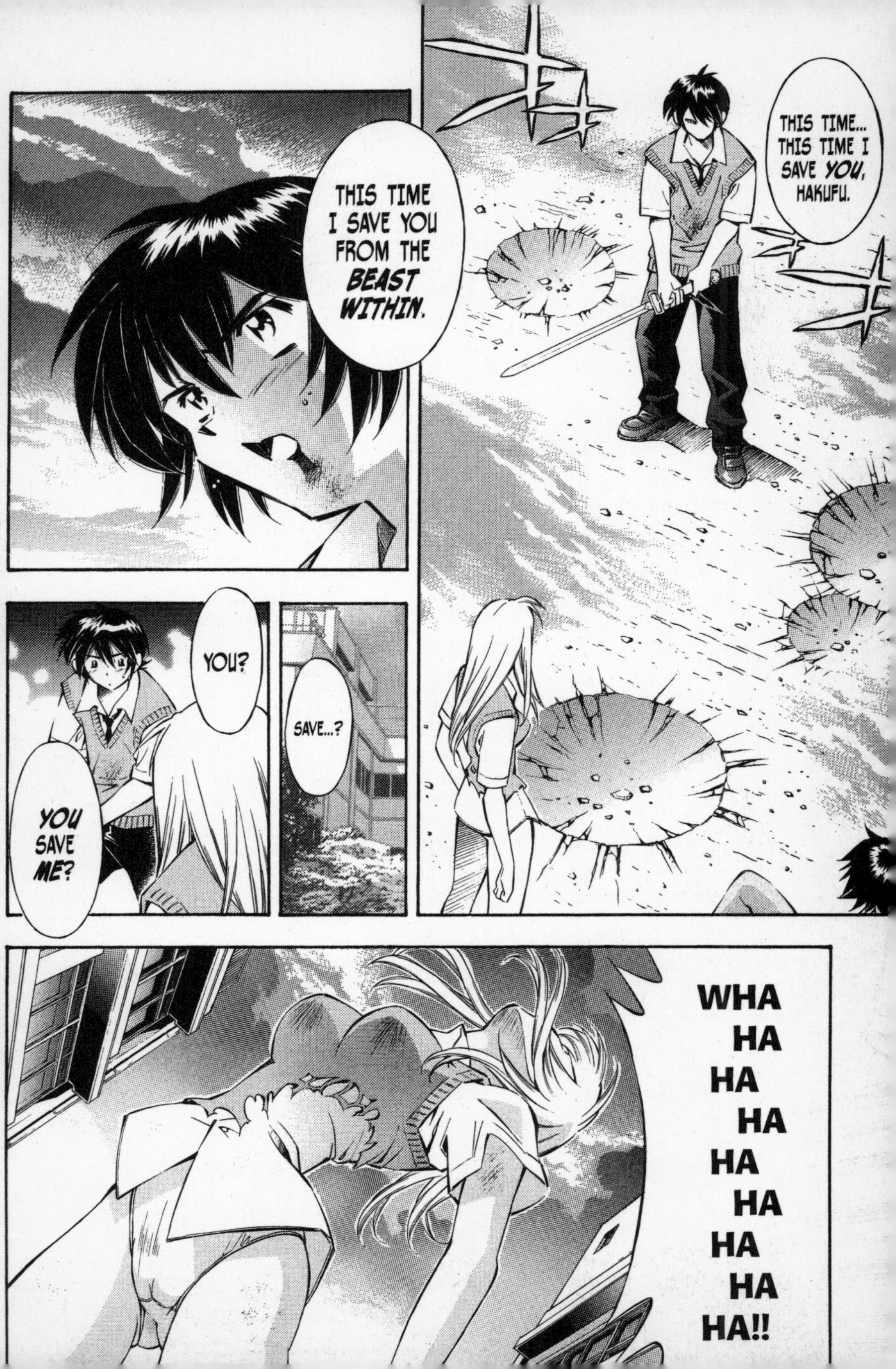

THIS TIME... THIS TIME I SAVE *YOU*, HAKUFU.
THIS TIME I SAVE YOU FROM THE *BEAST WITHIN*.
YOU?
SAVE...?
YOU SAVE *ME*?
WHA HA HA HA HA HA HA HA HA!!

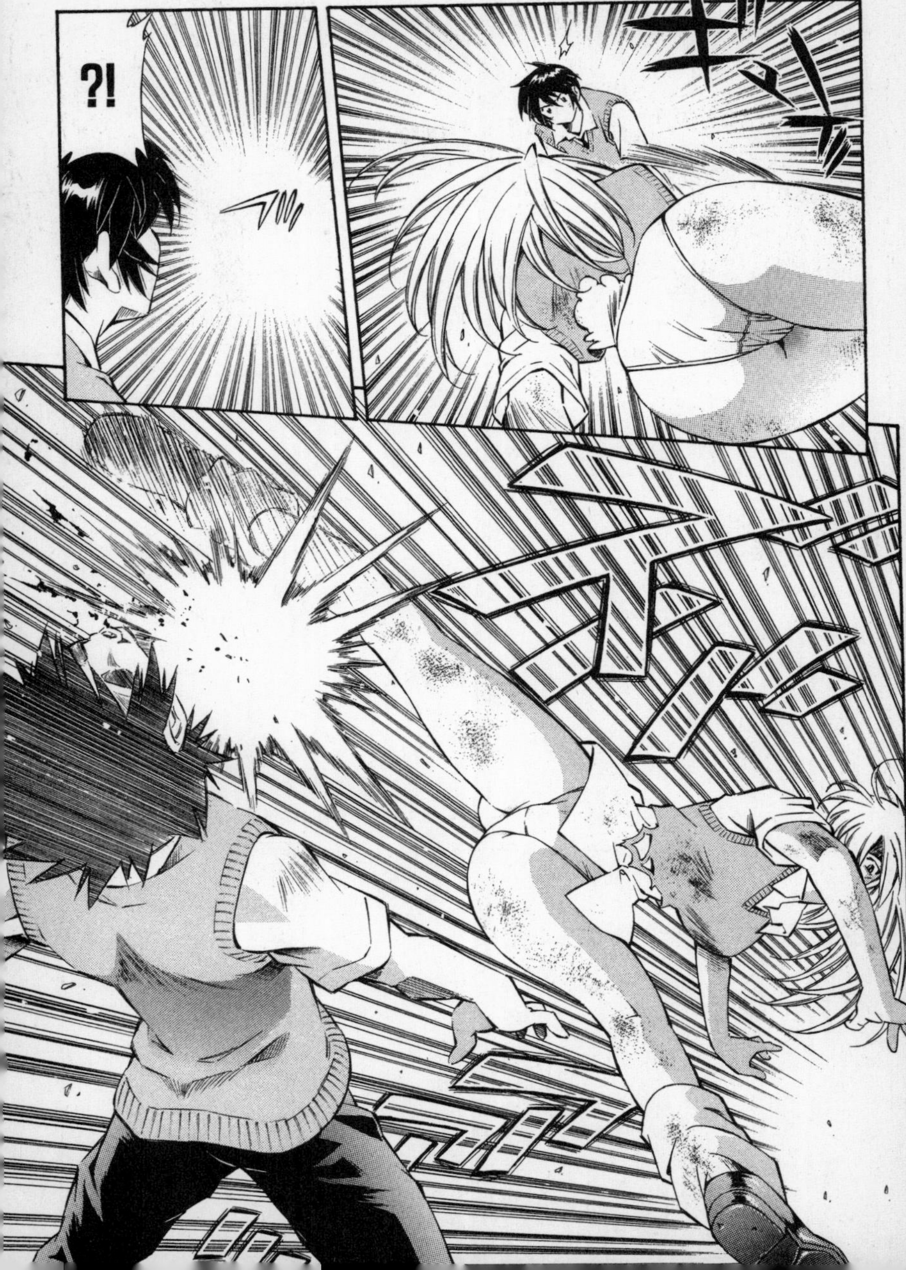
?!

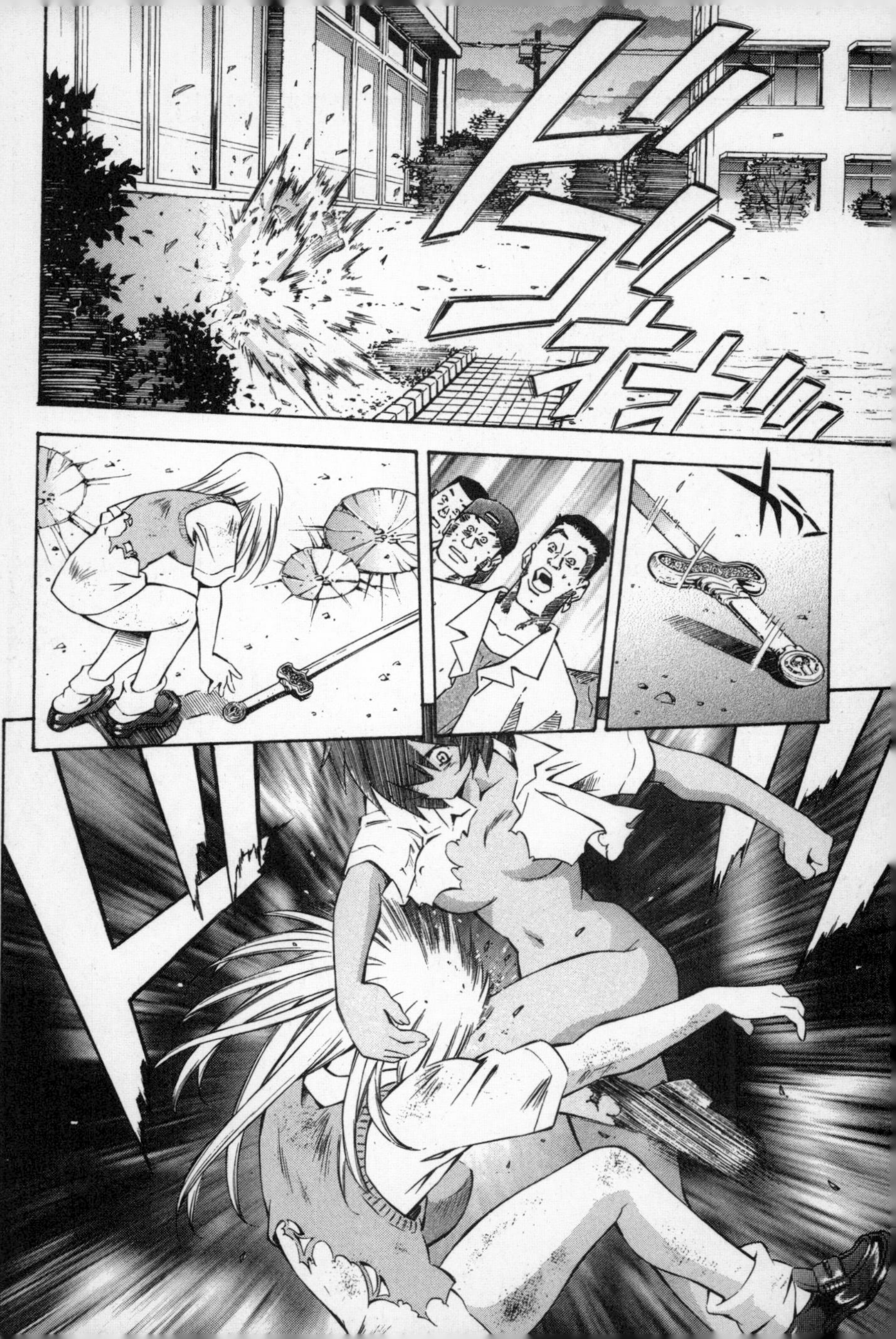
ドゴォォッ
ガッ

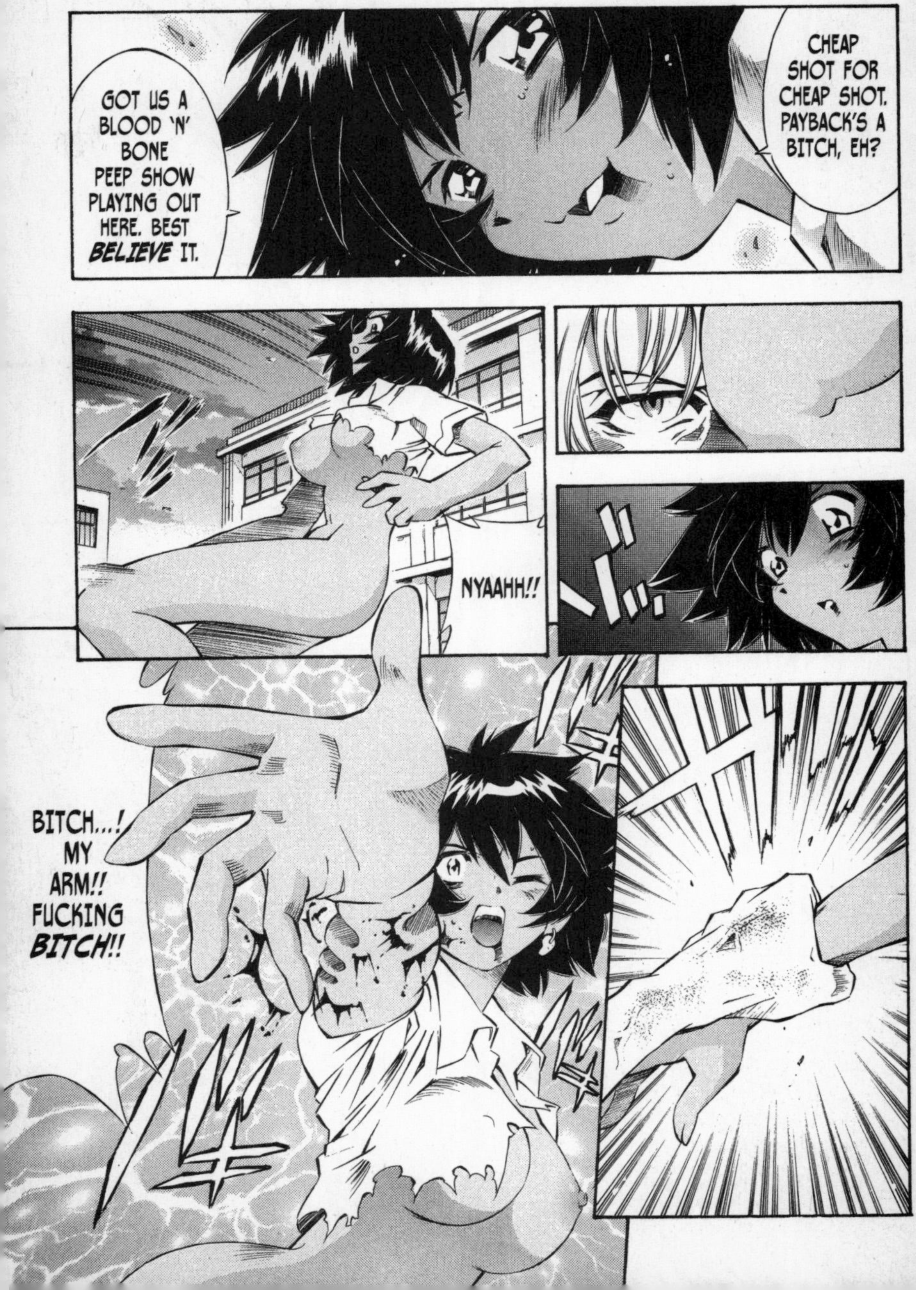
CHEAP SHOT FOR CHEAP SHOT. PAYBACK'S A BITCH, EH?
GOT US A BLOOD 'N' BONE PEEP SHOW PLAYING OUT HERE. BEST *BELIEVE* IT.
NYAAHH!!
BITCH...! MY ARM!! FUCKING *BITCH!!*

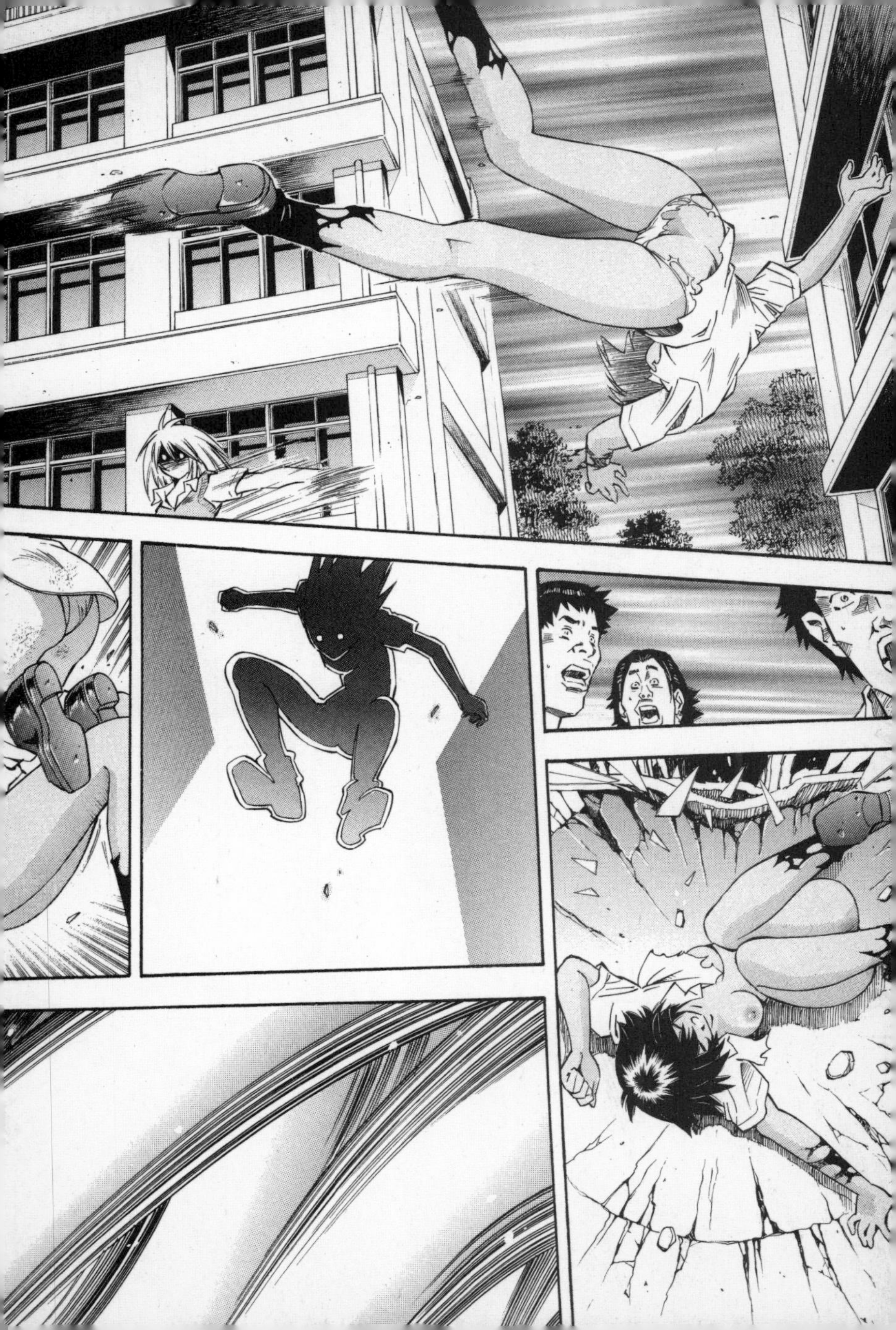

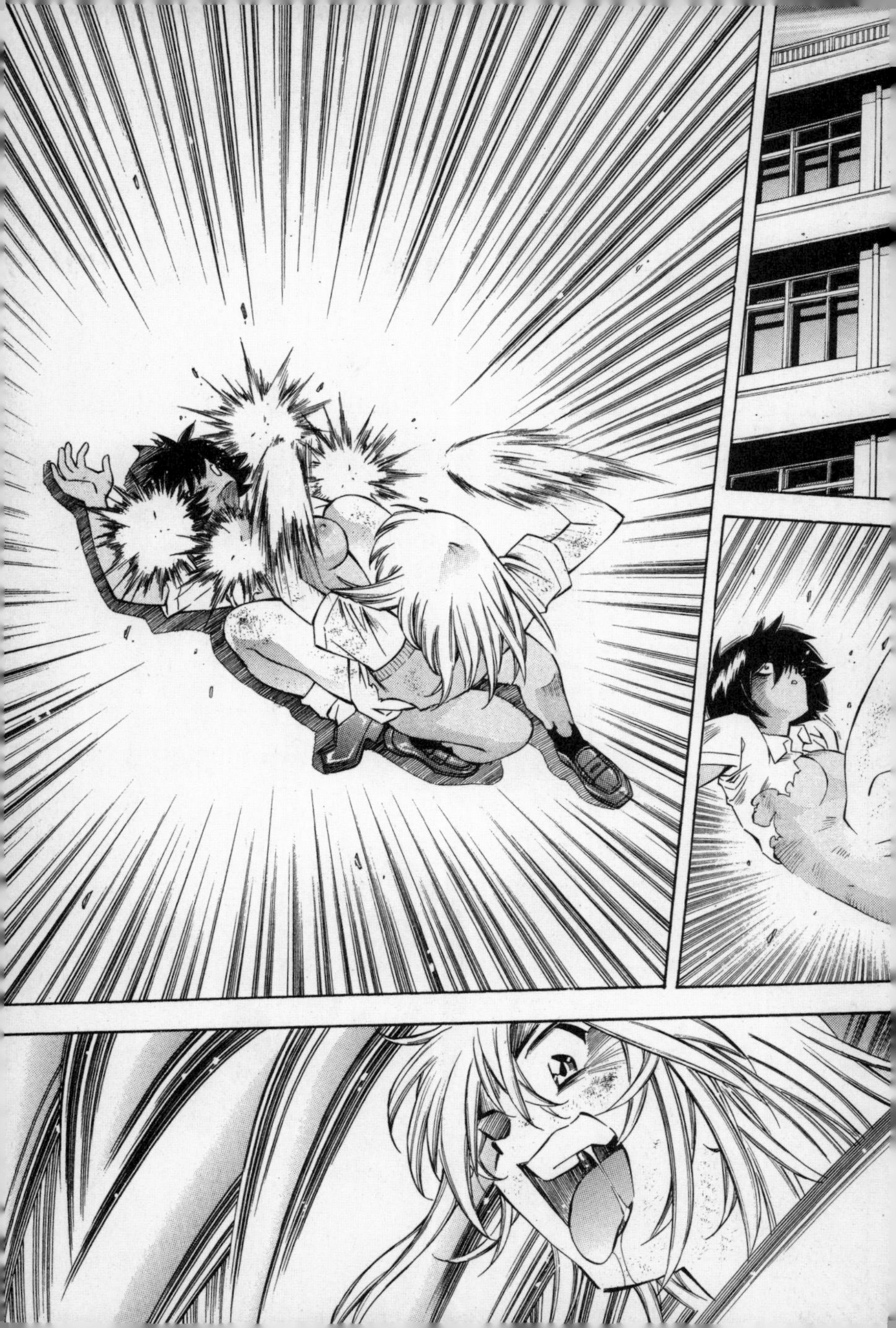

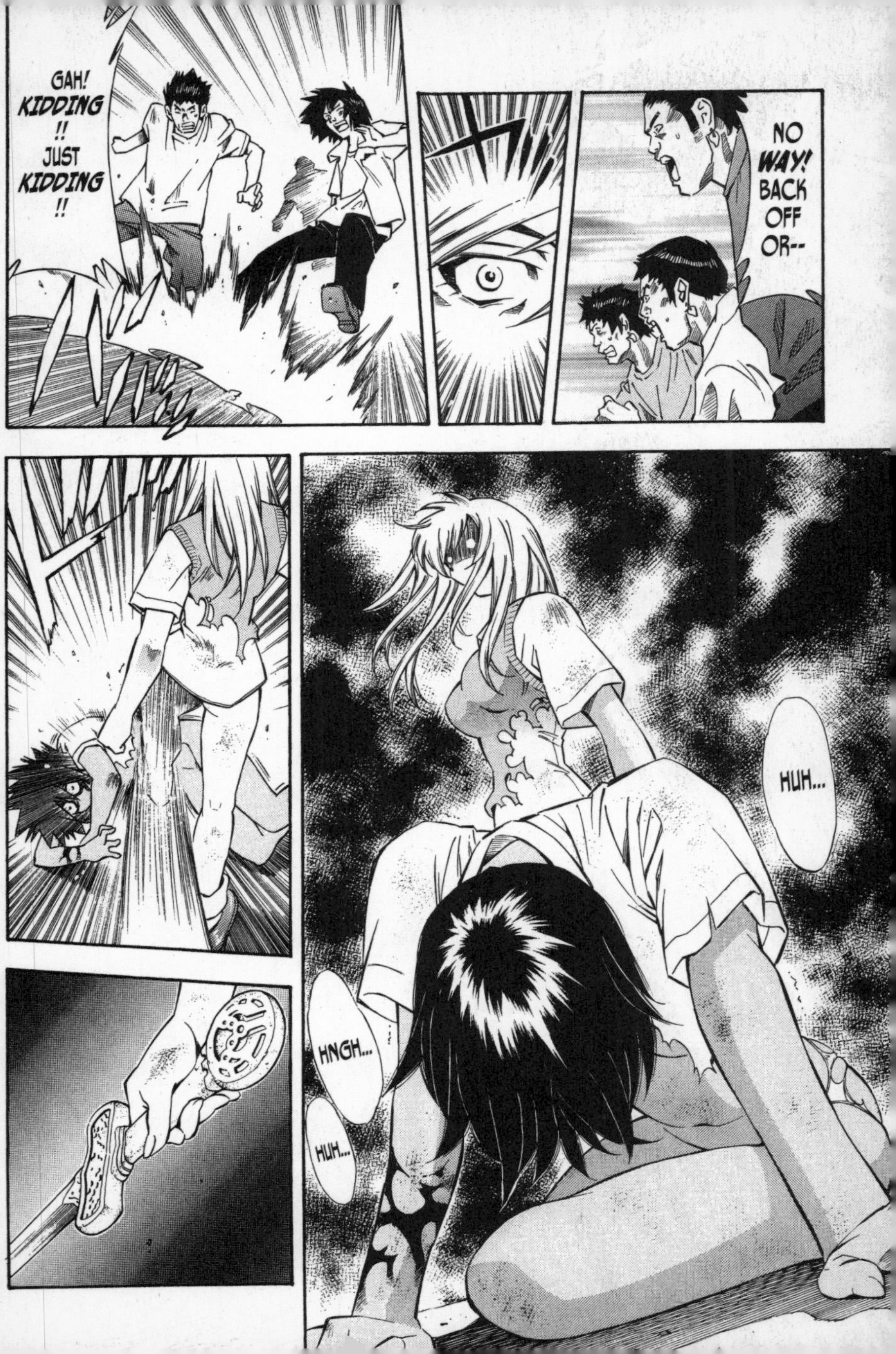
NO WAY! BACK OFF OR--
GAH! KIDDING!! JUST KIDDING!!
HUH...
HNGH...
HUH...

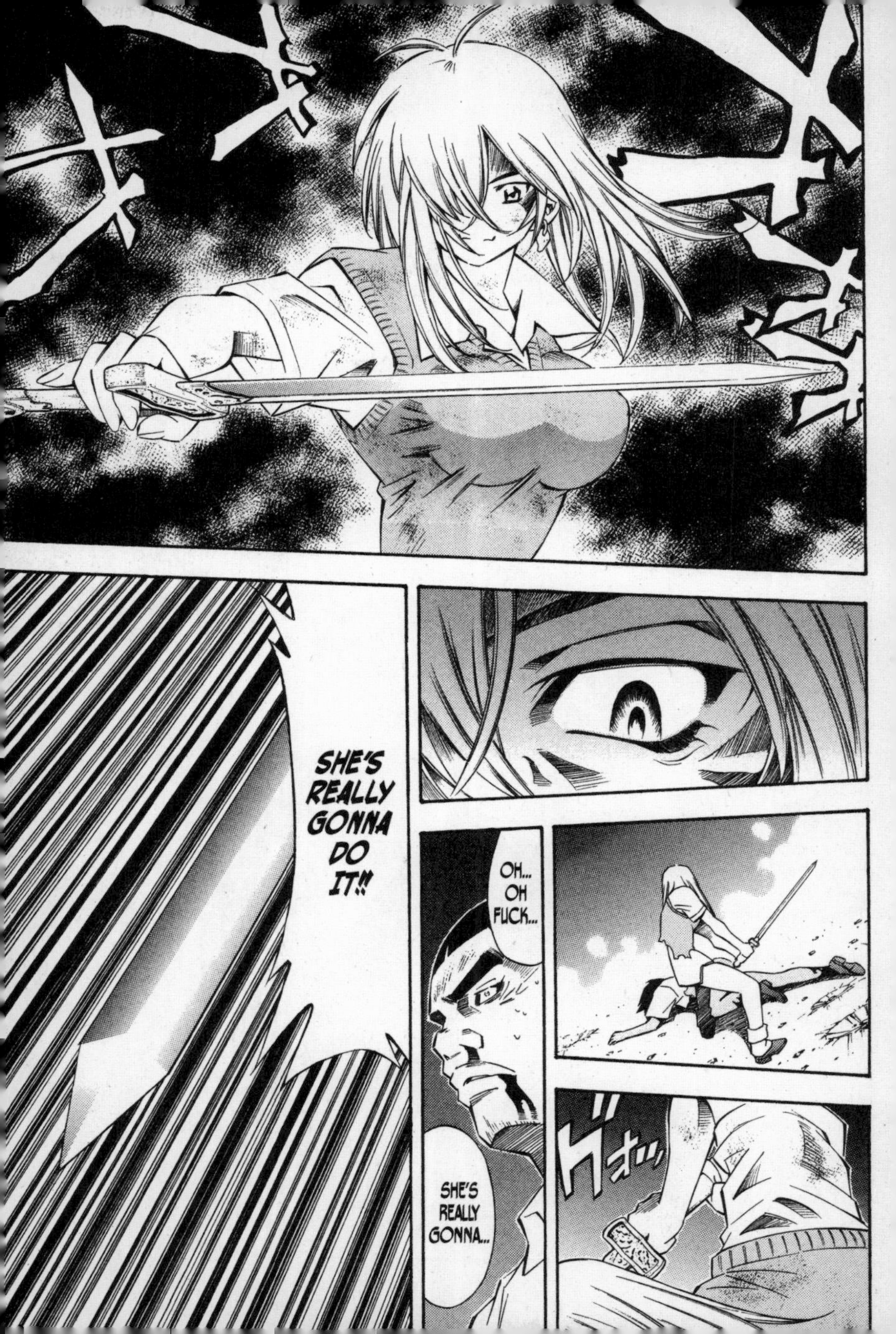
ゴォッ
OH... OH FUCK...
SHE'S REALLY GONNA...
SHE'S REALLY GONNA DO IT!!

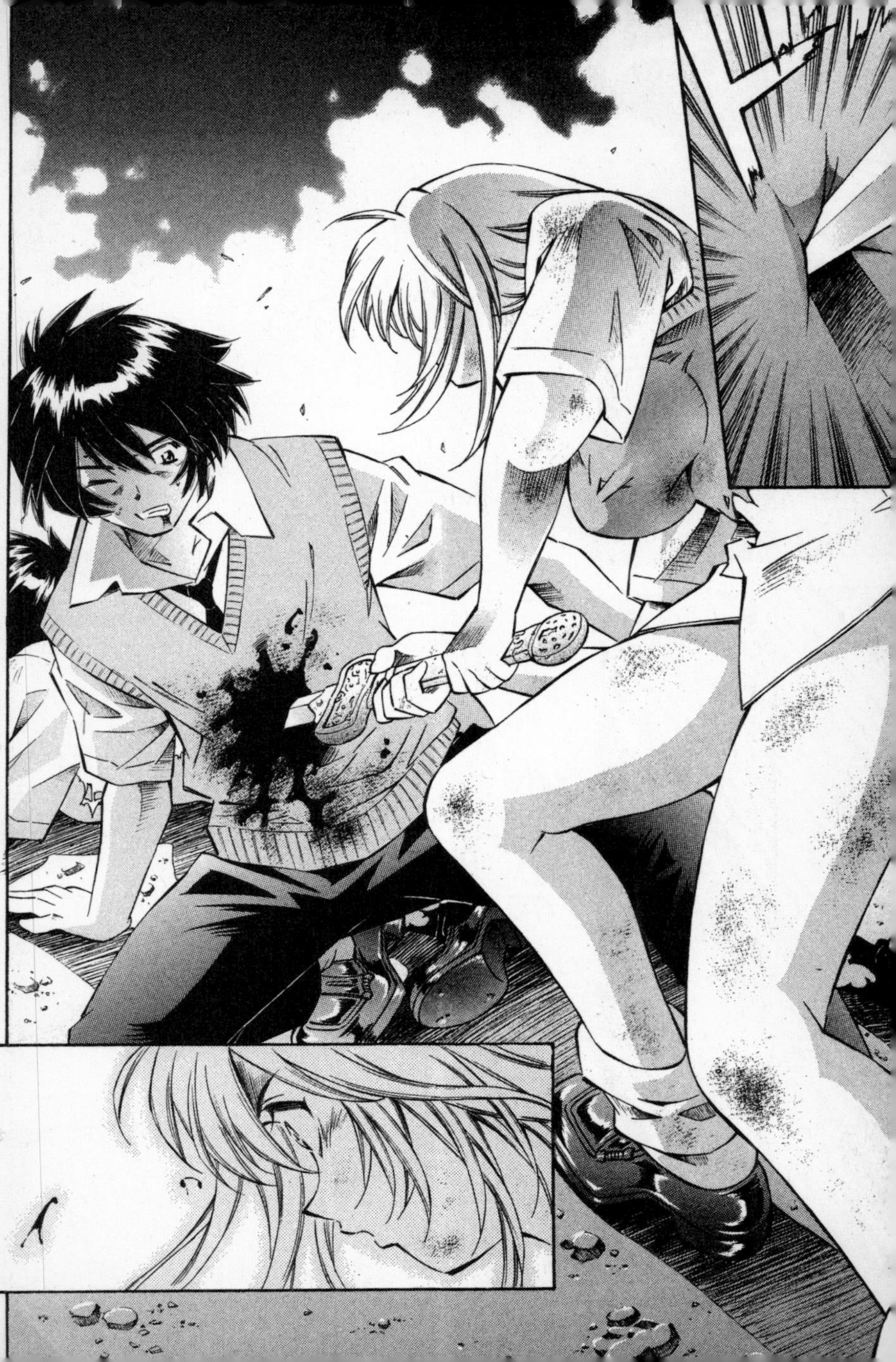

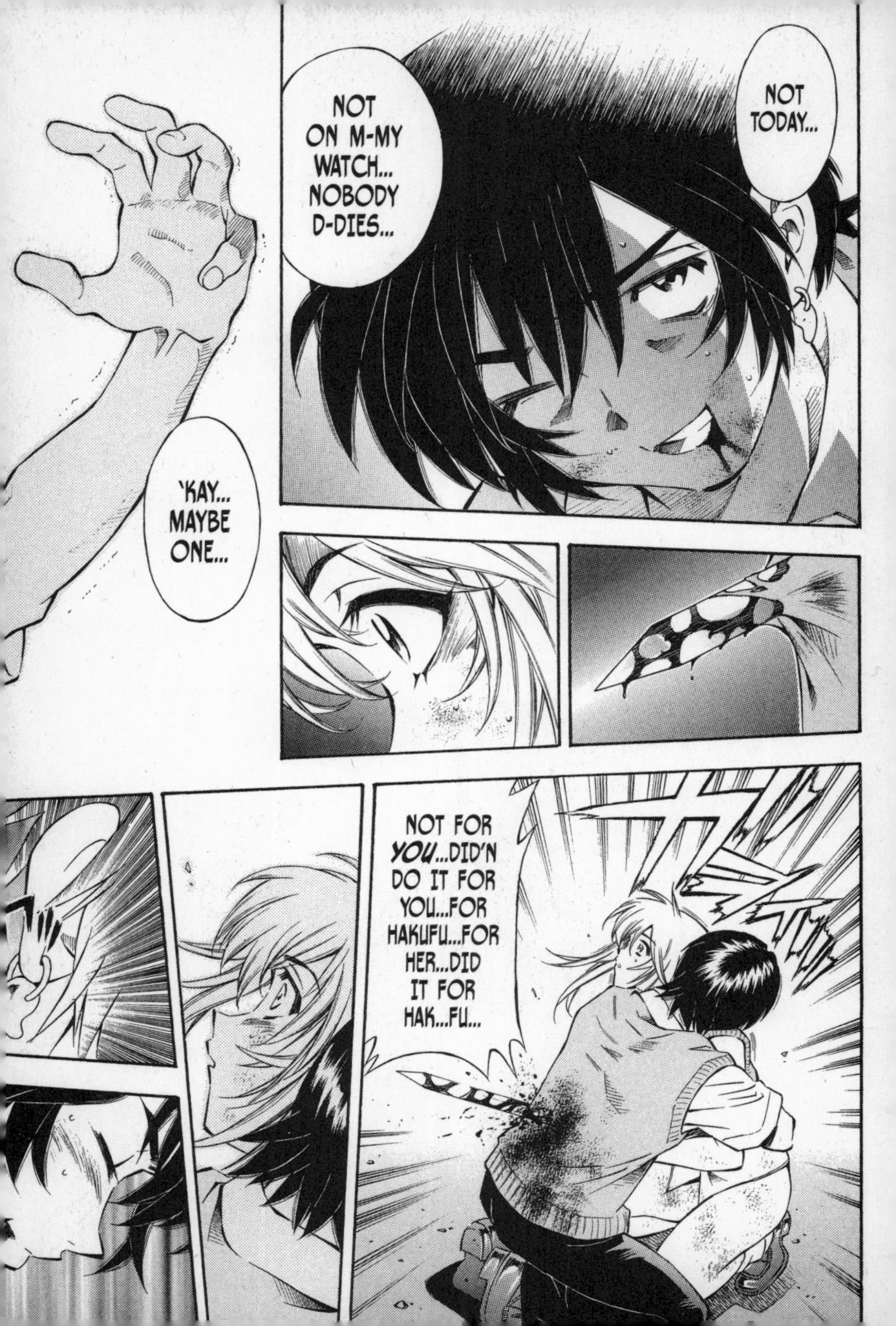
NOT TODAY...
NOT ON M-MY WATCH... NOBODY D-DIES...
'KAY... MAYBE ONE...
NOT FOR *YOU*...DID'N DO IT FOR YOU...FOR HAKUFU...FOR HER...DID IT FOR HAK...FU...

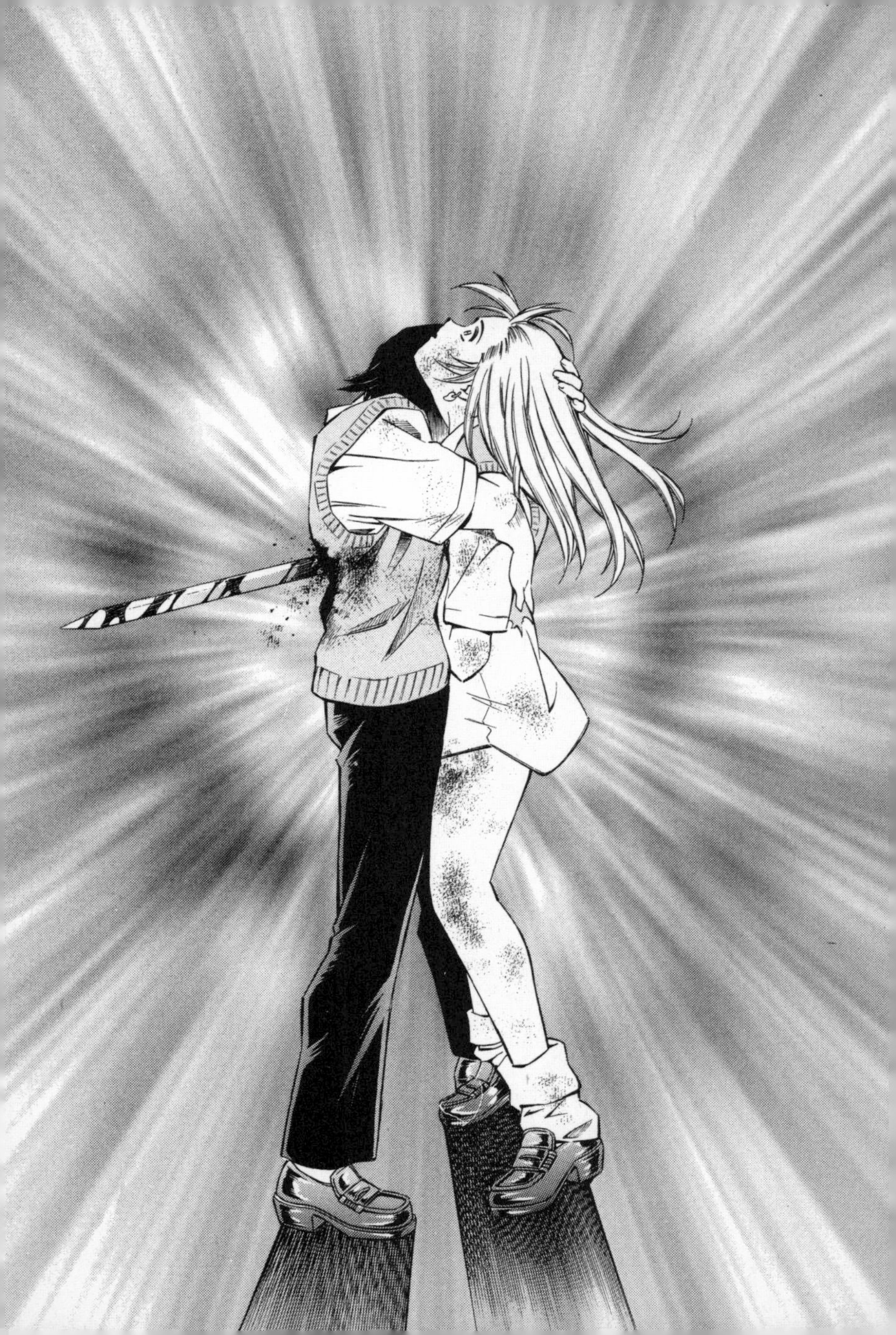

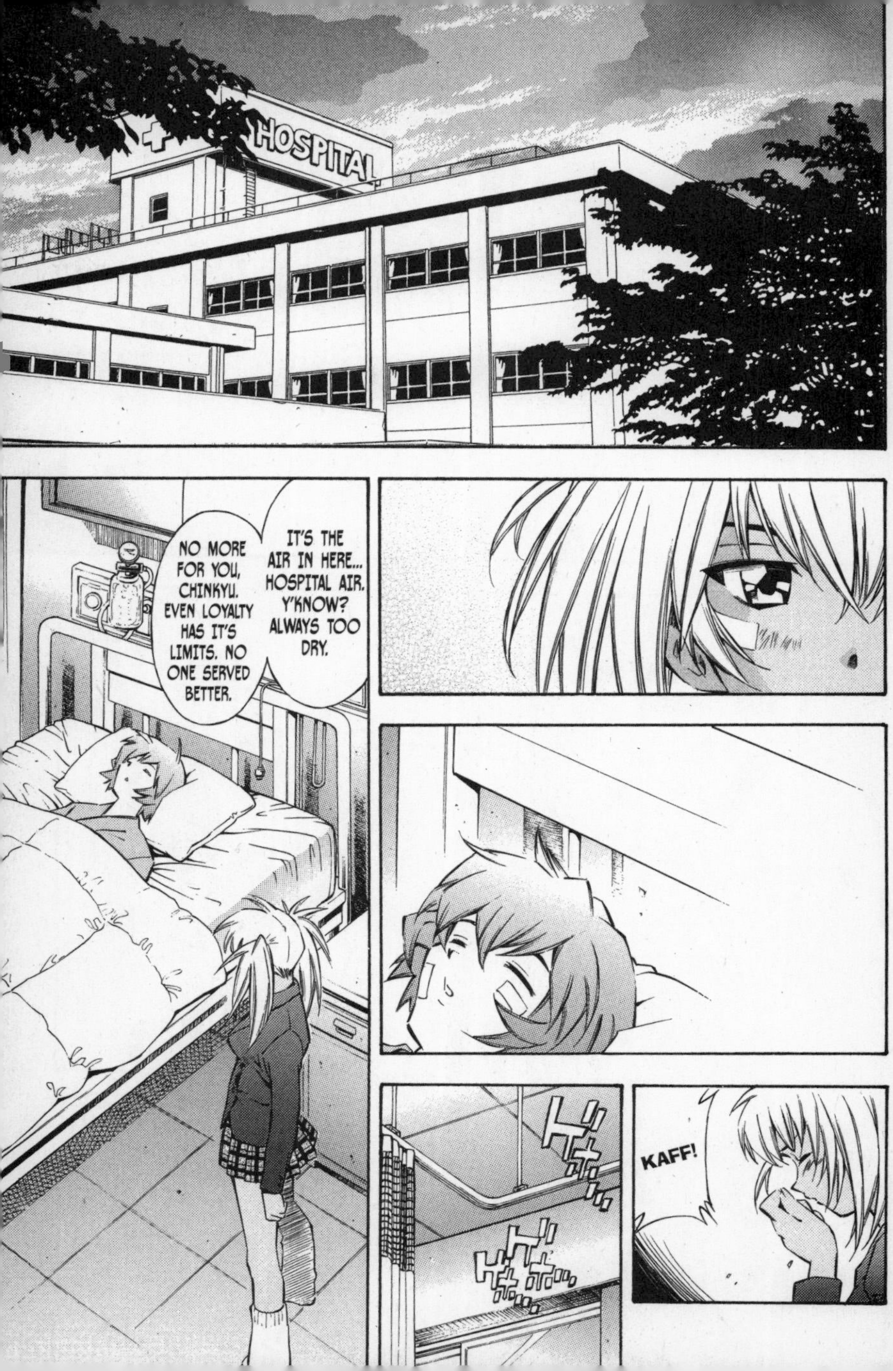
HOSPITAL
KAFF!
IT'S THE AIR IN HERE... HOSPITAL AIR. Y'KNOW? ALWAYS TOO DRY.
NO MORE FOR YOU, CHINKYU. EVEN LOYALTY HAS IT'S LIMITS. NO ONE SERVED BETTER.

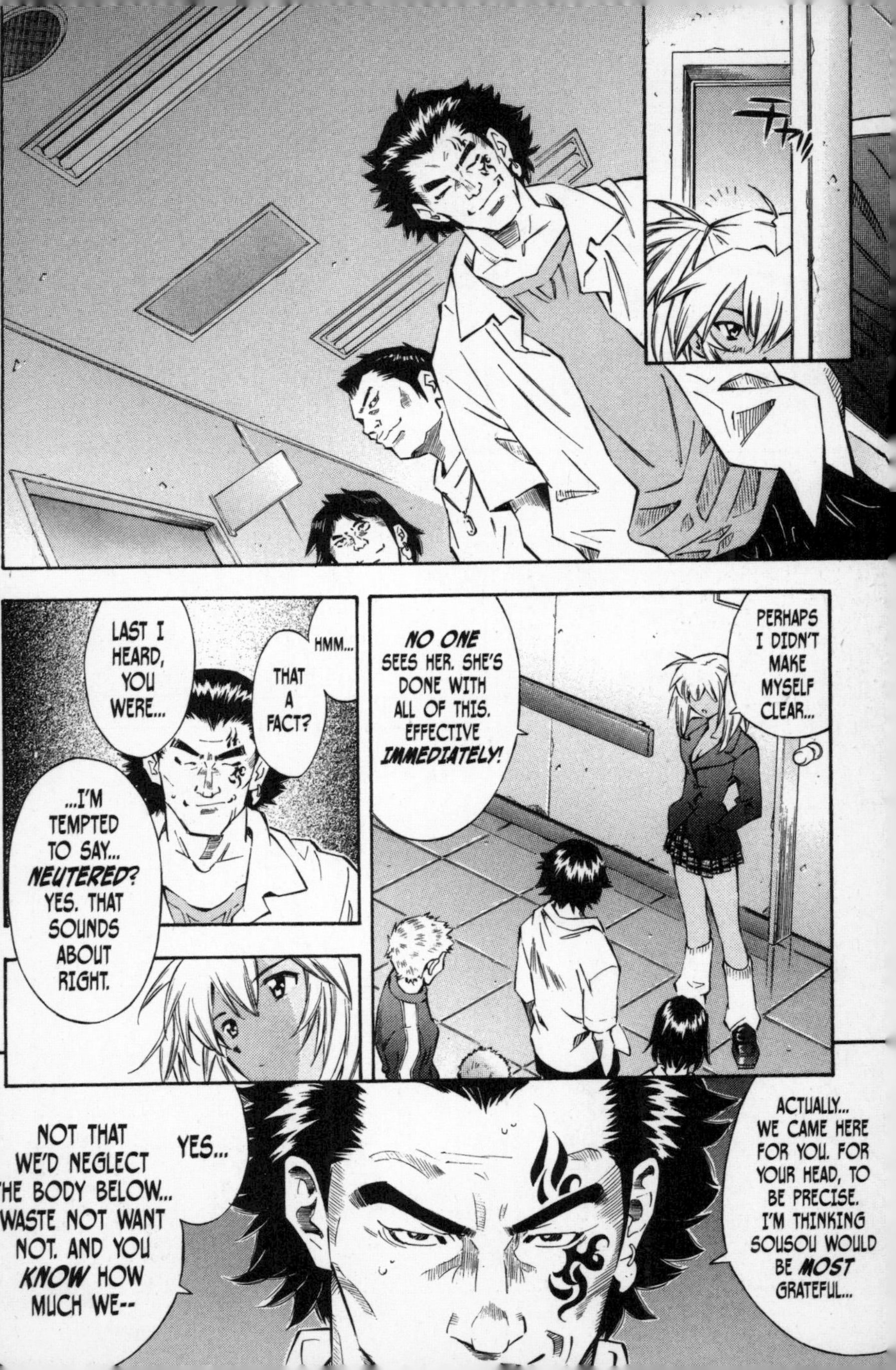
PERHAPS I DIDN'T MAKE MYSELF CLEAR...
NO ONE SEES HER. SHE'S DONE WITH ALL OF THIS. EFFECTIVE IMMEDIATELY!
HMM...
THAT A FACT?
LAST I HEARD, YOU WERE...
...I'M TEMPTED TO SAY... NEUTERED? YES. THAT SOUNDS ABOUT RIGHT.
ACTUALLY... WE CAME HERE FOR YOU. FOR YOUR HEAD, TO BE PRECISE. I'M THINKING SOUSOU WOULD BE MOST GRATEFUL...
YES...
NOT THAT WE'D NEGLECT THE BODY BELOW... WASTE NOT WANT NOT. AND YOU KNOW HOW MUCH WE--

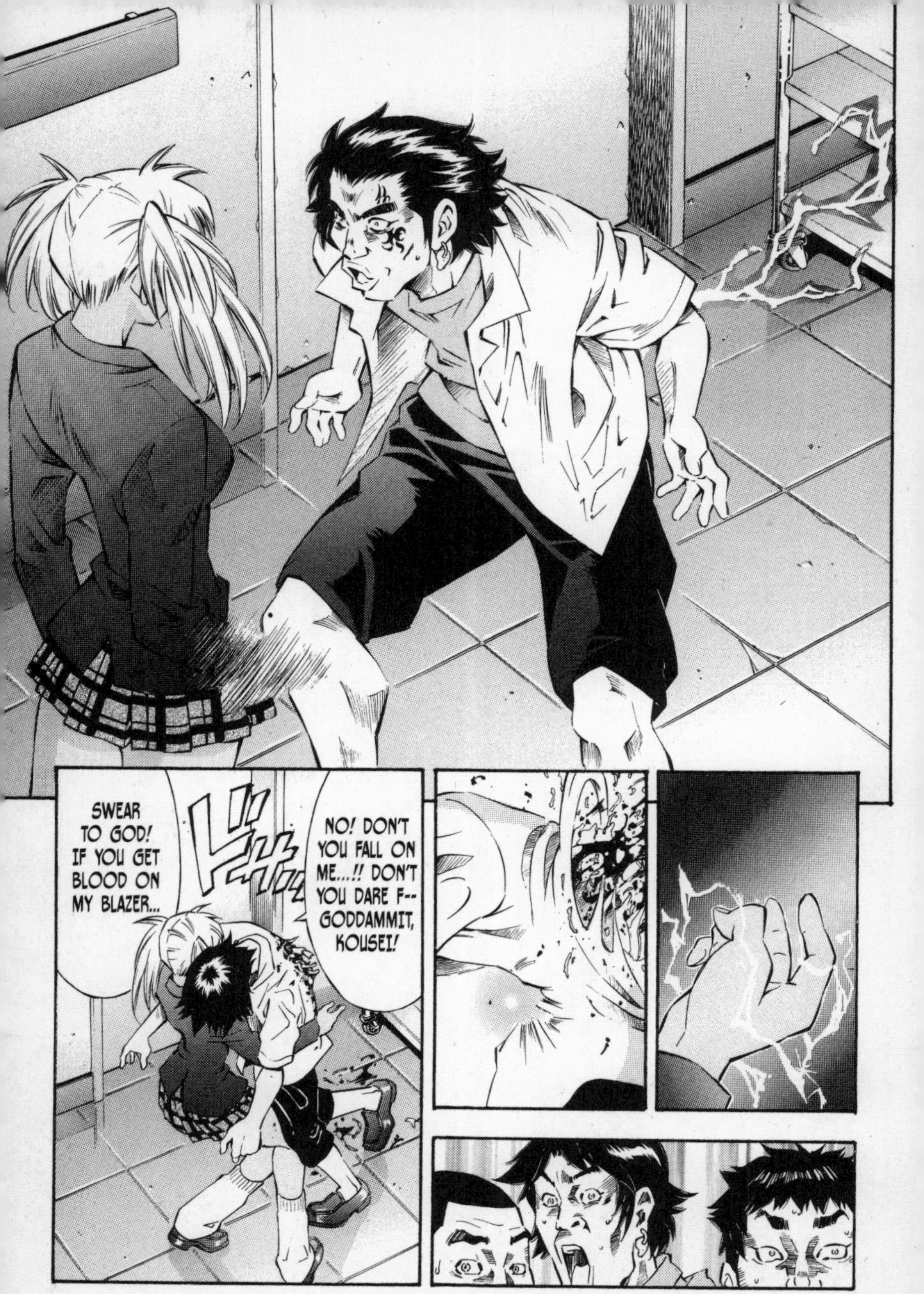
NO! DON'T YOU FALL ON ME...!! DON'T YOU DARE F-- GODDAMMIT, KOUSEI!
SWEAR TO GOD! IF YOU GET BLOOD ON MY BLAZER...

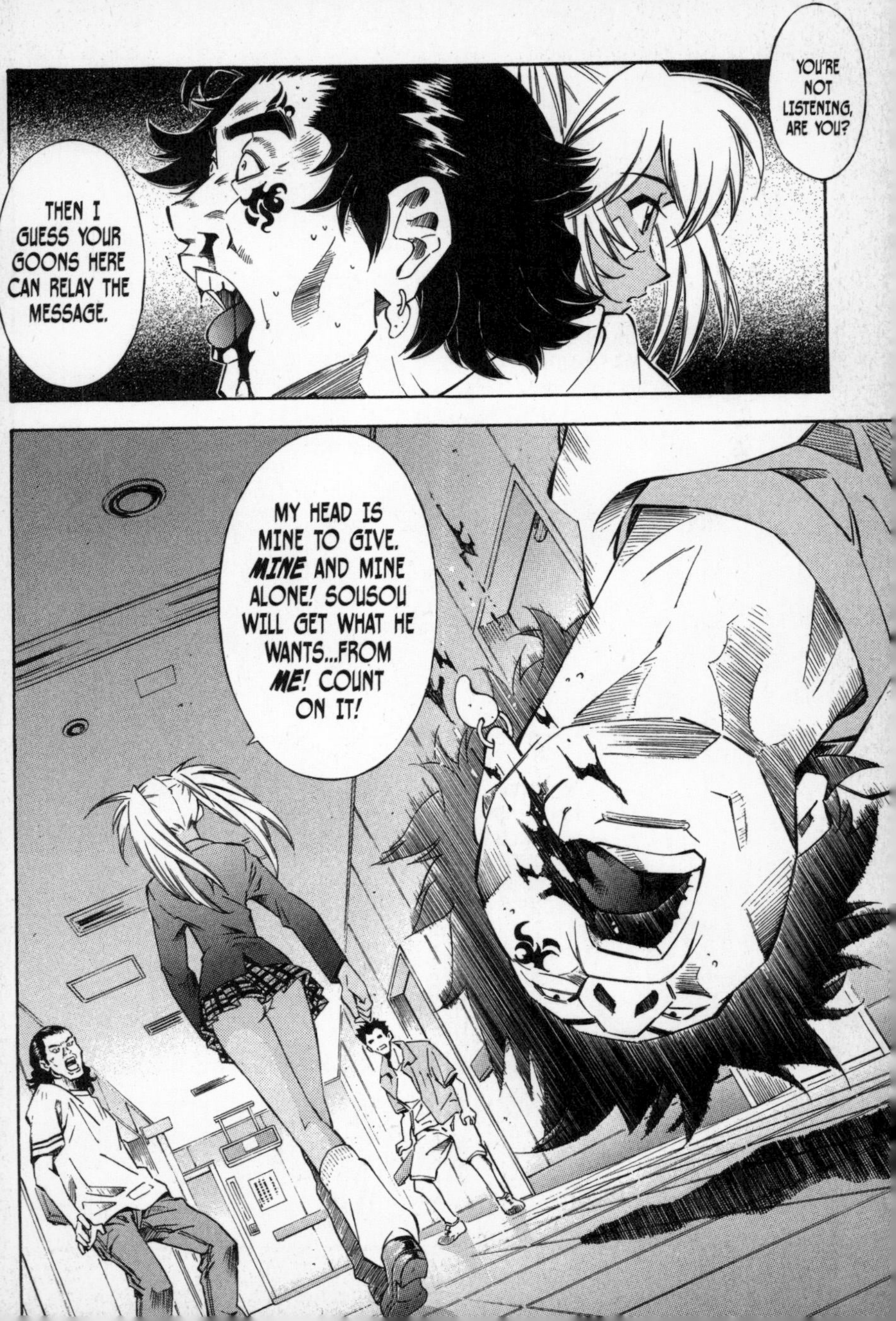
YOU'RE NOT LISTENING, ARE YOU?
THEN I GUESS YOUR GOONS HERE CAN RELAY THE MESSAGE.
MY HEAD IS MINE TO GIVE. MINE AND MINE ALONE! SOUSOU WILL GET WHAT HE WANTS...FROM ME! COUNT ON IT!

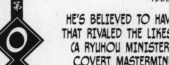

KAKU BUNWA

HE'S BELIEVED TO HAVE BEEN A MASTER STRATEGIST THAT RIVALED THE LIKES OF CHOURYOU AND CHINPEI (A RYUHOU MINISTER DURING THE HAN EMPIRE). A COVERT MASTERMIND, KAKU PLOTTED SOUSOU'S DEATH. THE KANTO WAR SAW KAKU SURRENDER TO SOUSOU. SOUSOU THEN CHOSE KAKU AS AN INNER CIRCLE ADVISOR (REF: NOT TOO BRIGHT). SOUSOU WAS KNOWN TO HAVE A SUSPICIOUS NATURE...BUT WHERE IT WAS WHEN SOUSOU ALLOWED KAKU INTO HIS INNER CIRCLE IS UNKNOWN.

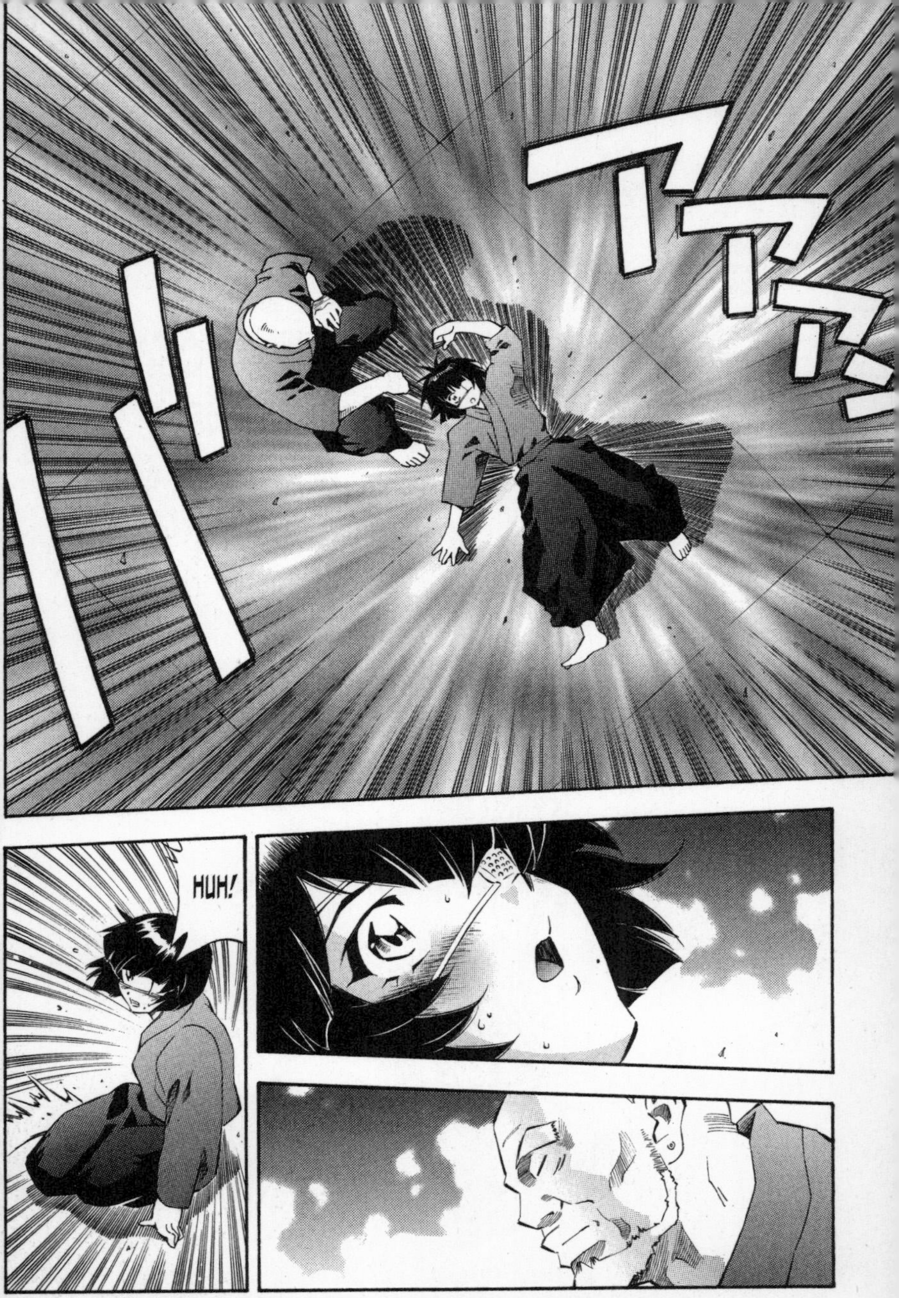
HUH!

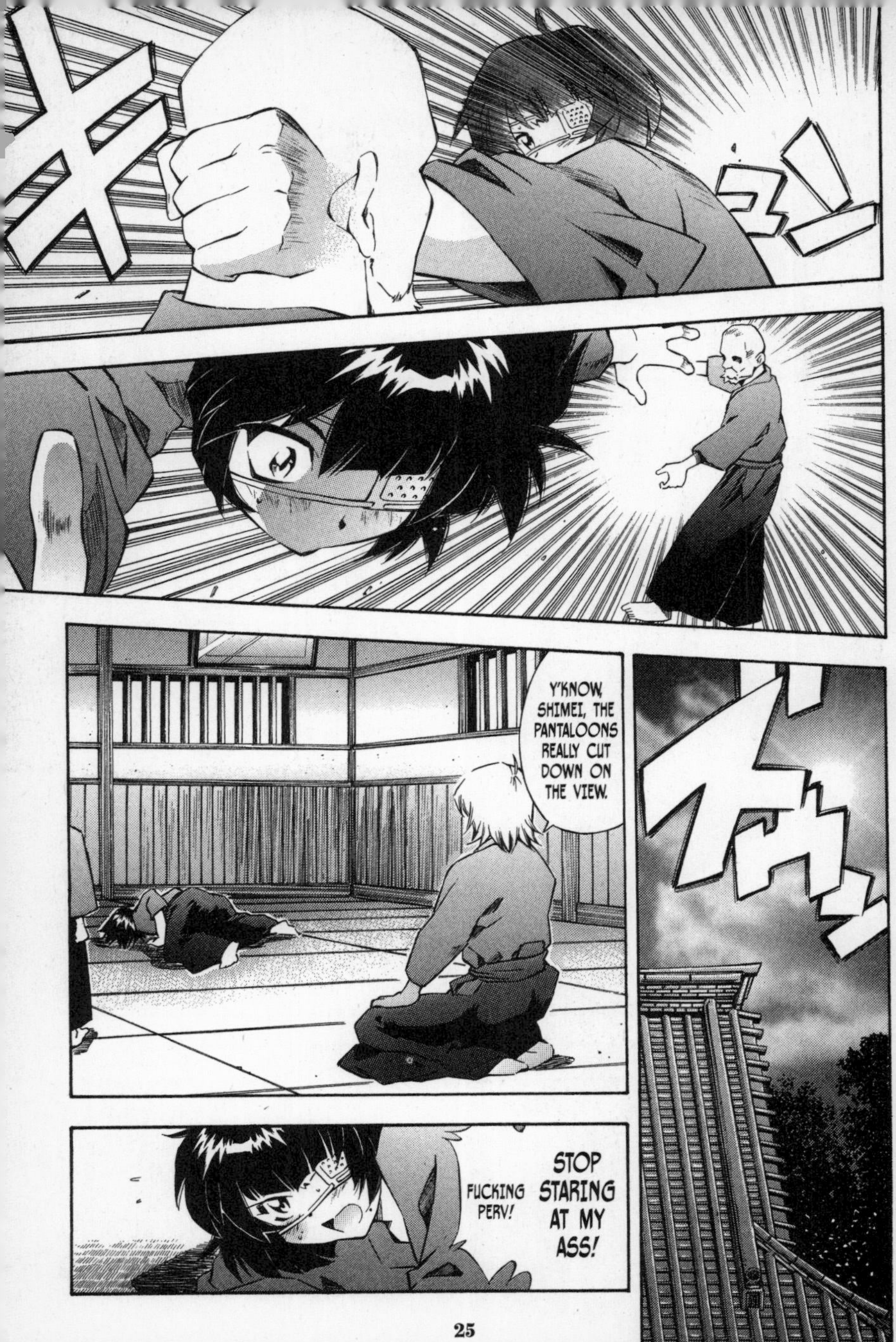
Y'KNOW, SHIMEI, THE PANTALOONS REALLY CUT DOWN ON THE VIEW.
STOP STARING AT MY ASS!
FUCKING PERV!

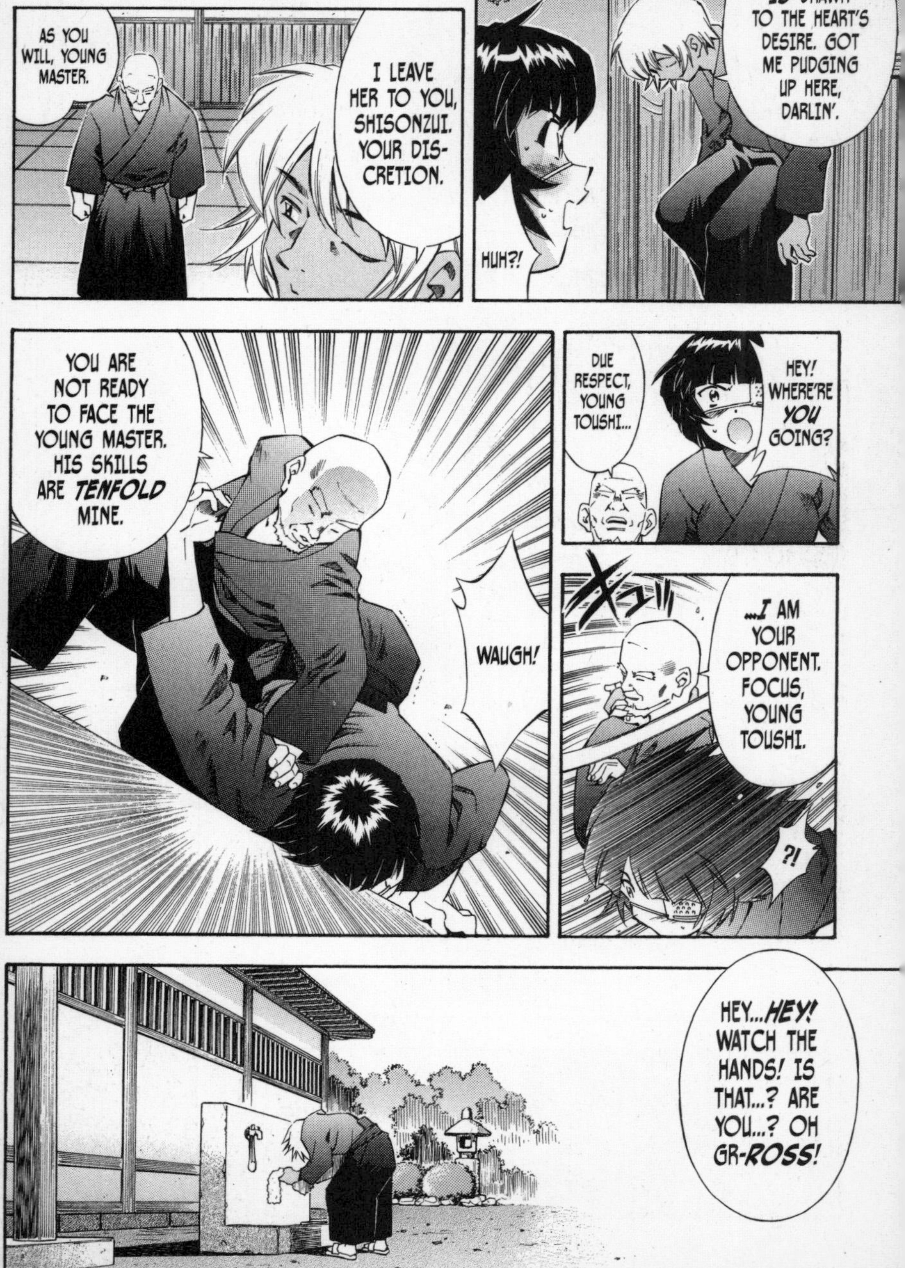
THE EYE *IS* DRAWN TO THE HEART'S DESIRE. GOT ME PUDGING UP HERE, DARLIN'.
HUH?!
I LEAVE HER TO YOU, SHISONZUI. YOUR DISCRETION.
AS YOU WILL, YOUNG MASTER.
HEY! WHERE'RE *YOU* GOING?
DUE RESPECT, YOUNG TOUSHI...
...*I* AM YOUR OPPONENT. FOCUS, YOUNG TOUSHI.
?!
WAUGH!
YOU ARE NOT READY TO FACE THE YOUNG MASTER. HIS SKILLS ARE *TENFOLD* MINE.
HEY...*HEY!* WATCH THE HANDS! IS THAT...? ARE YOU...? OH GR-*ROSS*!

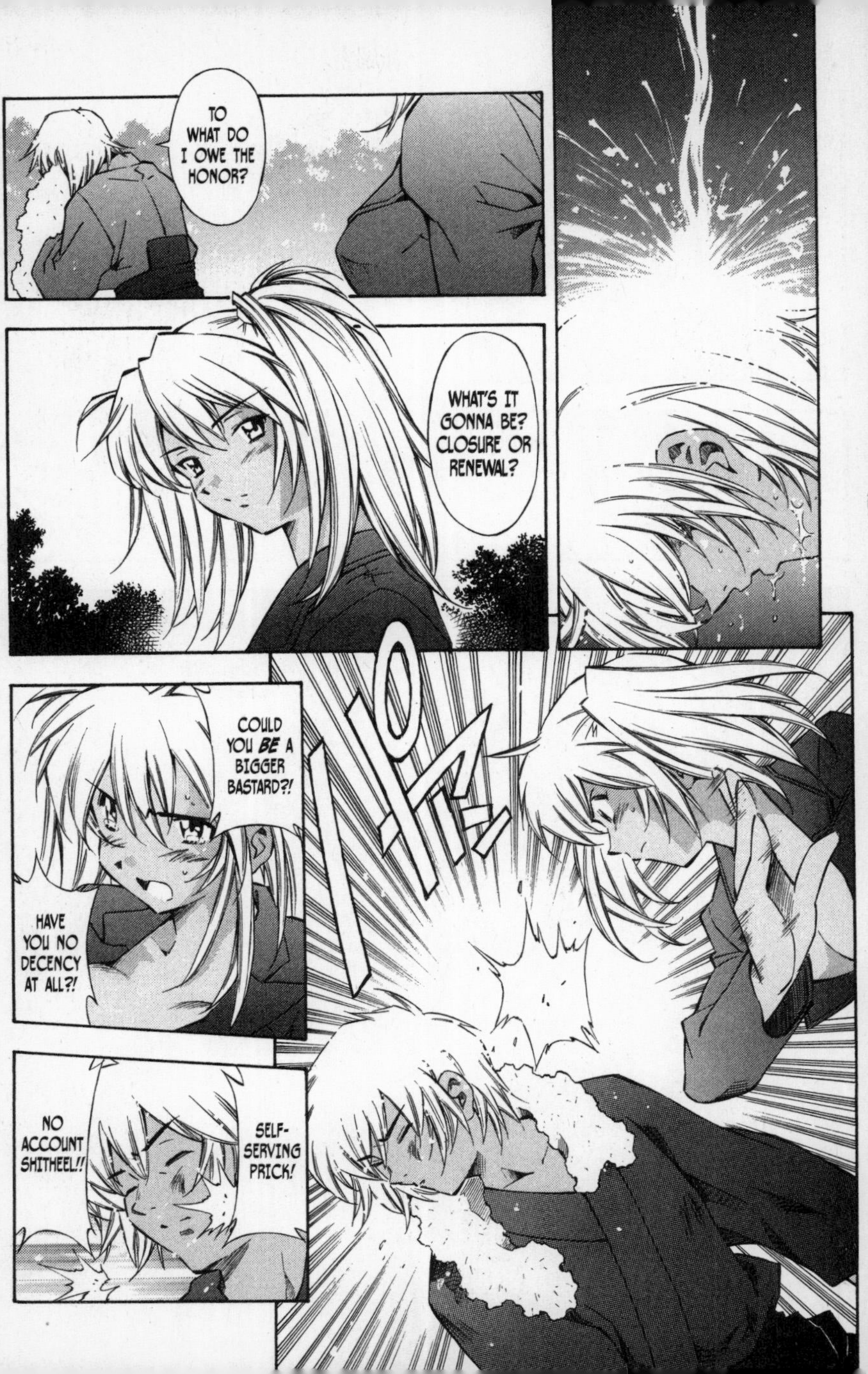
TO WHAT DO I OWE THE HONOR?
WHAT'S IT GONNA BE? CLOSURE OR RENEWAL?
COULD YOU *BE* A BIGGER BASTARD?!
HAVE YOU NO DECENCY AT ALL?!
SELF-SERVING PRICK!
NO ACCOUNT SHITHEEL!!

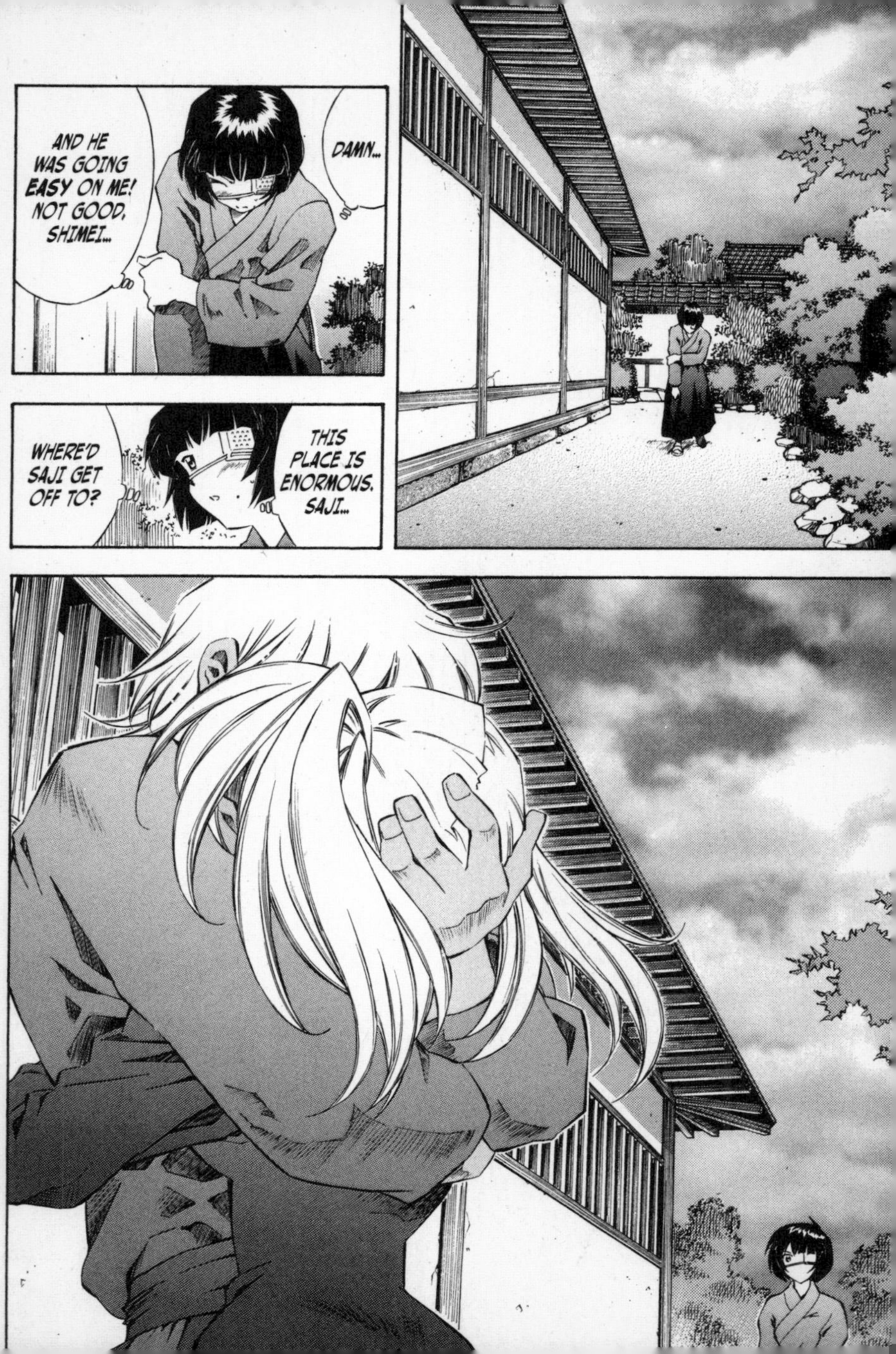
DAMN...
AND HE WAS GOING EASY ON ME! NOT GOOD, SHIMEI...
THIS PLACE IS ENORMOUS. SAJI...
WHERE'D SAJI GET OFF TO?

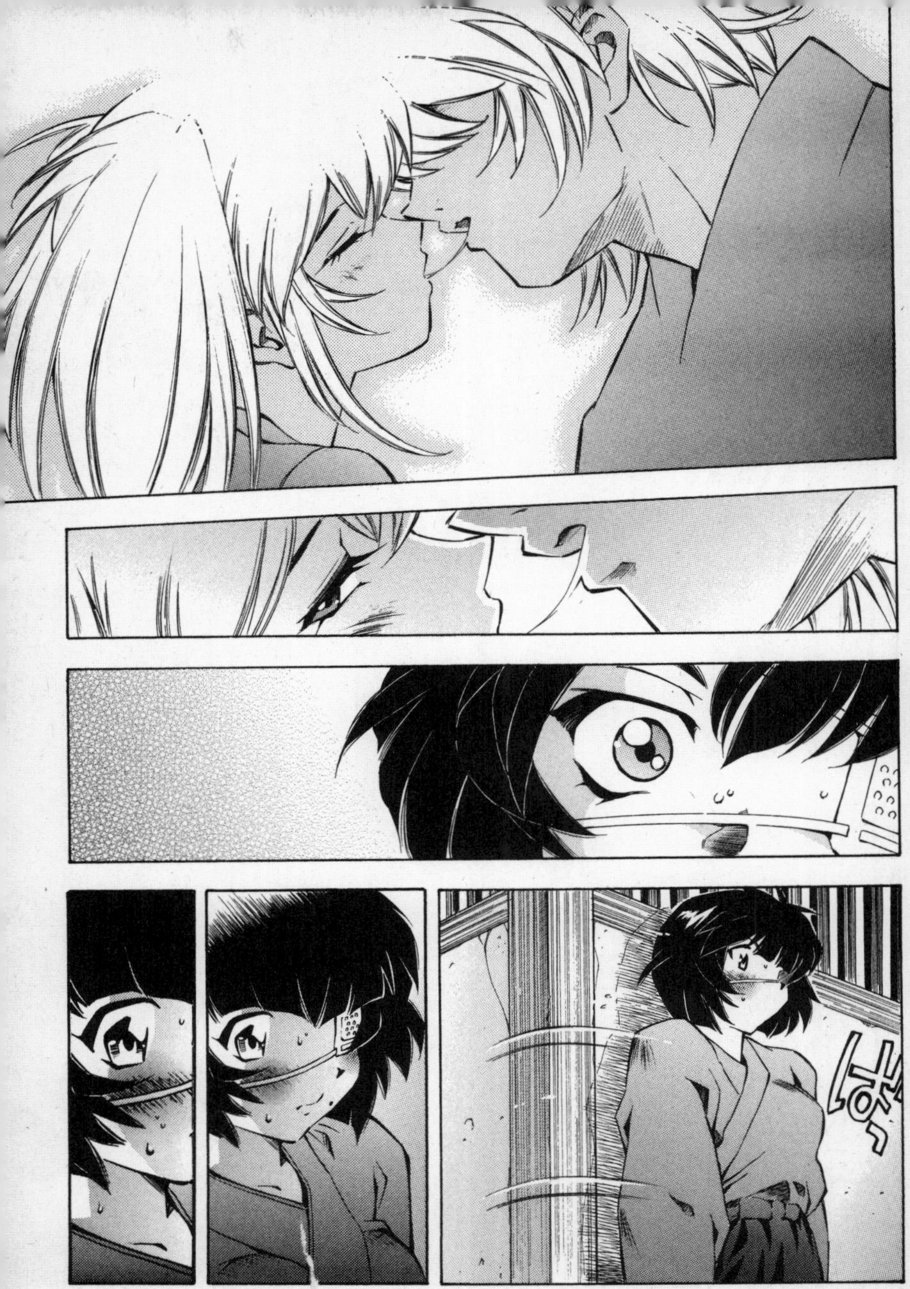
はっ

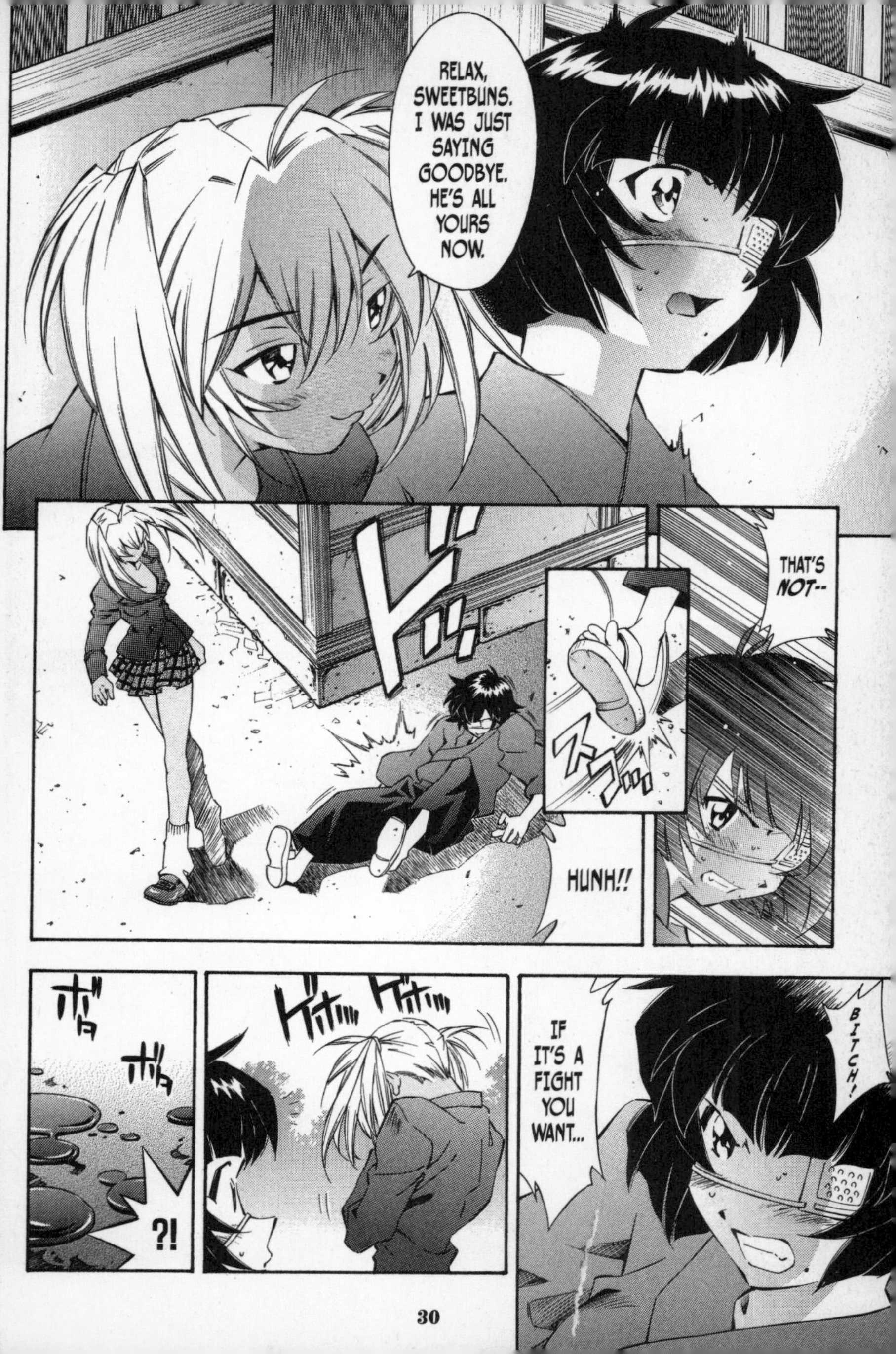
RELAX, SWEETBUNS. I WAS JUST SAYING GOODBYE. HE'S ALL YOURS NOW.
THAT'S *NOT*--
HUNH!!
BITCH!
IF IT'S A FIGHT YOU WANT...
?!

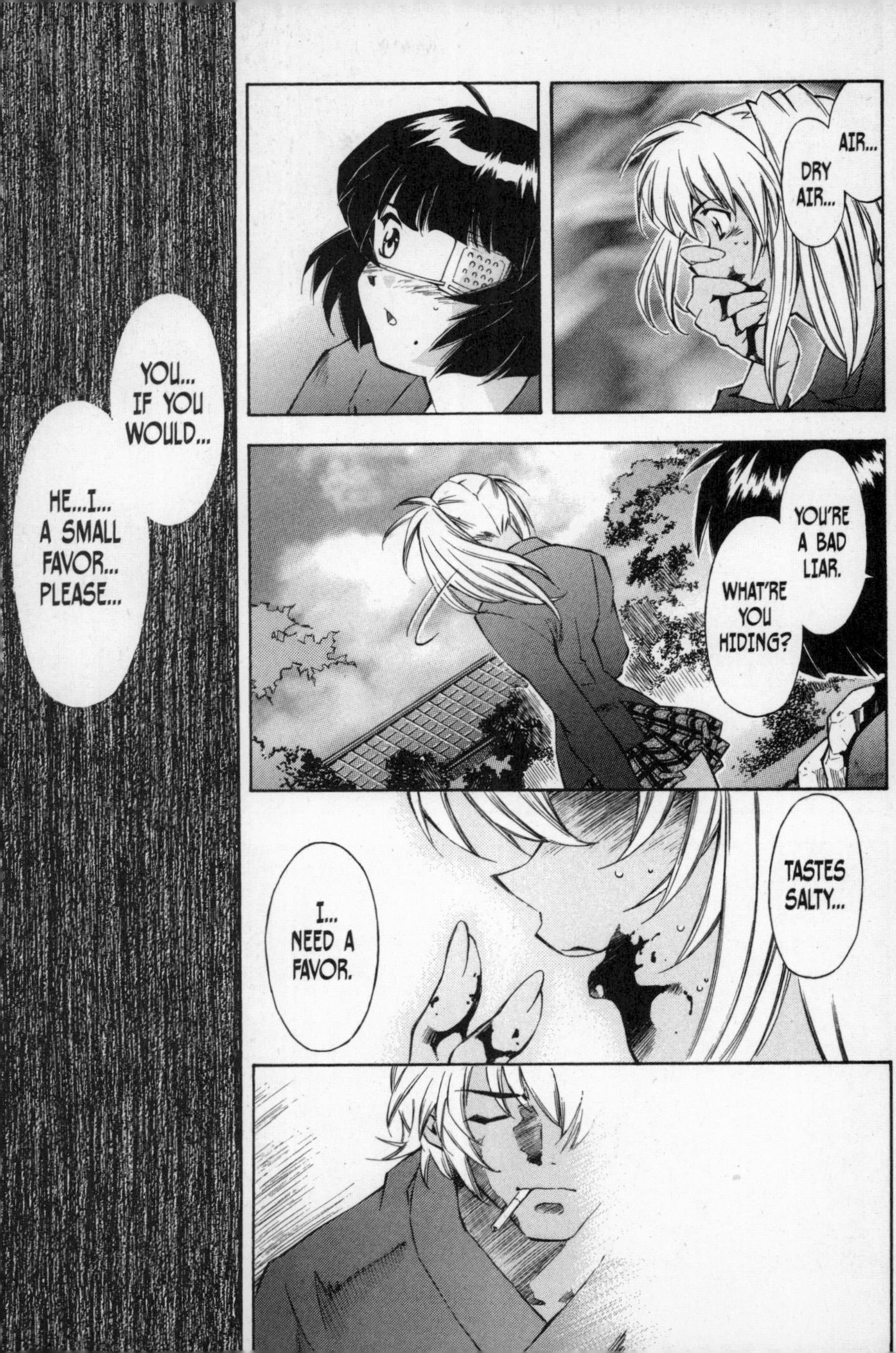
AIR... DRY AIR...
YOU'RE A BAD LIAR.
WHAT'RE YOU HIDING?
TASTES SALTY...
I... NEED A FAVOR.
YOU... IF YOU WOULD...
HE...I... A SMALL FAVOR... PLEASE...

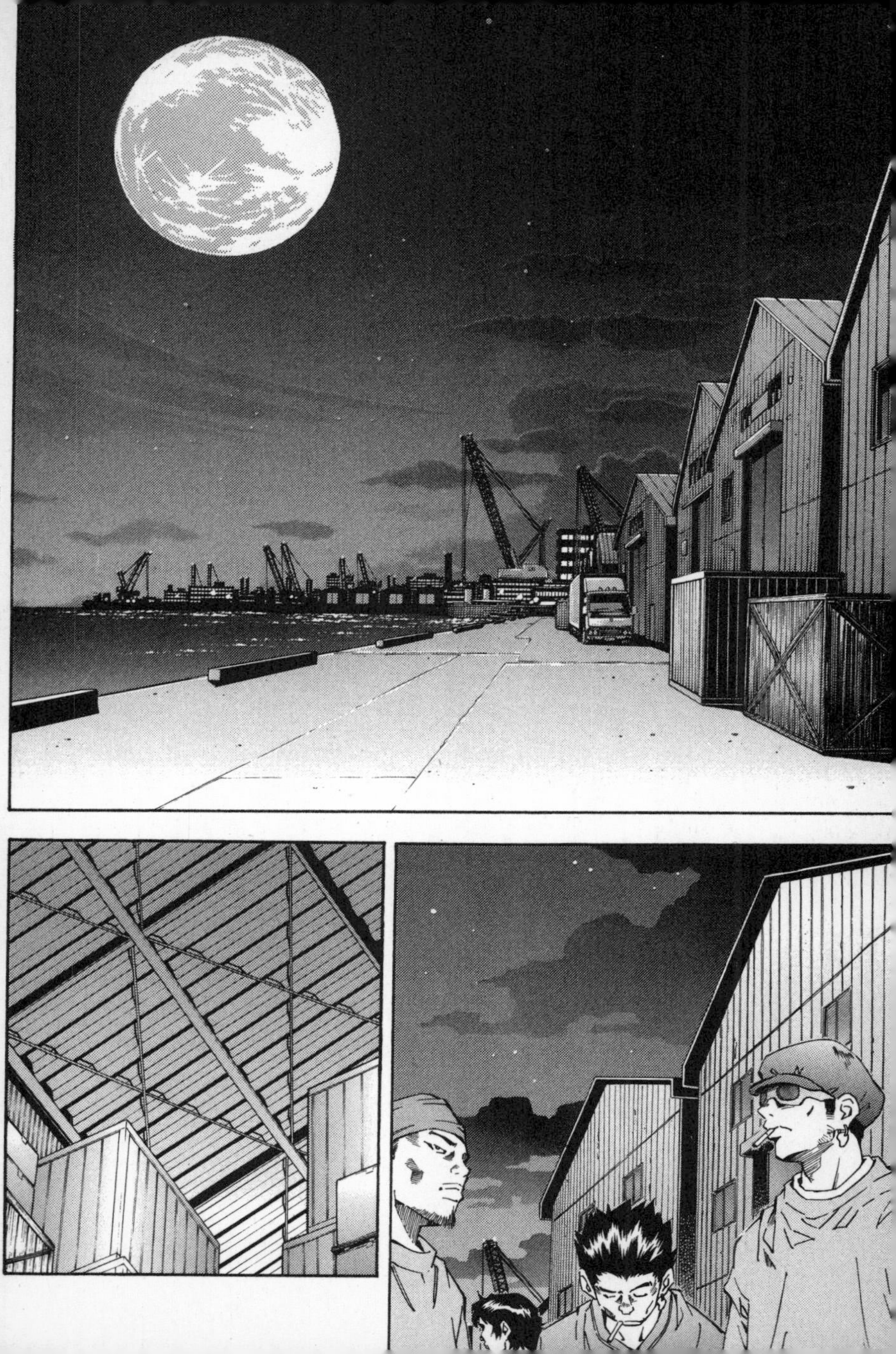

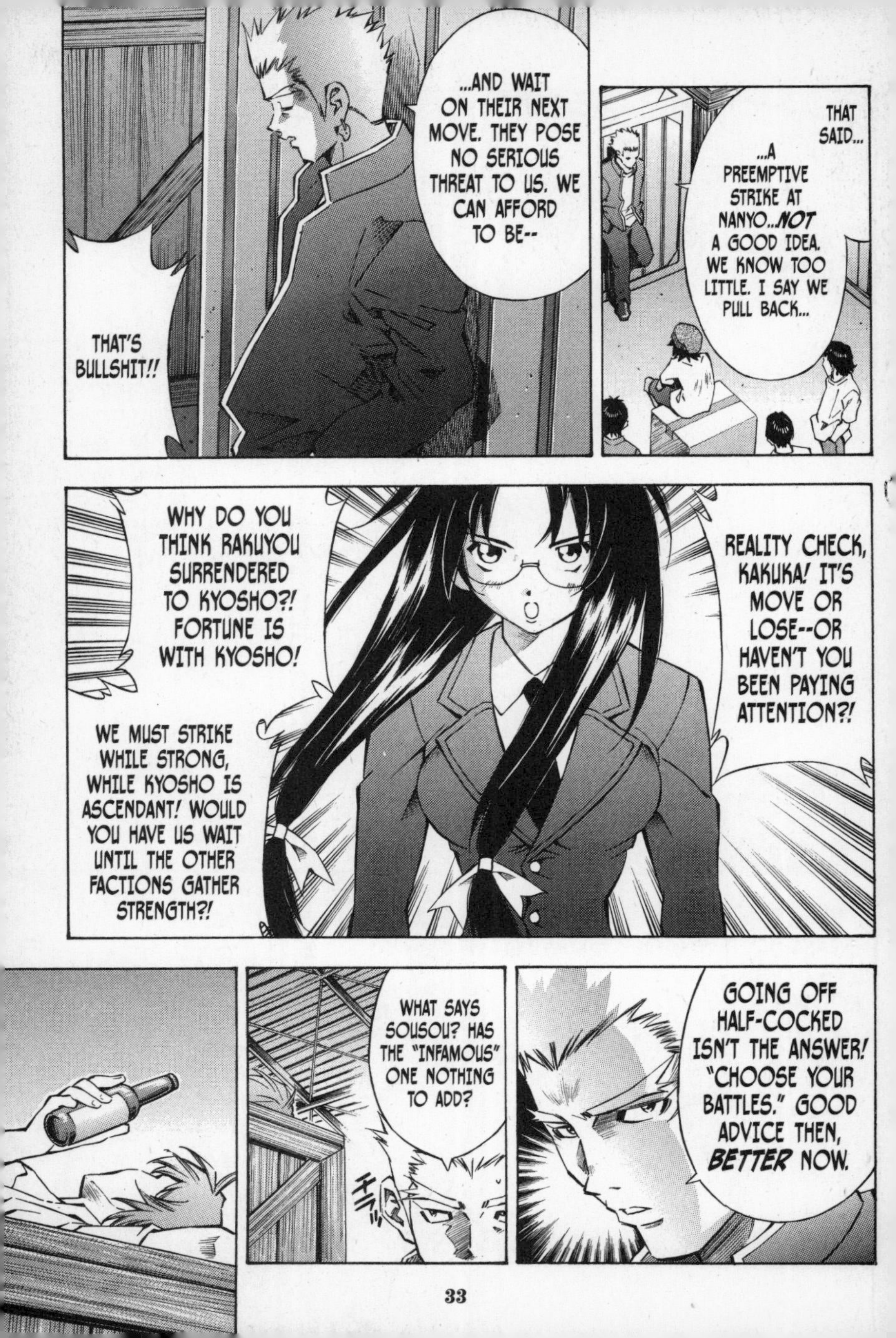
THAT SAID...
...A PREEMPTIVE STRIKE AT NANYO...NOT A GOOD IDEA. WE KNOW TOO LITTLE. I SAY WE PULL BACK...
...AND WAIT ON THEIR NEXT MOVE. THEY POSE NO SERIOUS THREAT TO US. WE CAN AFFORD TO BE--
THAT'S BULLSHIT!!
REALITY CHECK, KAKUKA! IT'S MOVE OR LOSE--OR HAVEN'T YOU BEEN PAYING ATTENTION?!
WHY DO YOU THINK RAKUYOU SURRENDERED TO KYOSHO?! FORTUNE IS WITH KYOSHO!
WE MUST STRIKE WHILE STRONG, WHILE KYOSHO IS ASCENDANT! WOULD YOU HAVE US WAIT UNTIL THE OTHER FACTIONS GATHER STRENGTH?!
GOING OFF HALF-COCKED ISN'T THE ANSWER! "CHOOSE YOUR BATTLES." GOOD ADVICE THEN, BETTER NOW.
WHAT SAYS SOUSOU? HAS THE "INFAMOUS" ONE NOTHING TO ADD?

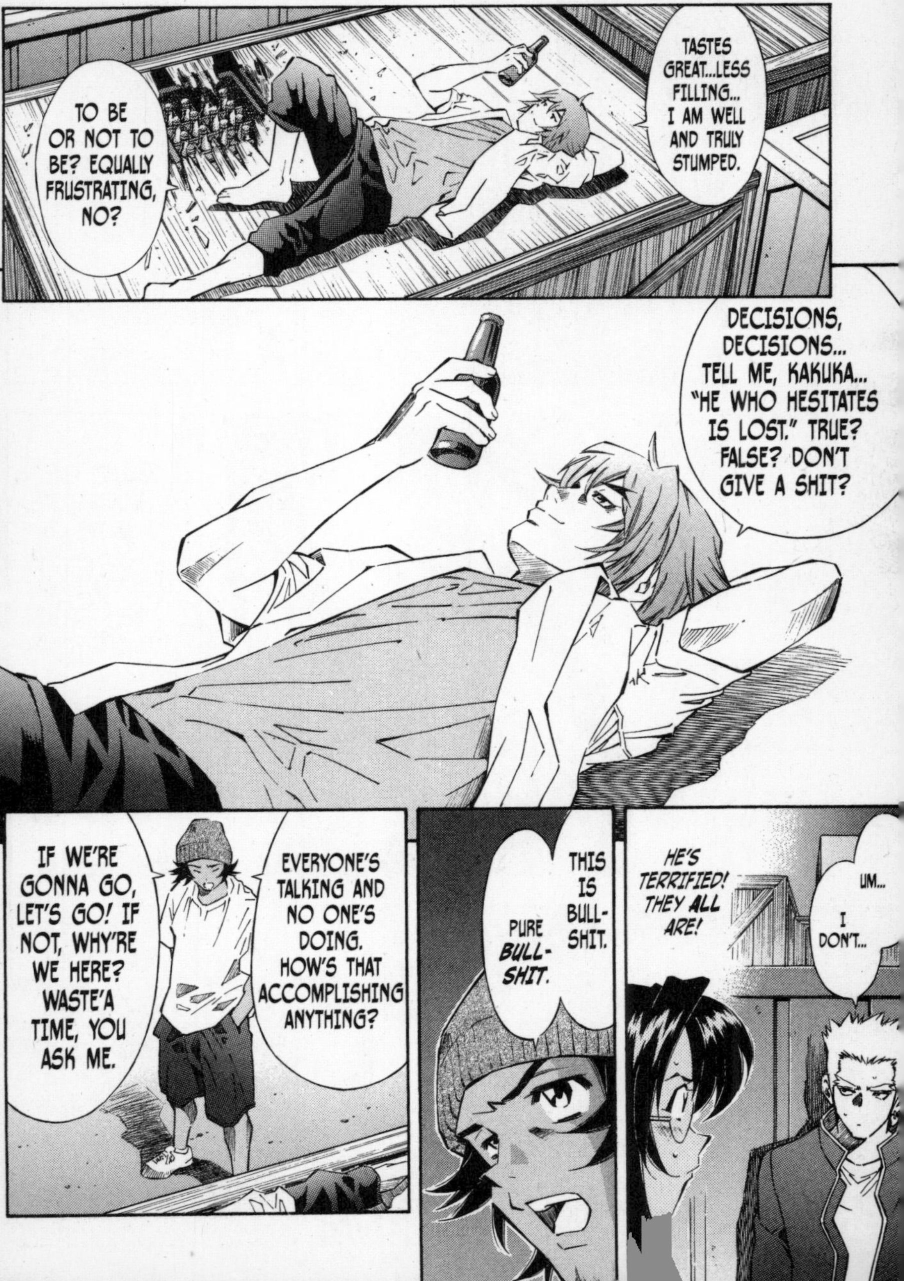
TASTES GREAT...LESS FILLING... I AM WELL AND TRULY STUMPED.
TO BE OR NOT TO BE? EQUALLY FRUSTRATING, NO?
DECISIONS, DECISIONS... TELL ME, KAKUKA... "HE WHO HESITATES IS LOST." TRUE? FALSE? DON'T GIVE A SHIT?
UM... I DON'T...
HE'S TERRIFIED! THEY ALL ARE!
THIS IS BULL-SHIT.
PURE BULL-SHIT.
EVERYONE'S TALKING AND NO ONE'S DOING. HOW'S THAT ACCOMPLISHING ANYTHING?
IF WE'RE GONNA GO, LET'S GO! IF NOT, WHY'RE WE HERE? WASTE'A TIME, YOU ASK ME.

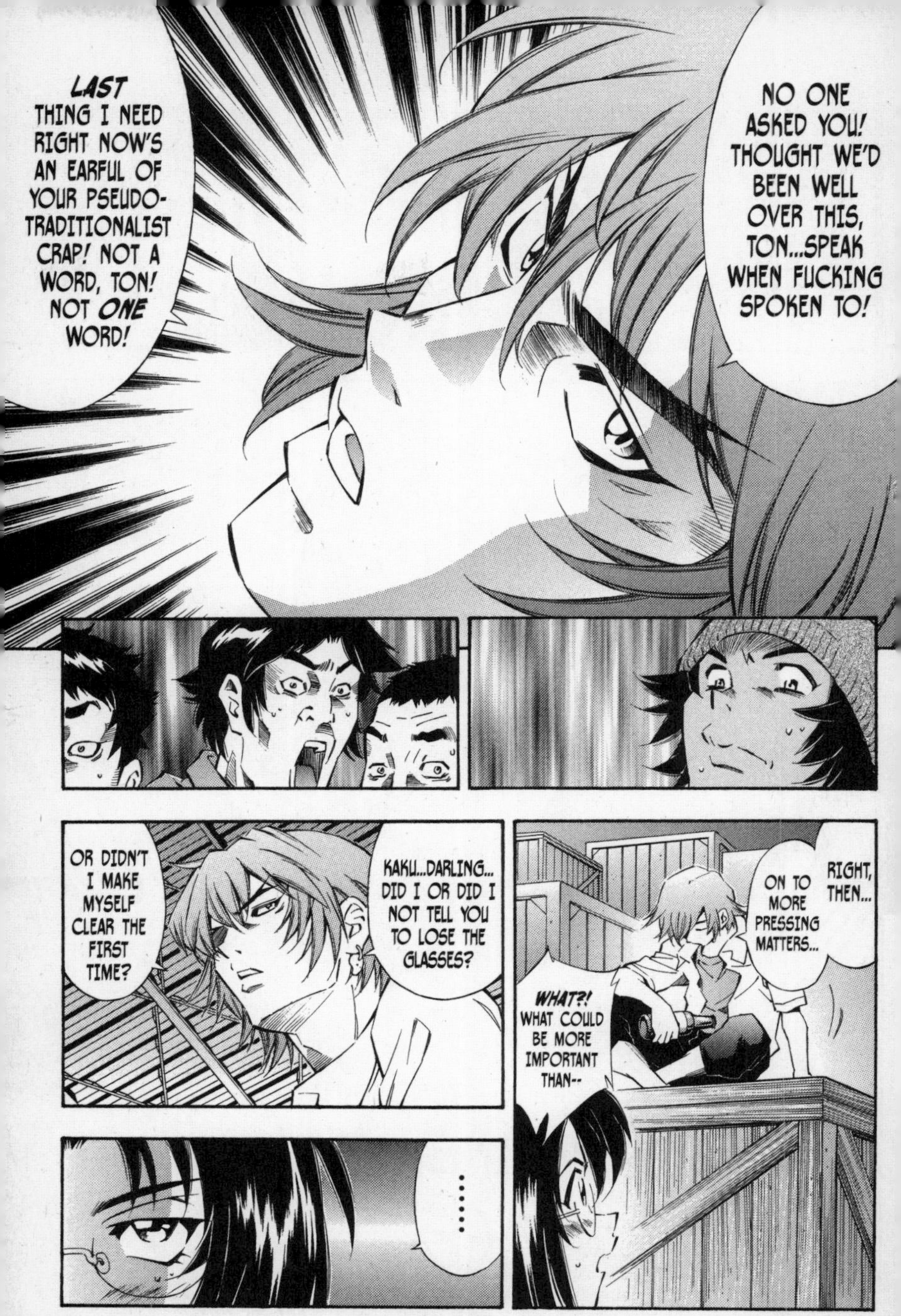
NO ONE ASKED YOU! THOUGHT WE'D BEEN WELL OVER THIS, TON...SPEAK WHEN FUCKING SPOKEN TO!
LAST THING I NEED RIGHT NOW'S AN EARFUL OF YOUR PSEUDO-TRADITIONALIST CRAP! NOT A WORD, TON! NOT ONE WORD!
RIGHT, THEN...
ON TO MORE PRESSING MATTERS...
WHAT?! WHAT COULD BE MORE IMPORTANT THAN--
KAKU...DARLING... DID I OR DID I NOT TELL YOU TO LOSE THE GLASSES?
OR DIDN'T I MAKE MYSELF CLEAR THE FIRST TIME?
......

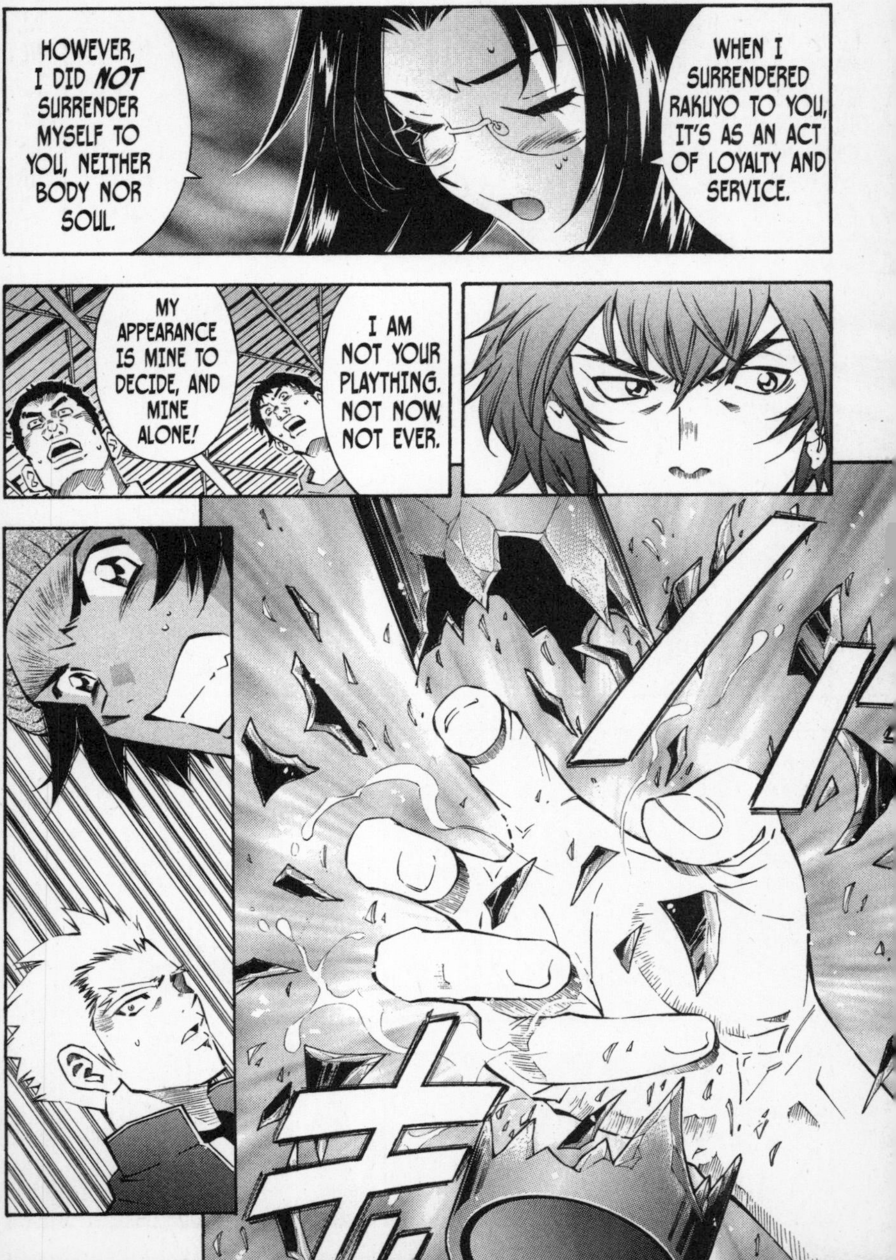
WHEN I SURRENDERED RAKUYO TO YOU, IT'S AS AN ACT OF LOYALTY AND SERVICE.
HOWEVER, I DID ***NOT*** SURRENDER MYSELF TO YOU, NEITHER BODY NOR SOUL.
I AM NOT YOUR PLAYTHING. NOT NOW, NOT EVER.
MY APPEARANCE IS MINE TO DECIDE, AND MINE ALONE!

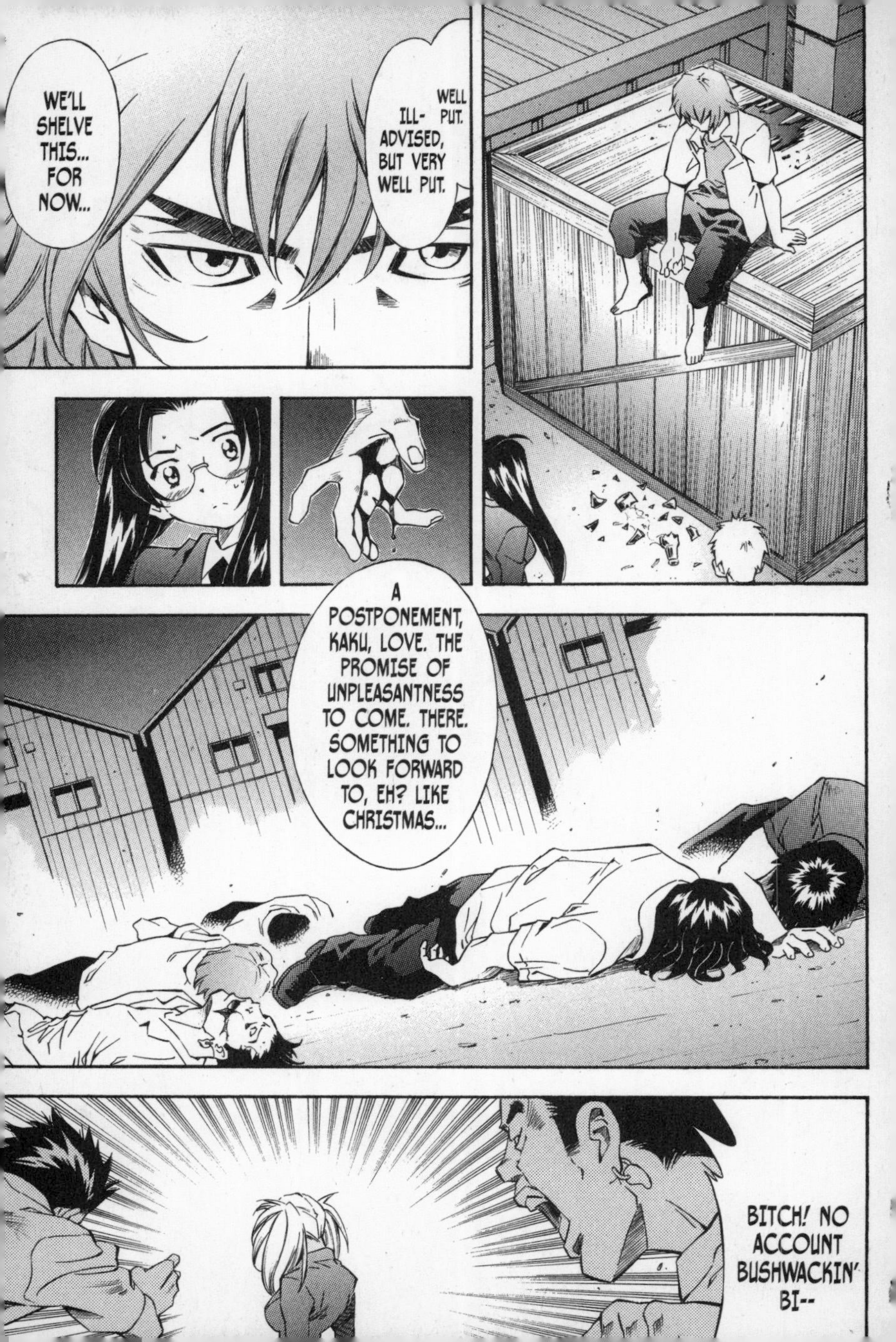
WELL PUT. ILL-ADVISED, BUT VERY WELL PUT.
WE'LL SHELVE THIS... FOR NOW...
A POSTPONEMENT, KAKU, LOVE. THE PROMISE OF UNPLEASANTNESS TO COME. THERE. SOMETHING TO LOOK FORWARD TO, EH? LIKE CHRISTMAS...
BITCH! NO ACCOUNT BUSHWACKIN' BI--

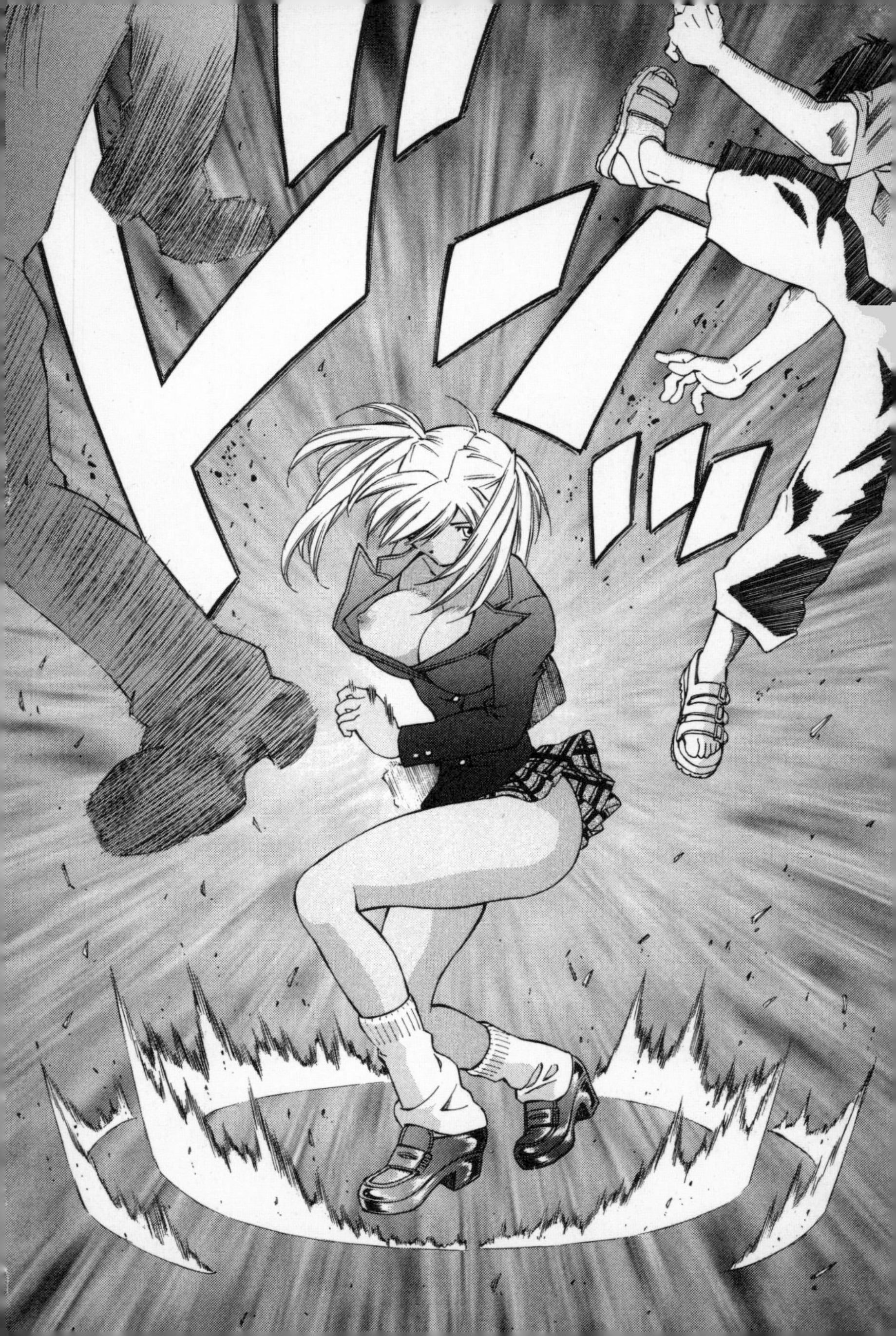

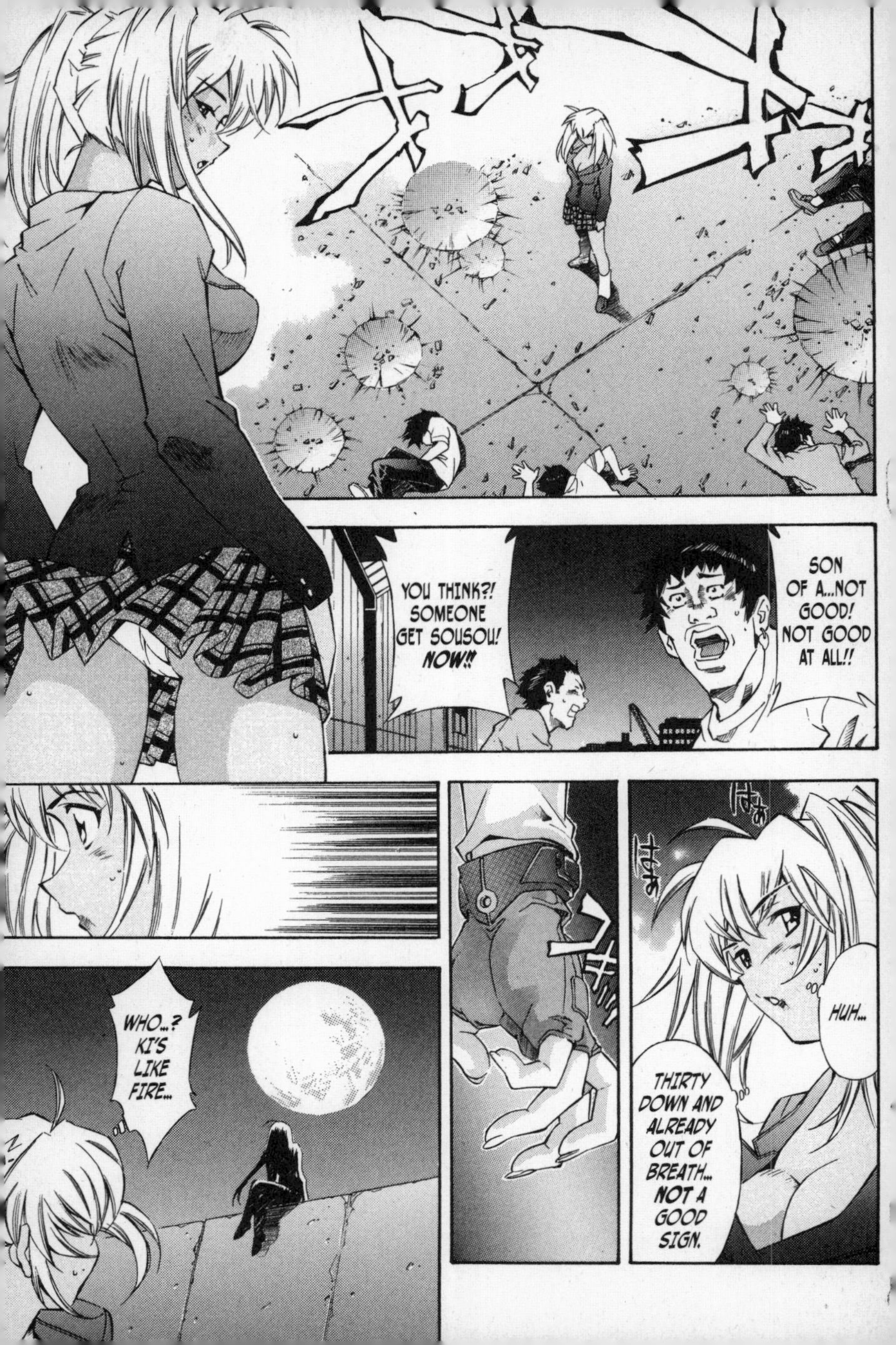
SON OF A...NOT GOOD! NOT GOOD AT ALL!!
YOU THINK?! SOMEONE GET SOUSOU! NOW!!
HUH...
THIRTY DOWN AND ALREADY OUT OF BREATH... NOT A GOOD SIGN.
WHO...? KI'S LIKE FIRE...

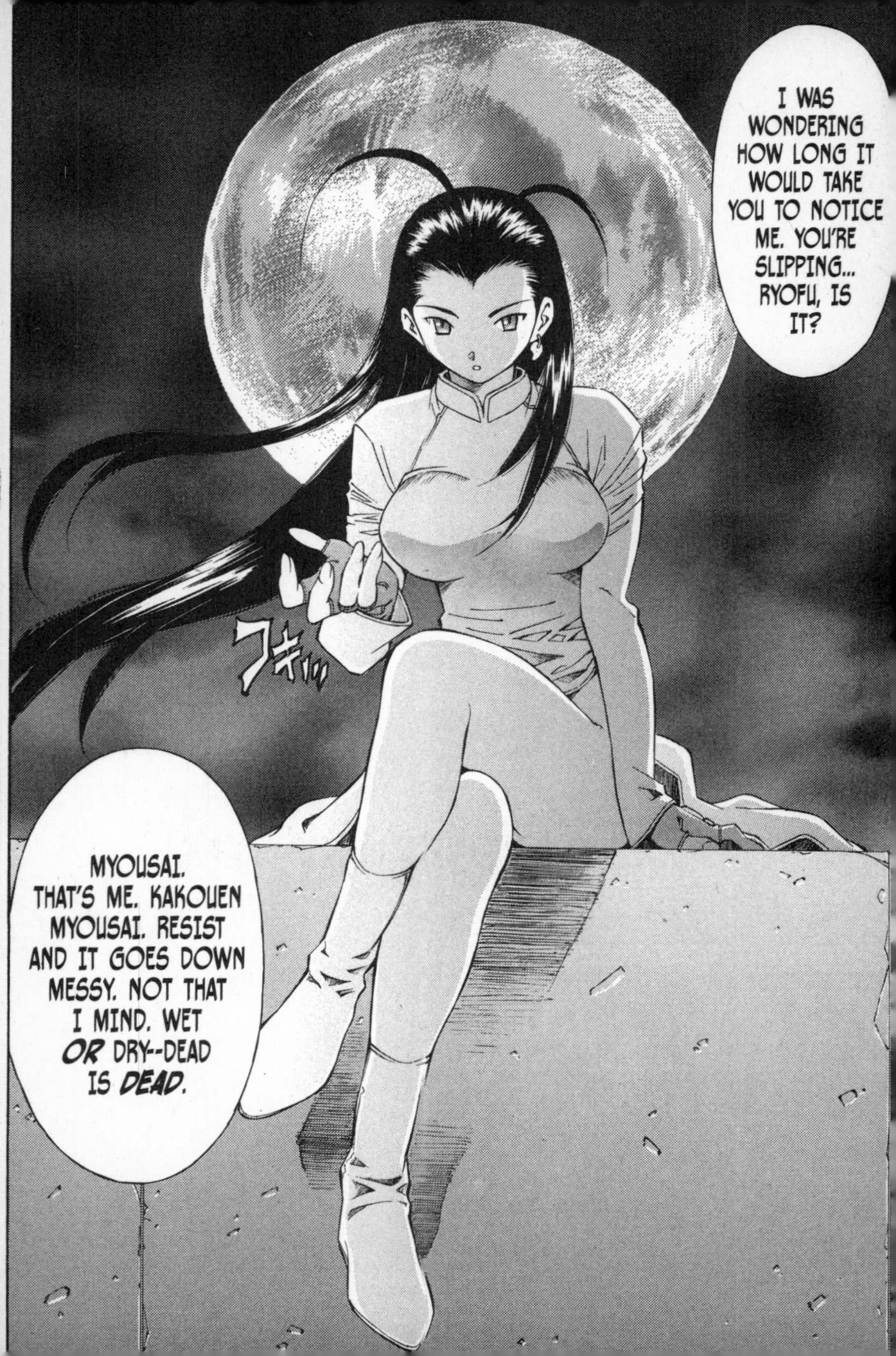
I WAS WONDERING HOW LONG IT WOULD TAKE YOU TO NOTICE ME. YOU'RE SLIPPING... RYOFU, IS IT?
MYOUSAI. THAT'S ME. KAKOUEN MYOUSAI. RESIST AND IT GOES DOWN MESSY. NOT THAT I MIND. WET *OR* DRY--DEAD IS *DEAD*.

KAKOUEN MYOUSAI

ONE OF THE ERA'S GREATEST WARRIORS, AND HIS LOYALTY TO SOUSOU WAS UNWAVERING. KAKOUEN AND SOUSOU BONDED AS YOUTHS--AND THE BLOOD BOND ONLY STRENGTHENED AS THEY GREW OLDER. KAKOUEN WOULD, AT TIMES, TAKE ON SOUSOU'S SINS. HE WOULD ESSENTIALLY ATONE BY PROXY FOR SOUSOU'S TRANSGRESSIONS. SWIFT AND MERCILESS, KAKOUEN WAS WIDELY FEARED AND RESPECTED.

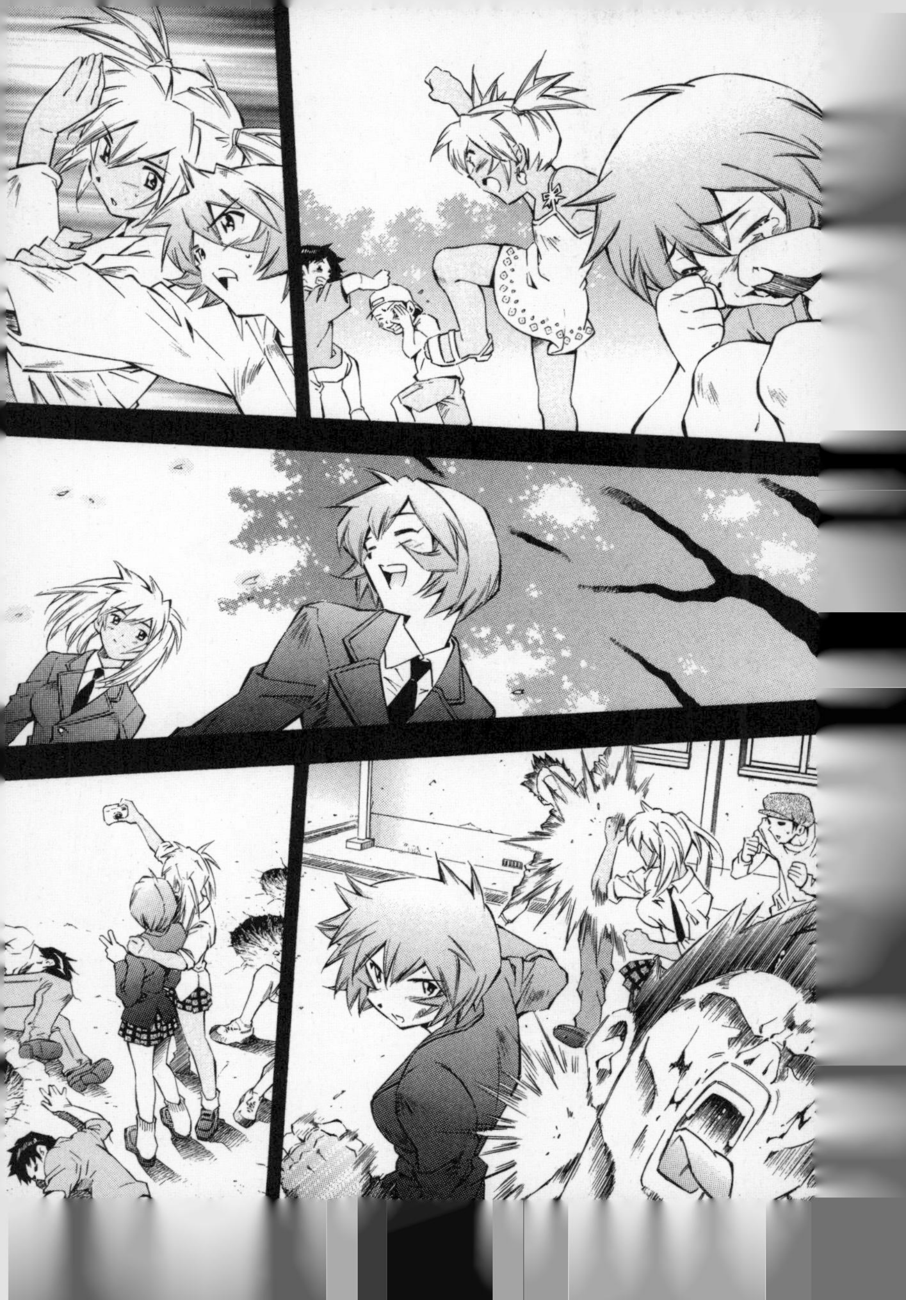

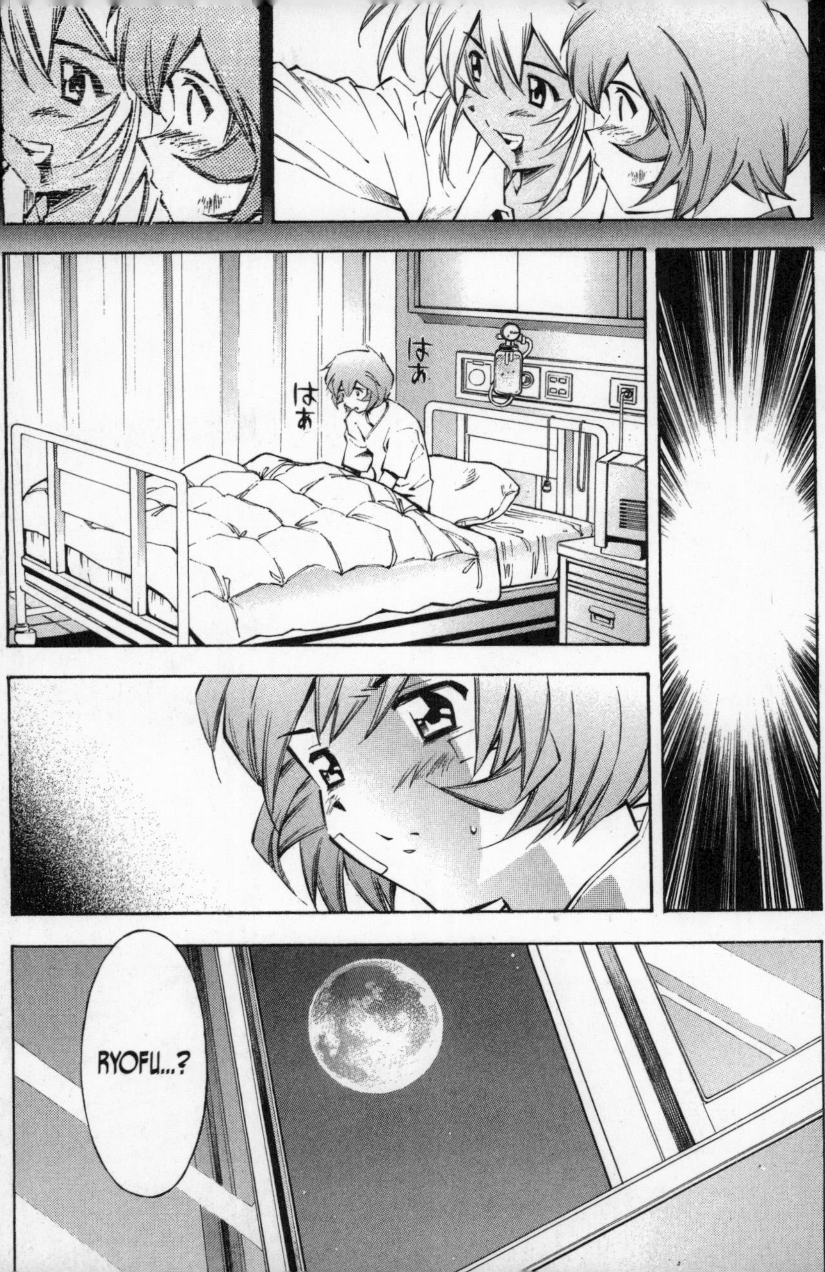
はぁ
はぁ
RYOFU...?

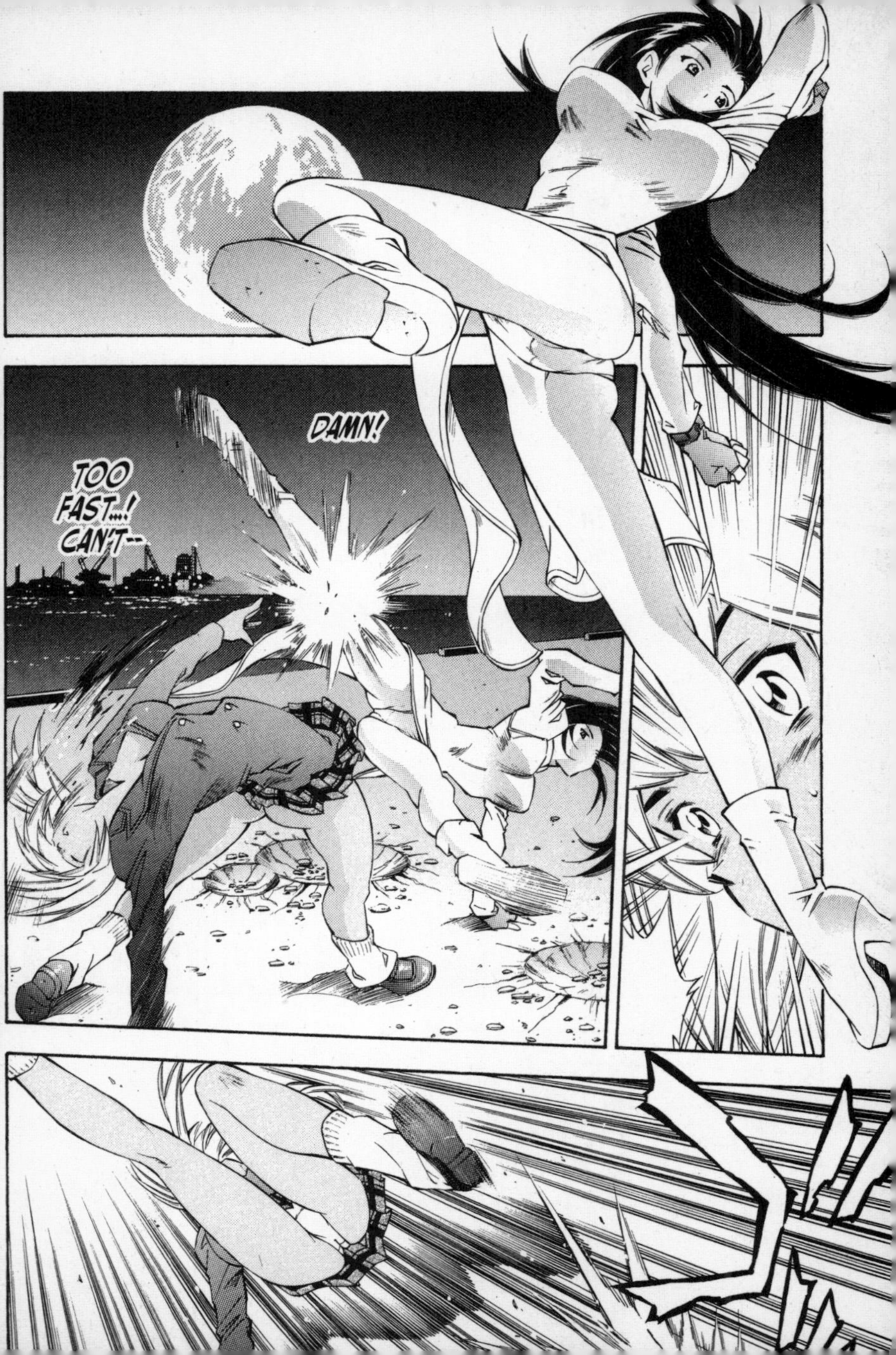
DAMN!
TOO FAST...! CAN'T--

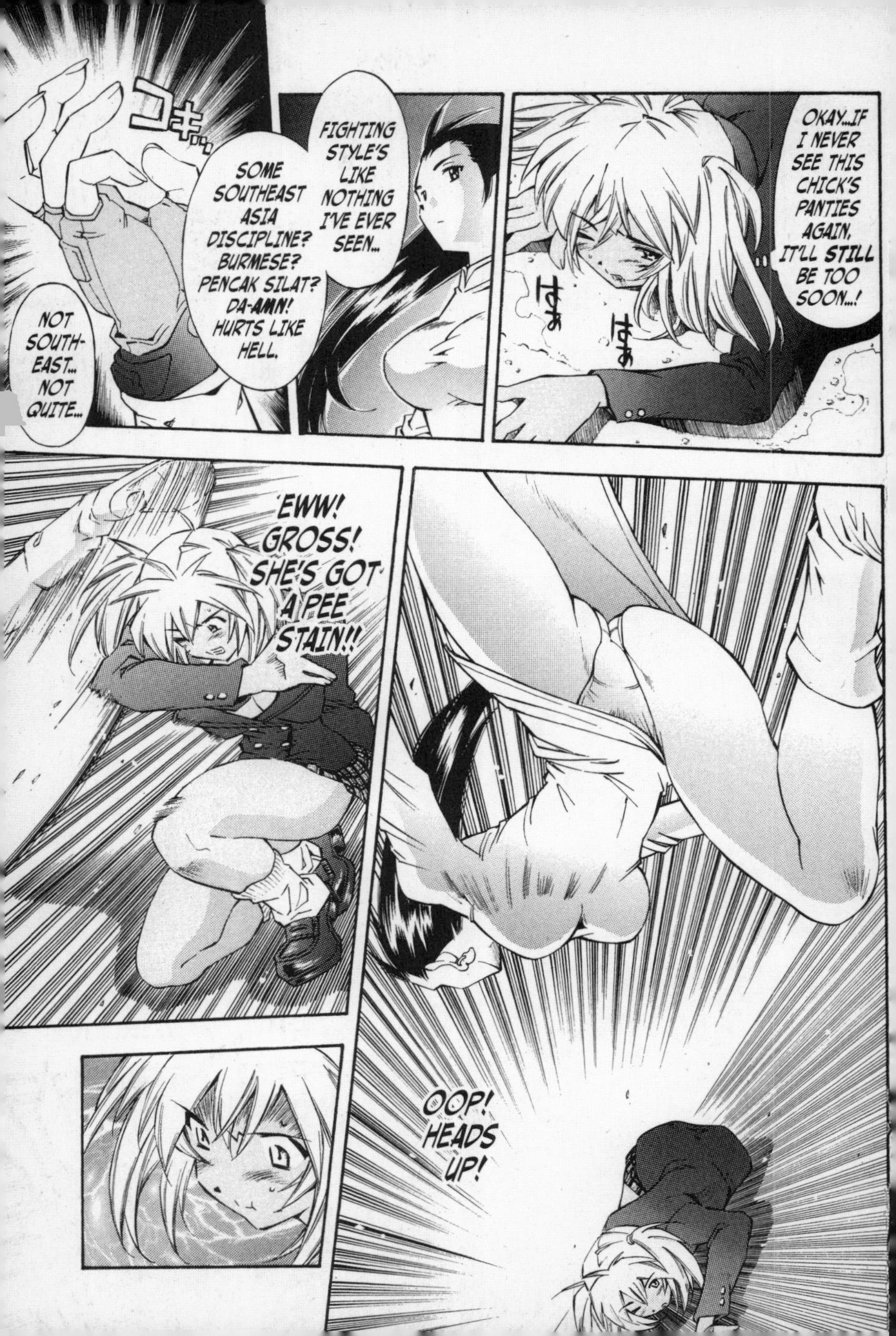
はぁ はぁ
OKAY...IF I NEVER SEE THIS CHICK'S PANTIES AGAIN, IT'LL **STILL** BE TOO SOON...!
FIGHTING STYLE'S LIKE NOTHING I'VE EVER SEEN...
コキ...
SOME SOUTHEAST ASIA DISCIPLINE? BURMESE? PENCAK SILAT? DA-**AMN**! HURTS LIKE HELL.
NOT SOUTH-EAST... NOT QUITE...
OOP! HEADS UP!
EWW! GROSS! SHE'S GOT A PEE STAIN!!

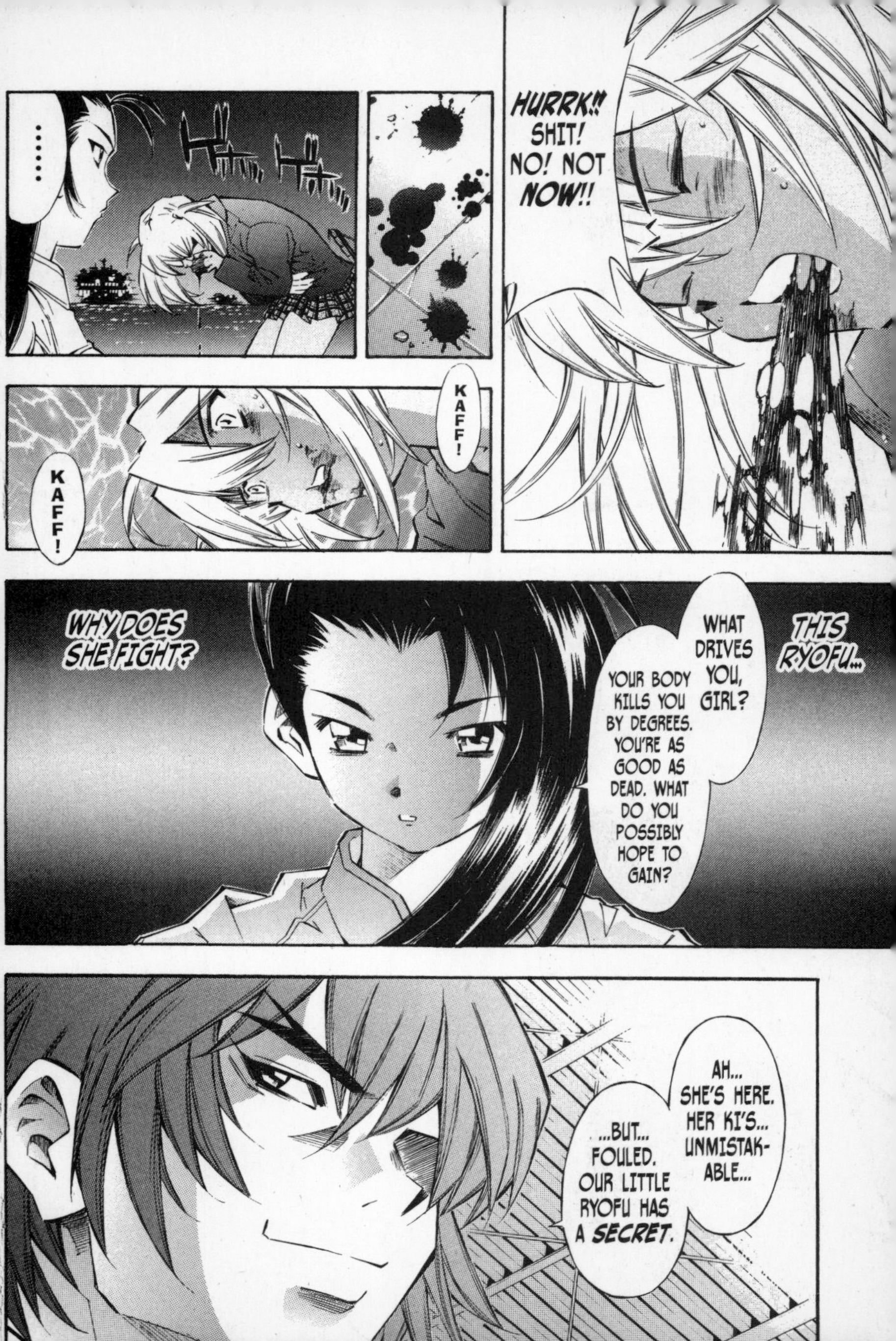
HURRK!! SHIT! NO! NOT NOW!!
......
KAFF!
KAFF!
THIS RYOFU...
WHAT DRIVES YOU, GIRL?
YOUR BODY KILLS YOU BY DEGREES. YOU'RE AS GOOD AS DEAD. WHAT DO YOU POSSIBLY HOPE TO GAIN?
WHY DOES SHE FIGHT?
AH... SHE'S HERE. HER KI'S... UNMISTAK-ABLE...
...BUT... FOULED. OUR LITTLE RYOFU HAS A SECRET.

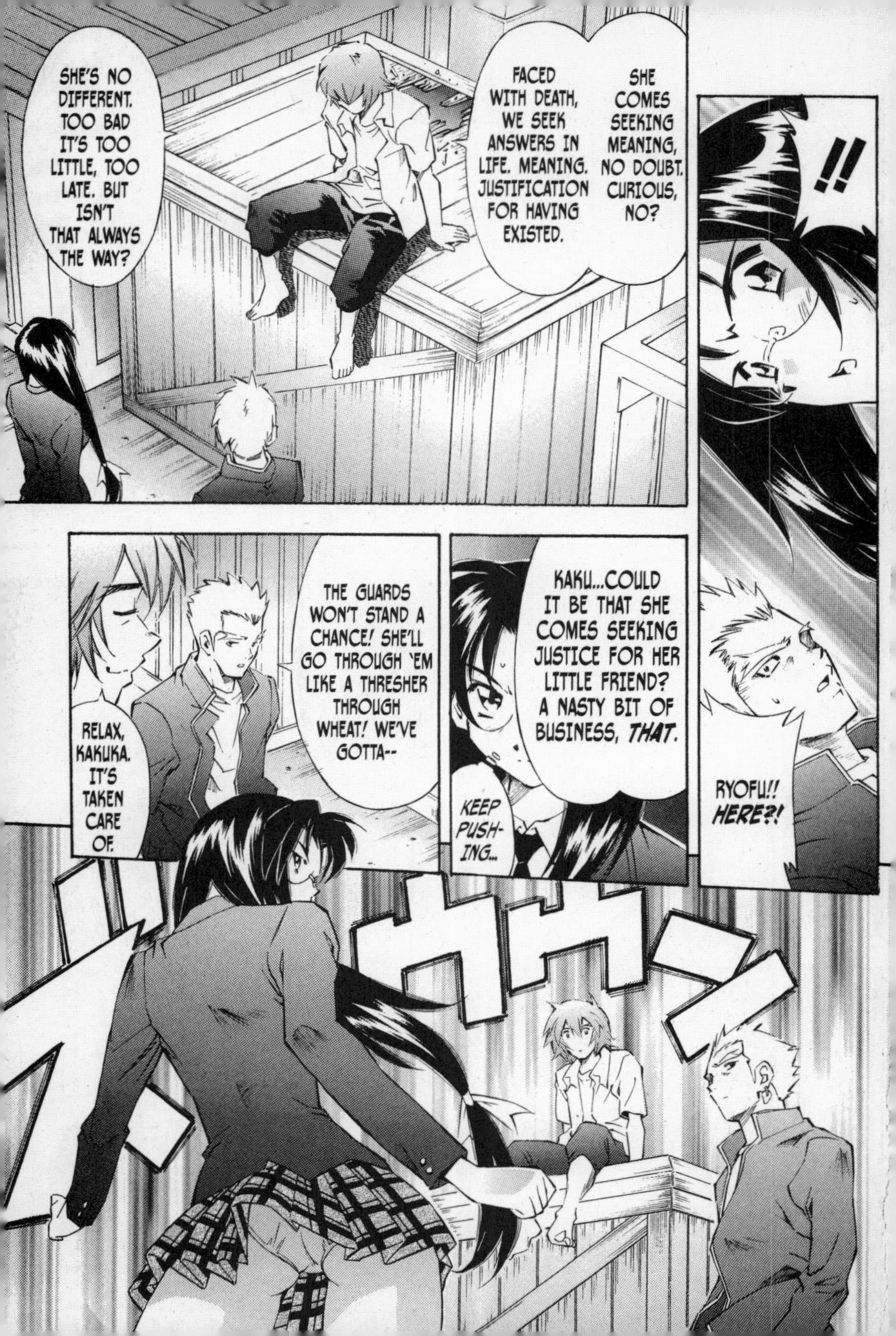
SHE COMES SEEKING MEANING, NO DOUBT. CURIOUS, NO?
FACED WITH DEATH, WE SEEK ANSWERS IN LIFE. MEANING. JUSTIFICATION FOR HAVING EXISTED.
SHE'S NO DIFFERENT. TOO BAD IT'S TOO LITTLE, TOO LATE. BUT ISN'T THAT ALWAYS THE WAY?
!!
RYOFU!! *HERE?!*
KAKU...COULD IT BE THAT SHE COMES SEEKING JUSTICE FOR HER LITTLE FRIEND? A NASTY BIT OF BUSINESS, *THAT*.
KEEP PUSH-ING...
THE GUARDS WON'T STAND A CHANCE! SHE'LL GO THROUGH 'EM LIKE A THRESHER THROUGH WHEAT! WE'VE GOTTA--
RELAX, KAKUKA. IT'S TAKEN CARE OF.

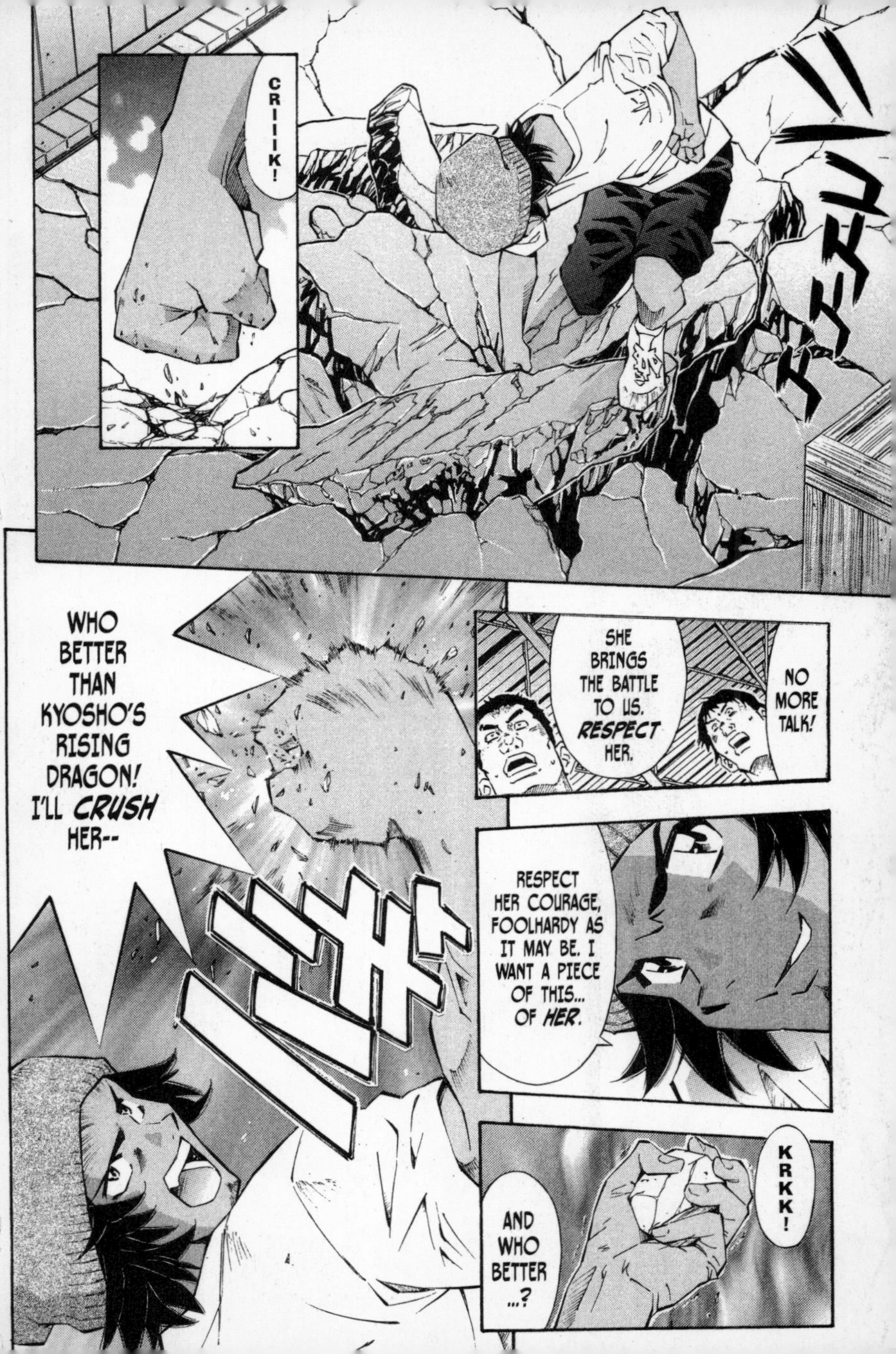
CRIIIK!
NO MORE TALK!
SHE BRINGS THE BATTLE TO US. RESPECT HER.
RESPECT HER COURAGE, FOOLHARDY AS IT MAY BE. I WANT A PIECE OF THIS... OF HER.
KRKK!
AND WHO BETTER ...?
WHO BETTER THAN KYOSHO'S RISING DRAGON! I'LL CRUSH HER--

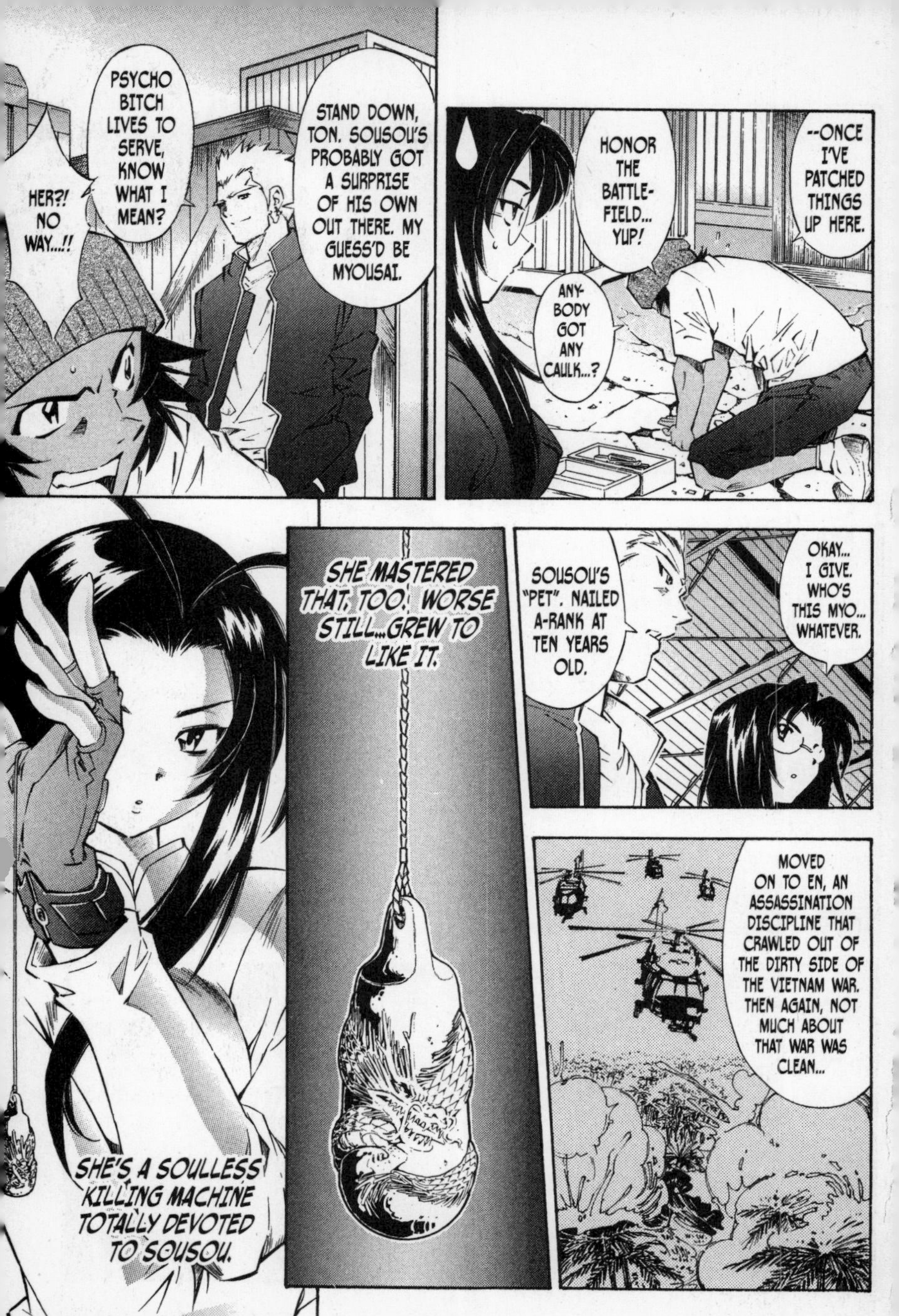
--ONCE I'VE PATCHED THINGS UP HERE.
HONOR THE BATTLE-FIELD... YUP!
ANY-BODY GOT ANY CAULK...?
STAND DOWN, TON. SOUSOU'S PROBABLY GOT A SURPRISE OF HIS OWN OUT THERE. MY GUESS'D BE MYOUSAI.
PSYCHO BITCH LIVES TO SERVE, KNOW WHAT I MEAN?
HER?! NO WAY...!!
OKAY... I GIVE. WHO'S THIS MYO... WHATEVER.
SOUSOU'S "PET". NAILED A-RANK AT TEN YEARS OLD.
MOVED ON TO EN, AN ASSASSINATION DISCIPLINE THAT CRAWLED OUT OF THE DIRTY SIDE OF THE VIETNAM WAR. THEN AGAIN, NOT MUCH ABOUT THAT WAR WAS CLEAN...
SHE MASTERED THAT, TOO. WORSE STILL...GREW TO LIKE IT.
SHE'S A SOULLESS KILLING MACHINE TOTALLY DEVOTED TO SOUSOU.

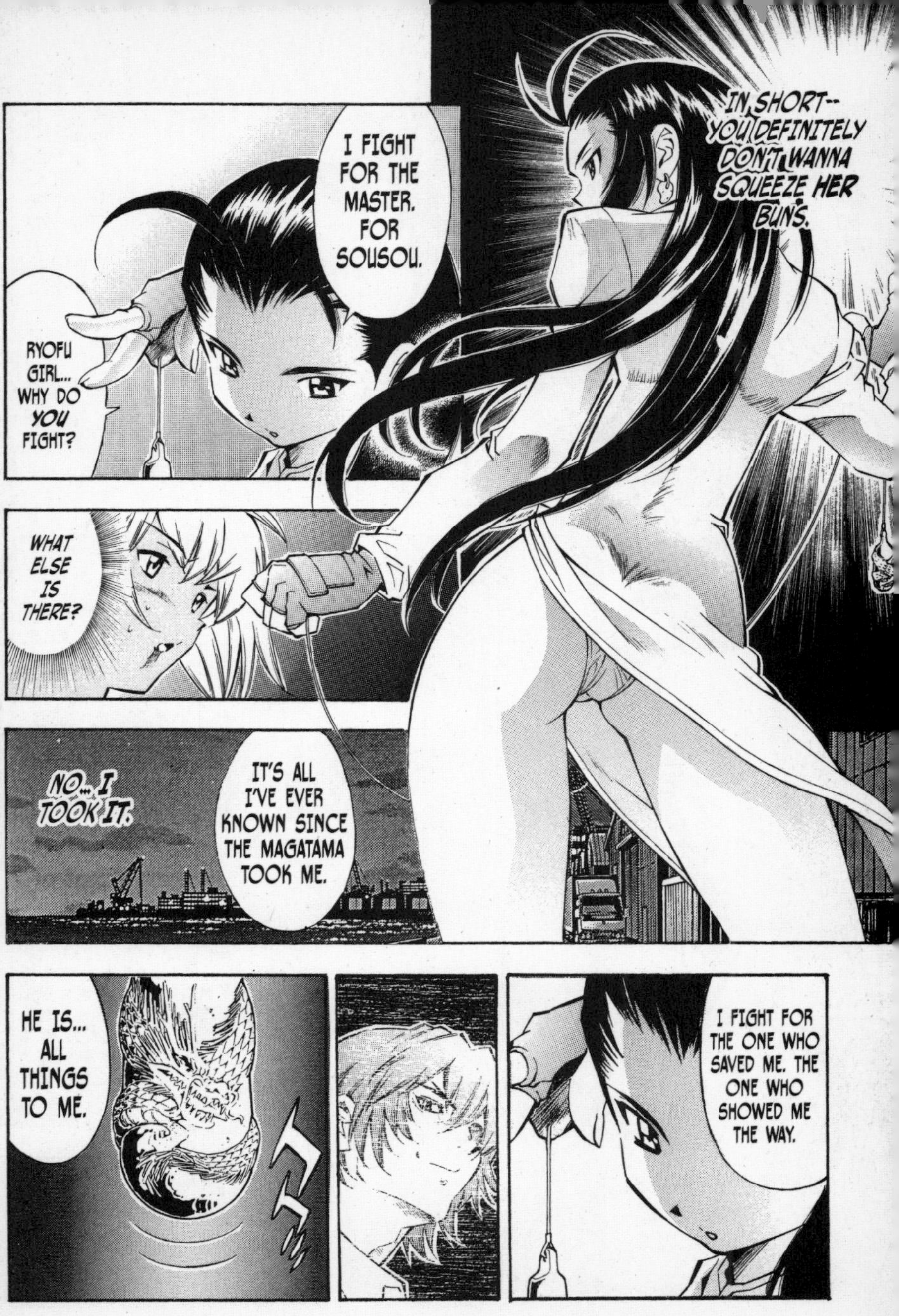
IN SHORT-- YOU DEFINITELY DON'T WANNA SQUEEZE HER BUNS.
I FIGHT FOR THE MASTER. FOR SOUSOU.
RYOFU GIRL... WHY DO YOU FIGHT?
WHAT ELSE IS THERE?
IT'S ALL I'VE EVER KNOWN SINCE THE MAGATAMA TOOK ME.
NO... I TOOK IT.
I FIGHT FOR THE ONE WHO SAVED ME. THE ONE WHO SHOWED ME THE WAY.
HE IS... ALL THINGS TO ME.

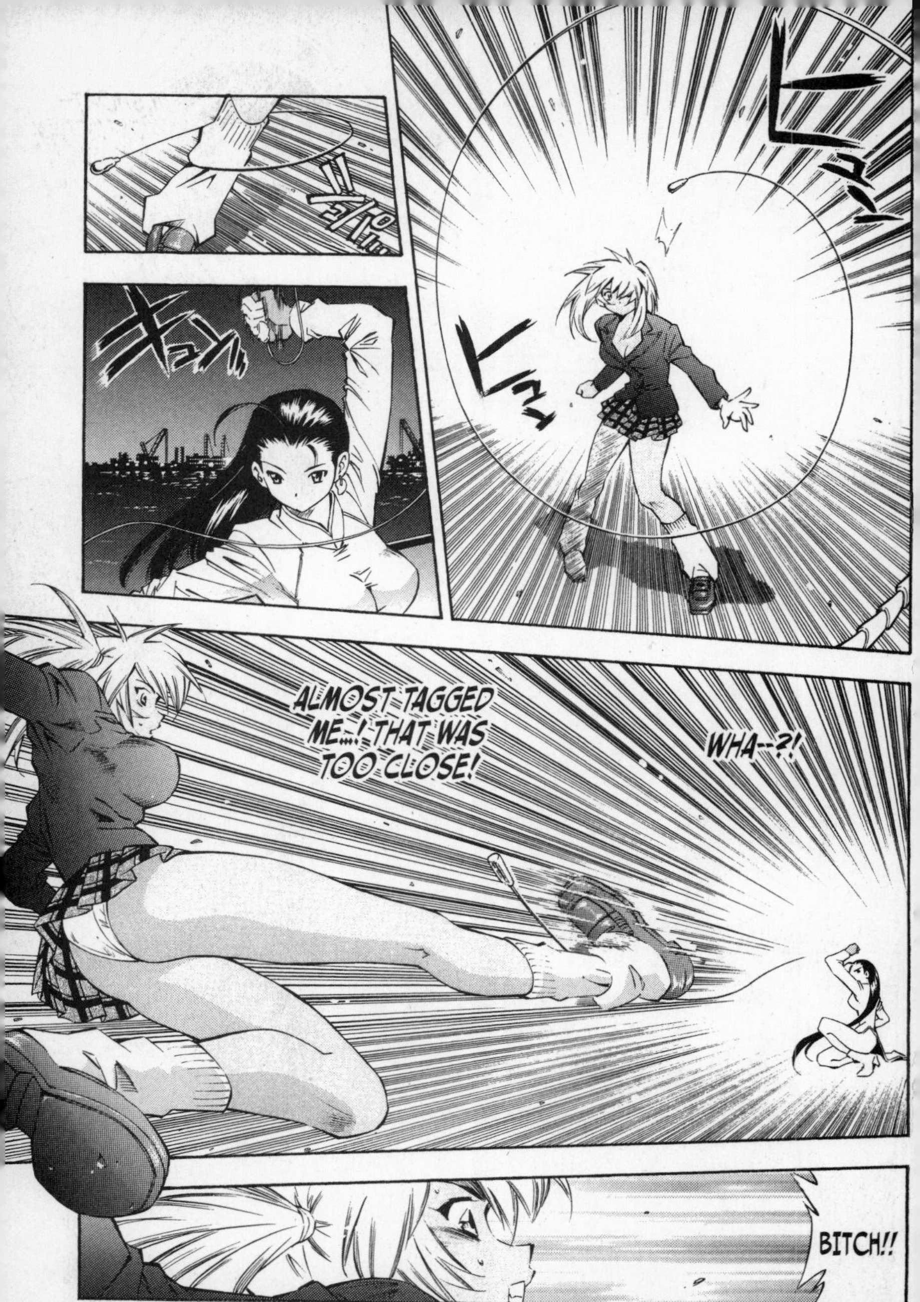
WHA--?!
ALMOST TAGGED ME...! THAT WAS TOO CLOSE!
BITCH!!

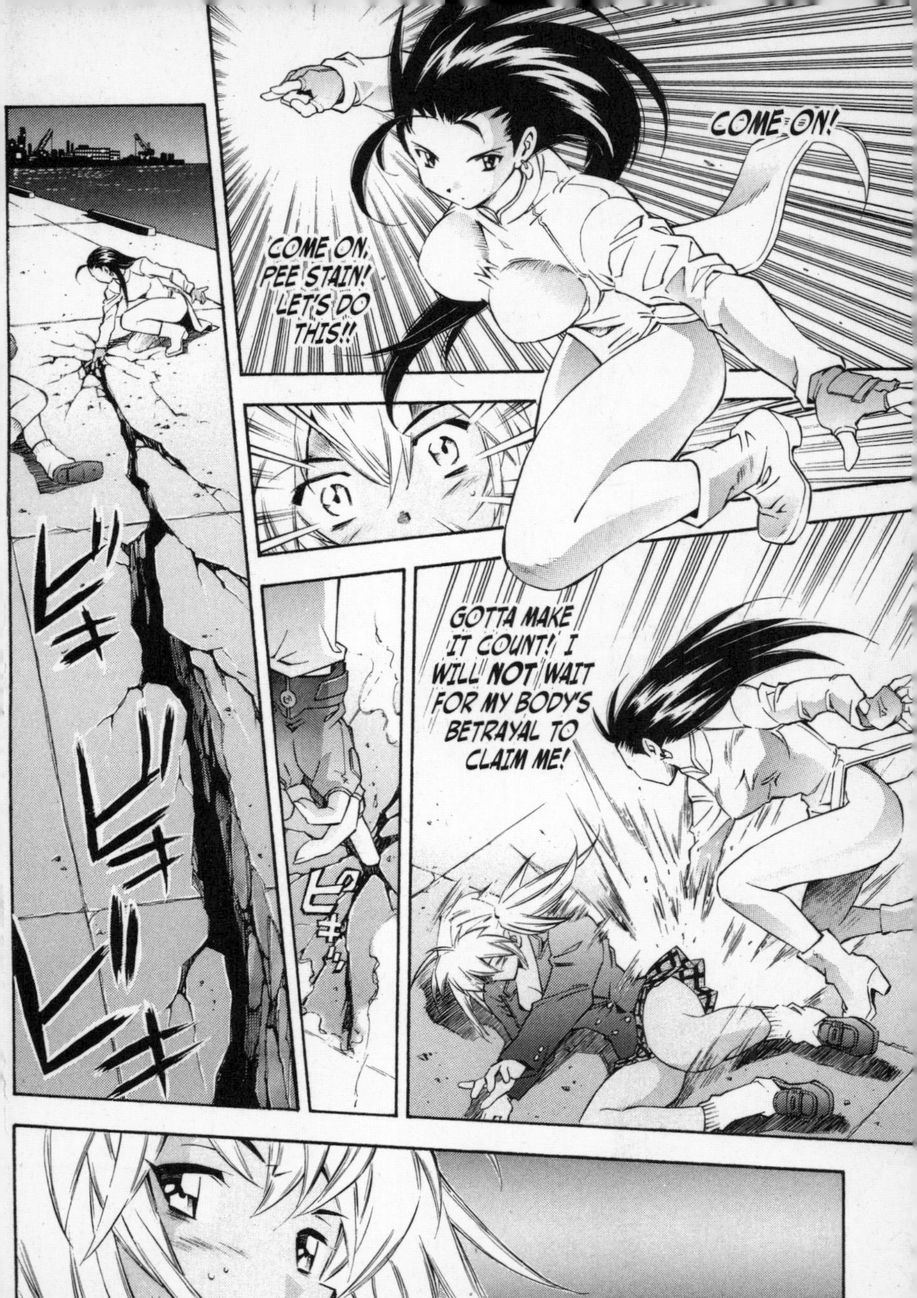

COME ON!
COME ON, PEE STAIN! LET'S DO THIS!!
GOTTA MAKE IT COUNT! I WILL NOT WAIT FOR MY BODY'S BETRAYAL TO CLAIM ME!

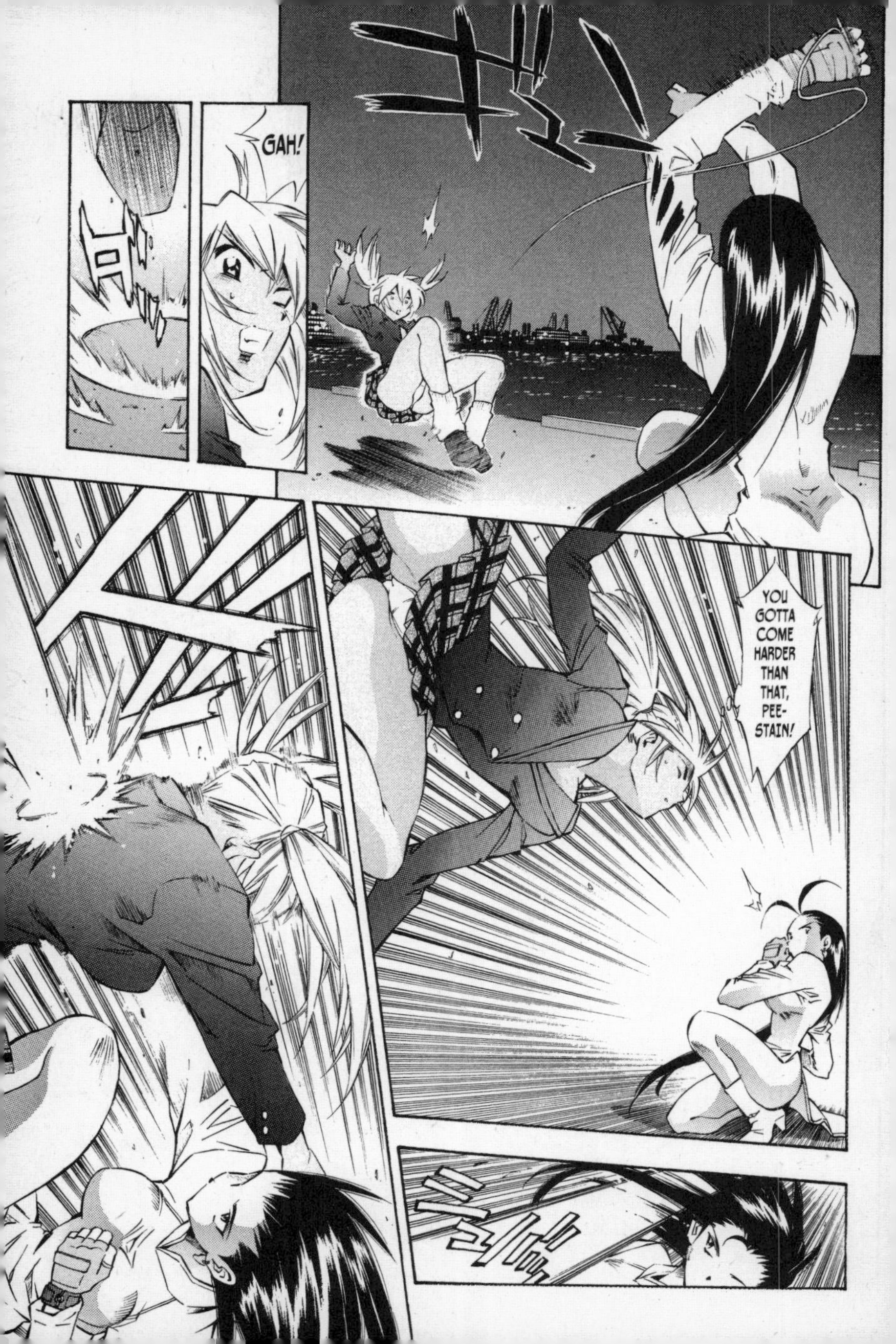
GAH!
YOU GOTTA COME HARDER THAN THAT, PEE-STAIN!

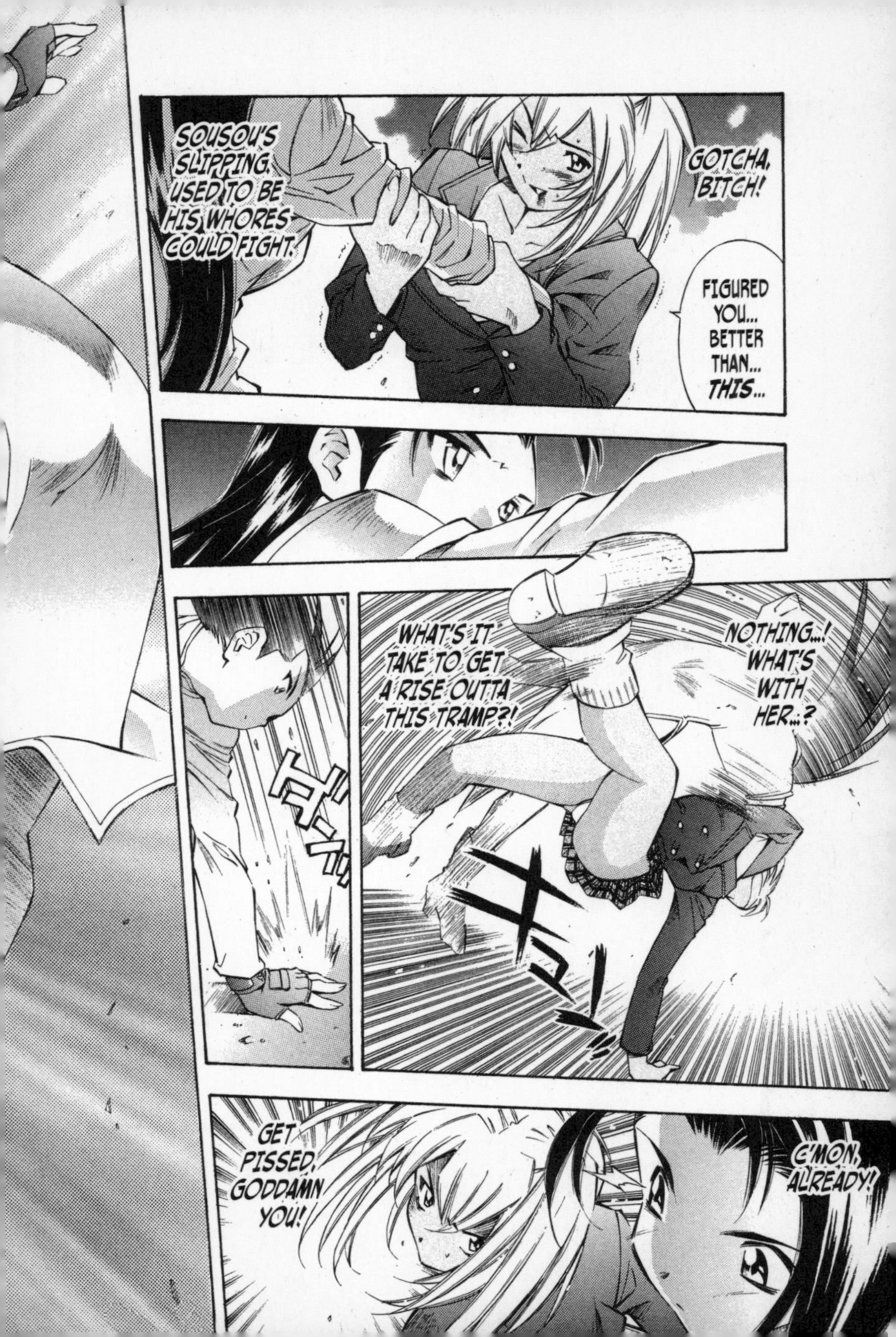
GOTCHA, BITCH!
SOUSOU'S SLIPPING. USED TO BE HIS WHORES COULD FIGHT.
FIGURED YOU... BETTER THAN... THIS...
NOTHING...! WHAT'S WITH HER...?
WHAT'S IT TAKE TO GET A RISE OUTTA THIS TRAMP?!
C'MON, ALREADY!
GET PISSED, GODDAMN YOU!

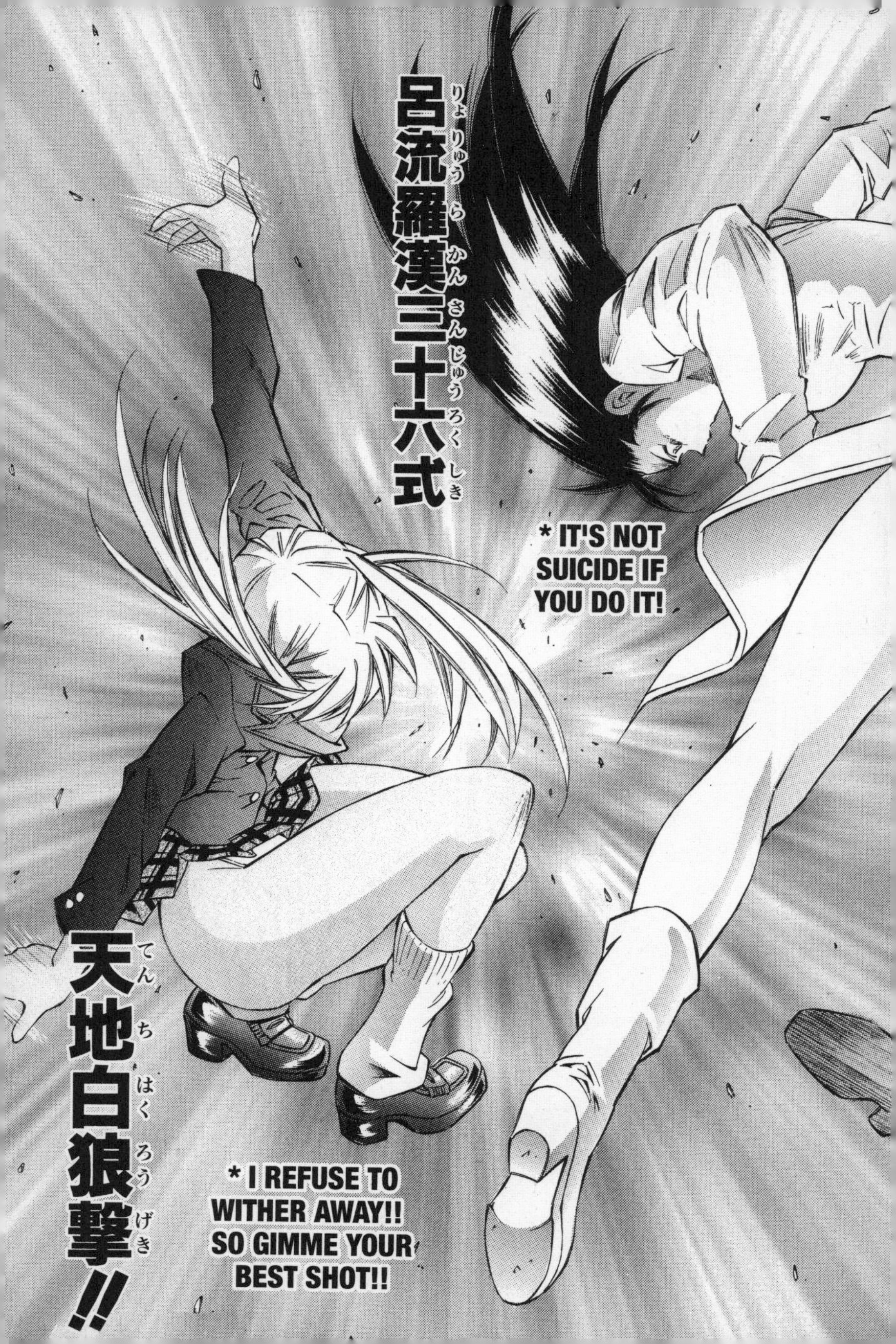
呂流羅漢三十六式
りょりゅうらかんさんじゅうろくしき
* IT'S NOT SUICIDE IF YOU DO IT!
天地白狼撃!!
てんちはくろうげき
* I REFUSE TO WITHER AWAY!! SO GIMME YOUR BEST SHOT!!

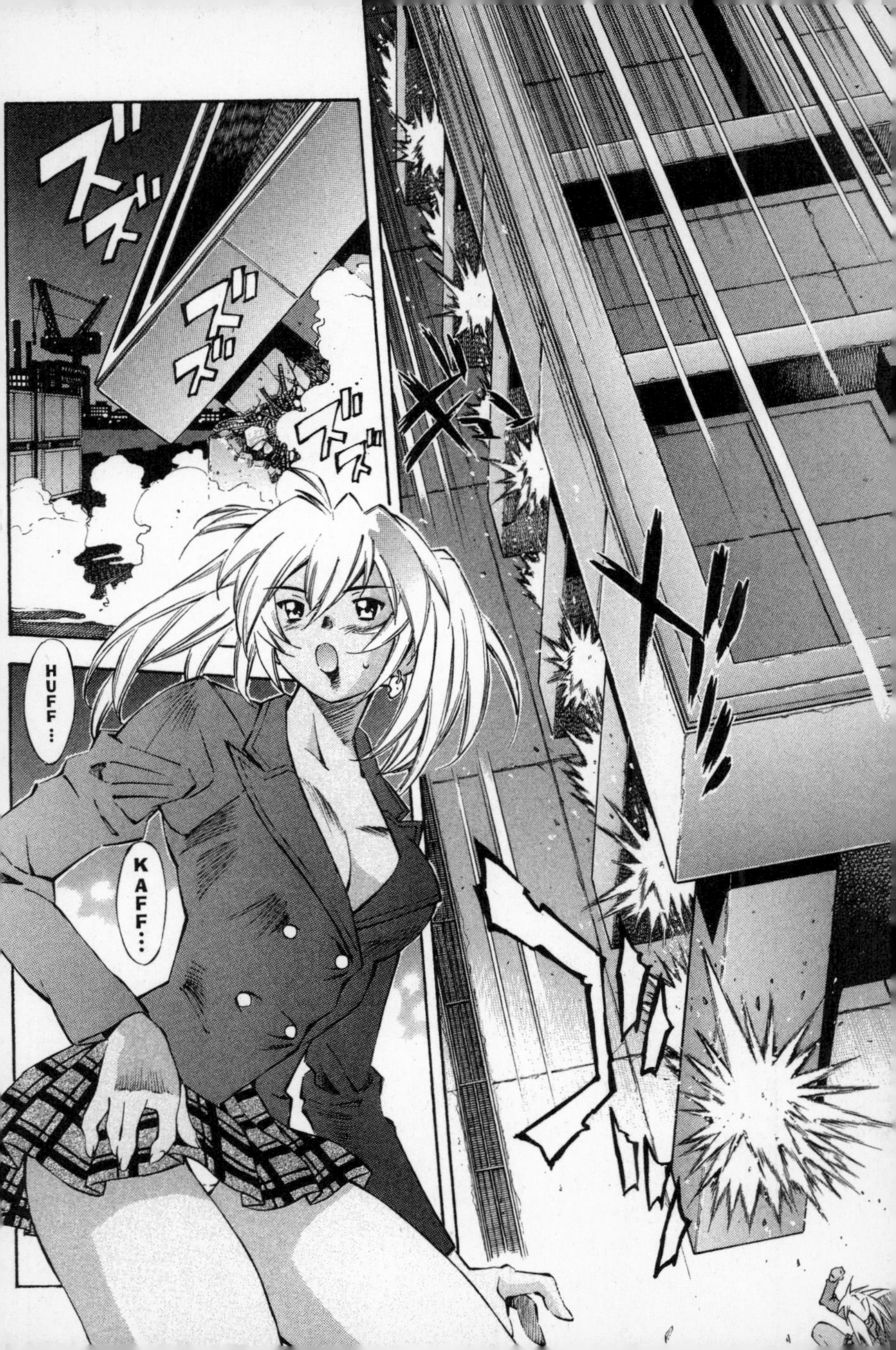
HUFF...
KAFF...

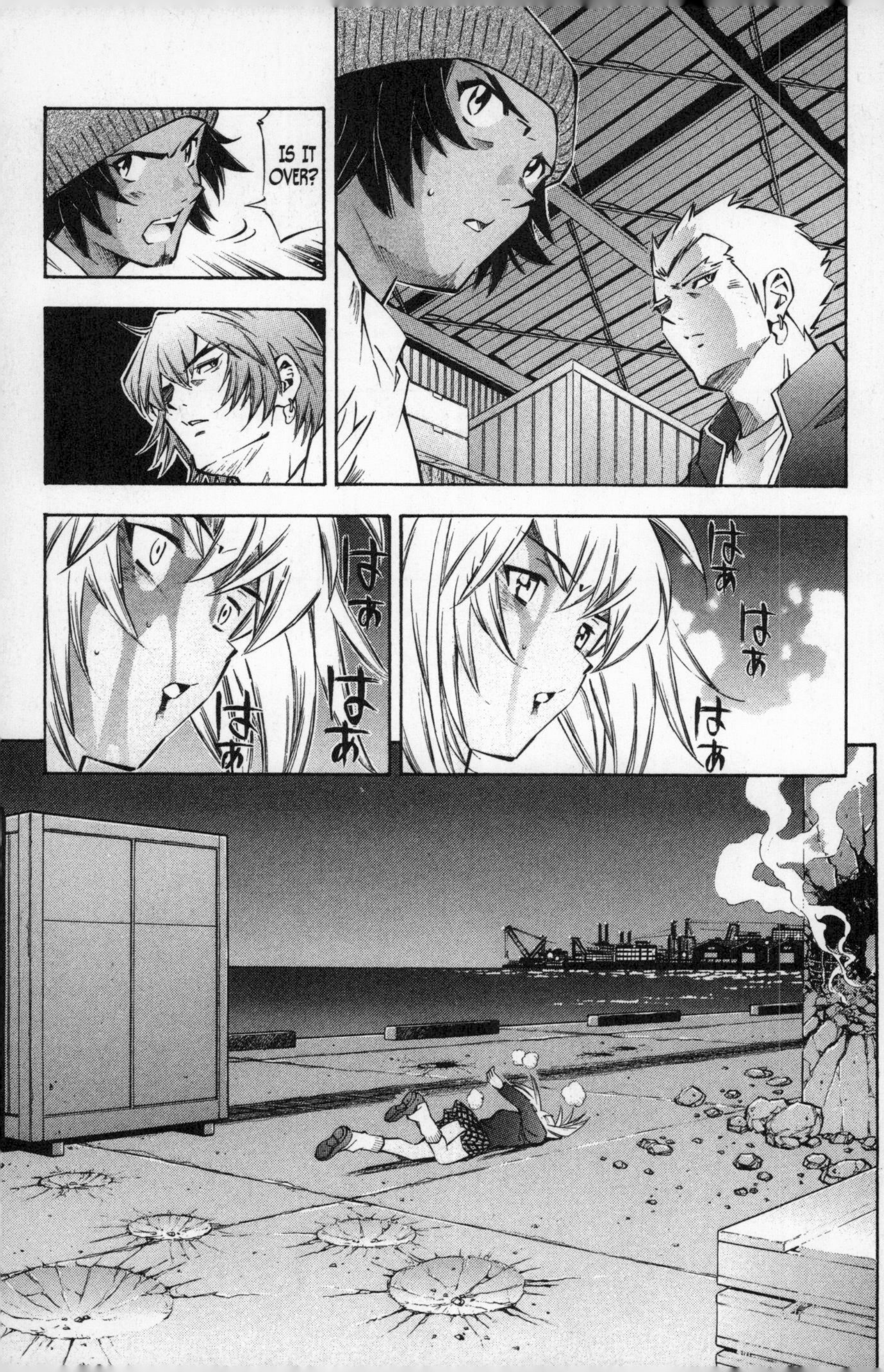
IS IT OVER?
はぁ はぁ はぁ
はぁ はぁ はぁ

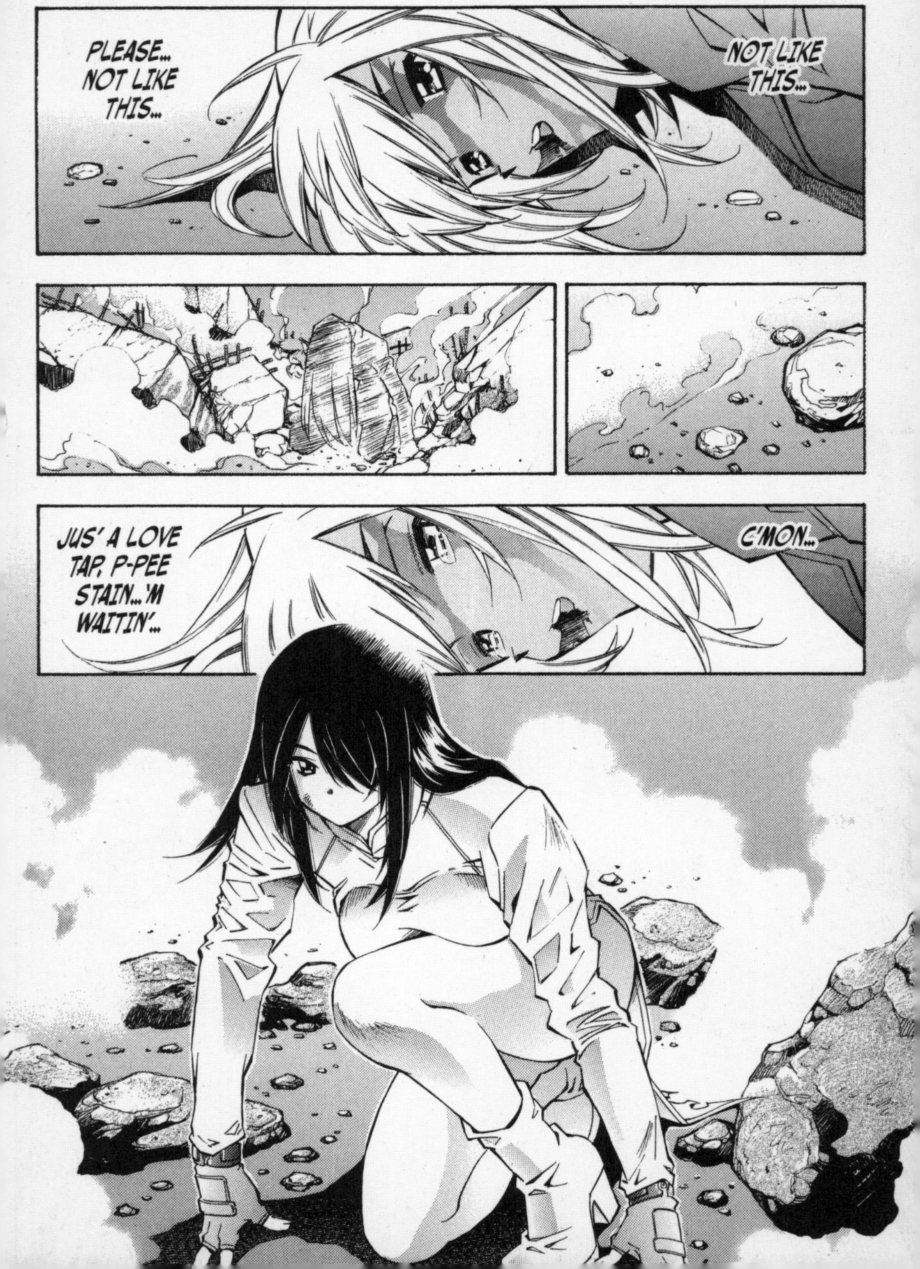
NOT LIKE THIS...
PLEASE... NOT LIKE THIS...
C'MON...
JUS' A LOVE TAP, P-PEE STAIN...'M WAITIN'...

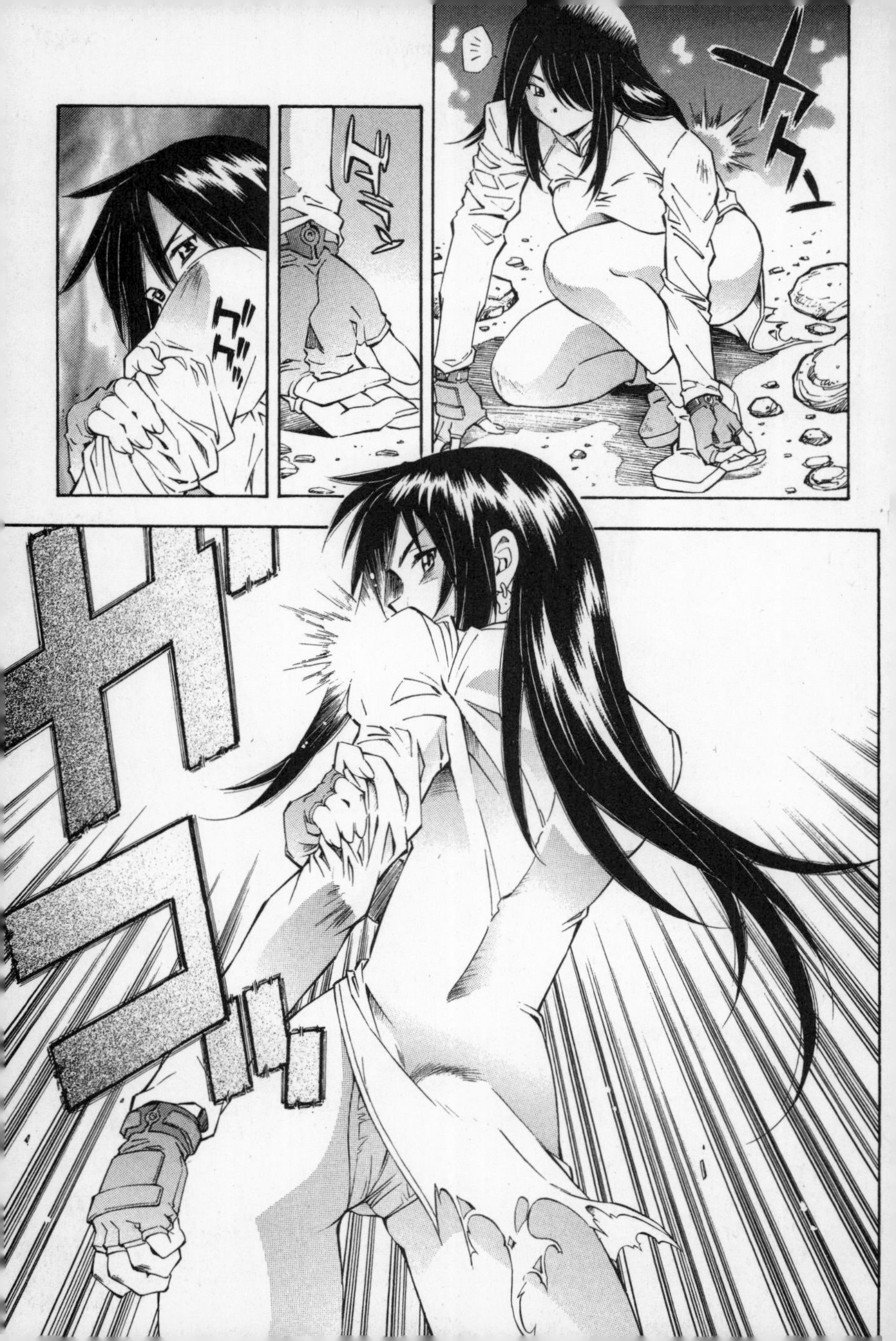
ゴゴ

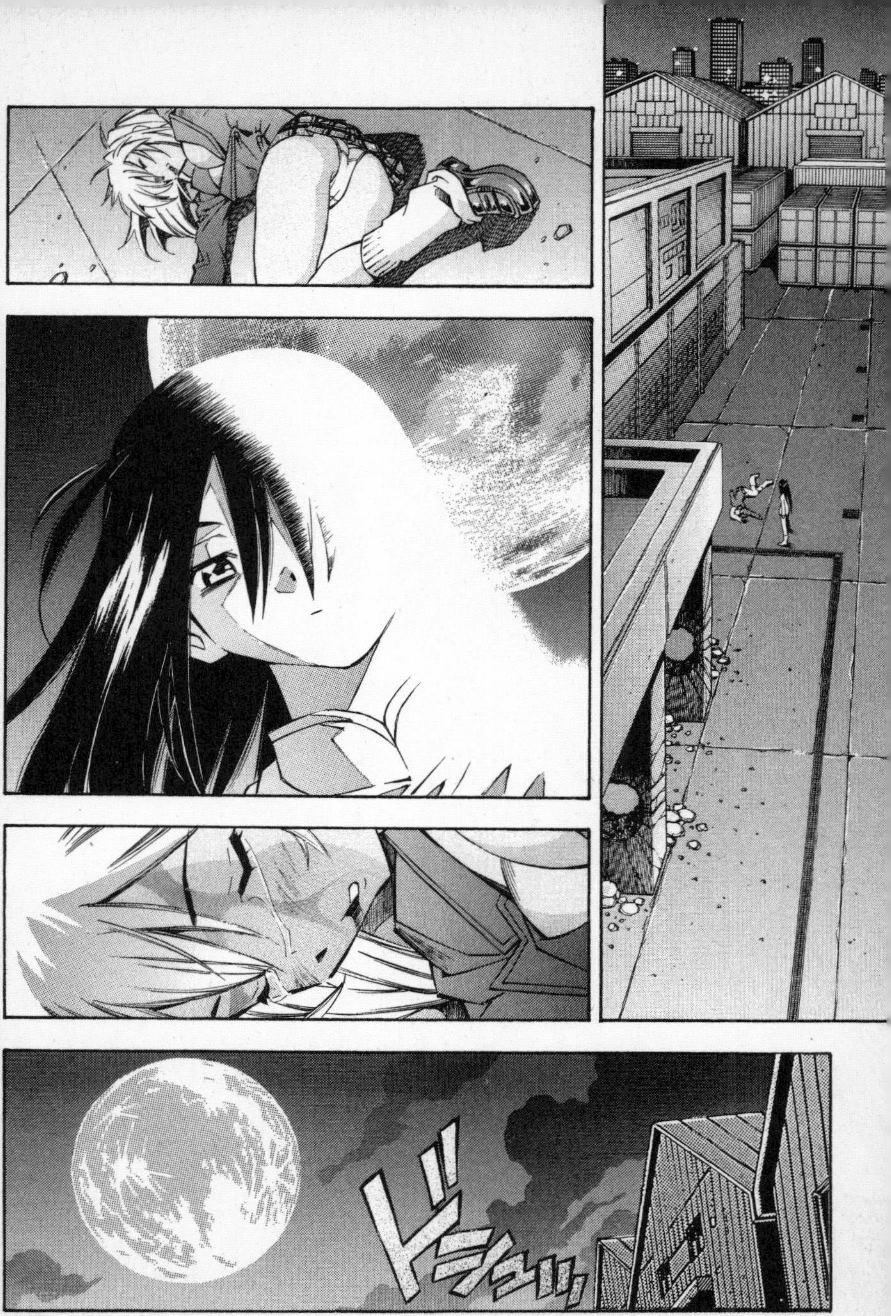
ドシュッ

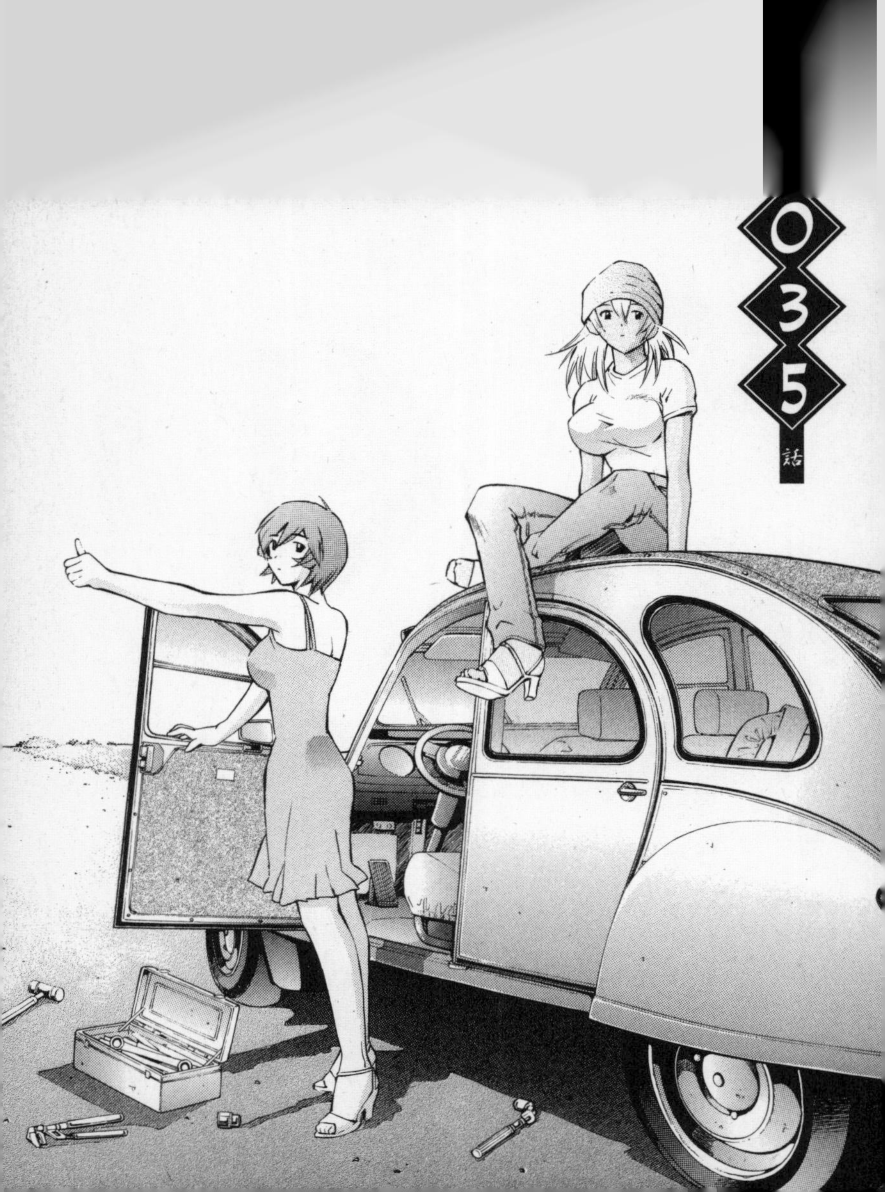
035
話

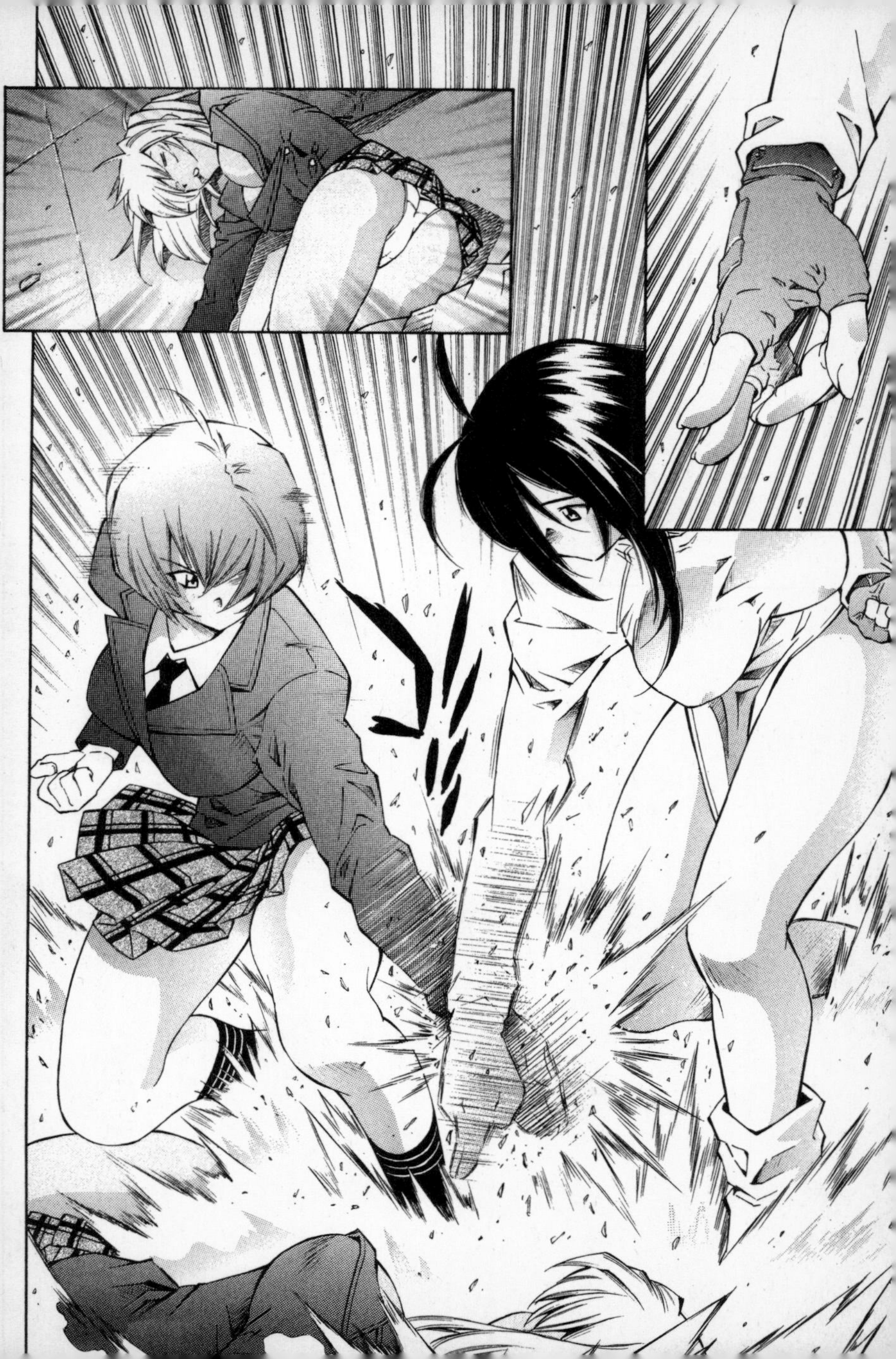

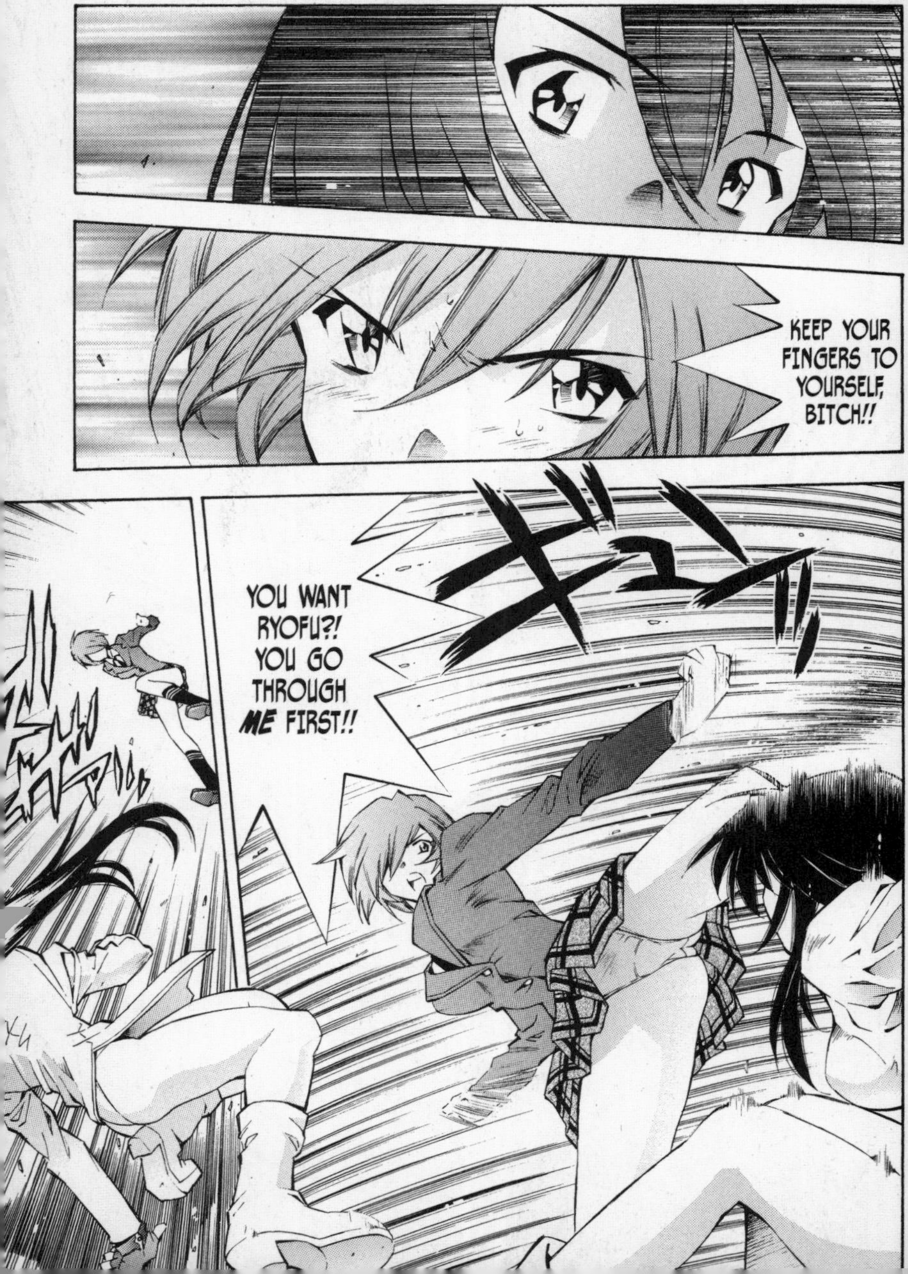
KEEP YOUR FINGERS TO YOURSELF, BITCH!!
YOU WANT RYOFU?! YOU GO THROUGH ME FIRST!!

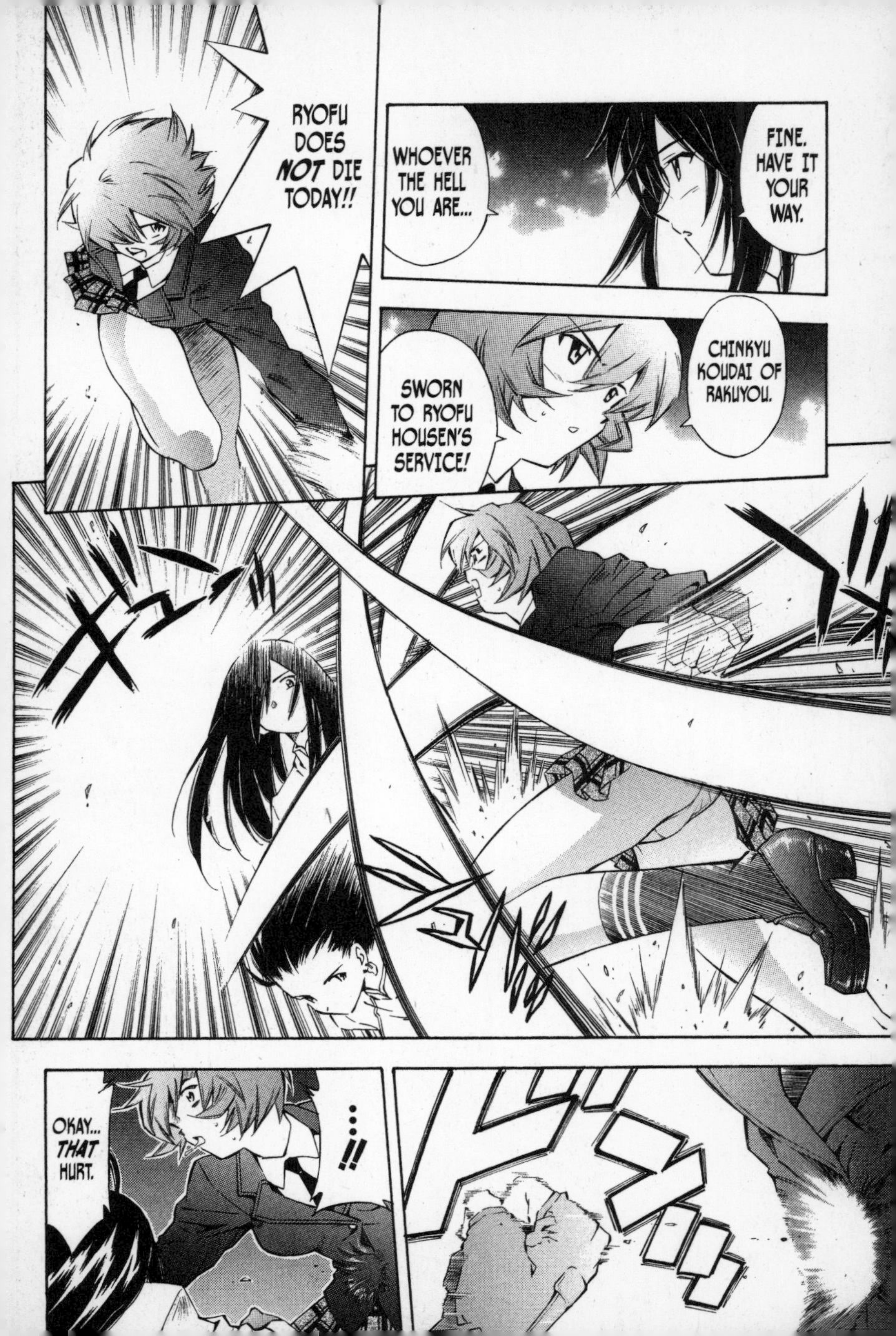
FINE. HAVE IT YOUR WAY.
WHOEVER THE HELL YOU ARE...
CHINKYU KOUDAI OF RAKUYOU.
SWORN TO RYOFU HOUSEN'S SERVICE!
RYOFU DOES NOT DIE TODAY!!
...!!
OKAY... THAT HURT.

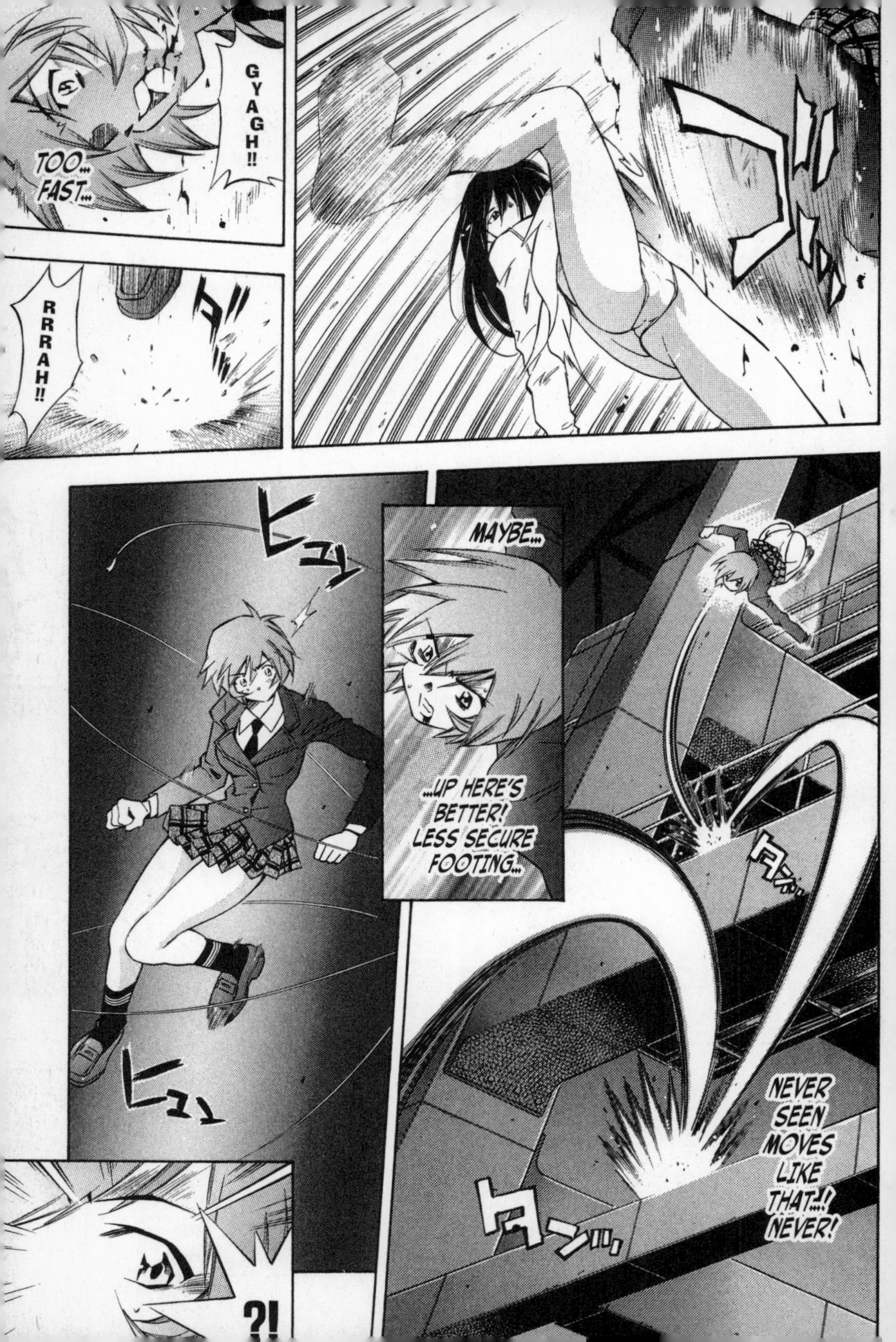
GYAGH!!
TOO... FAST...
RRRAH!!
ダッ
MAYBE...
...UP HERE'S BETTER! LESS SECURE FOOTING...
タンッ
タンッ
NEVER SEEN MOVES LIKE THAT...! NEVER!
ヒュッ
ヒュッ
?!

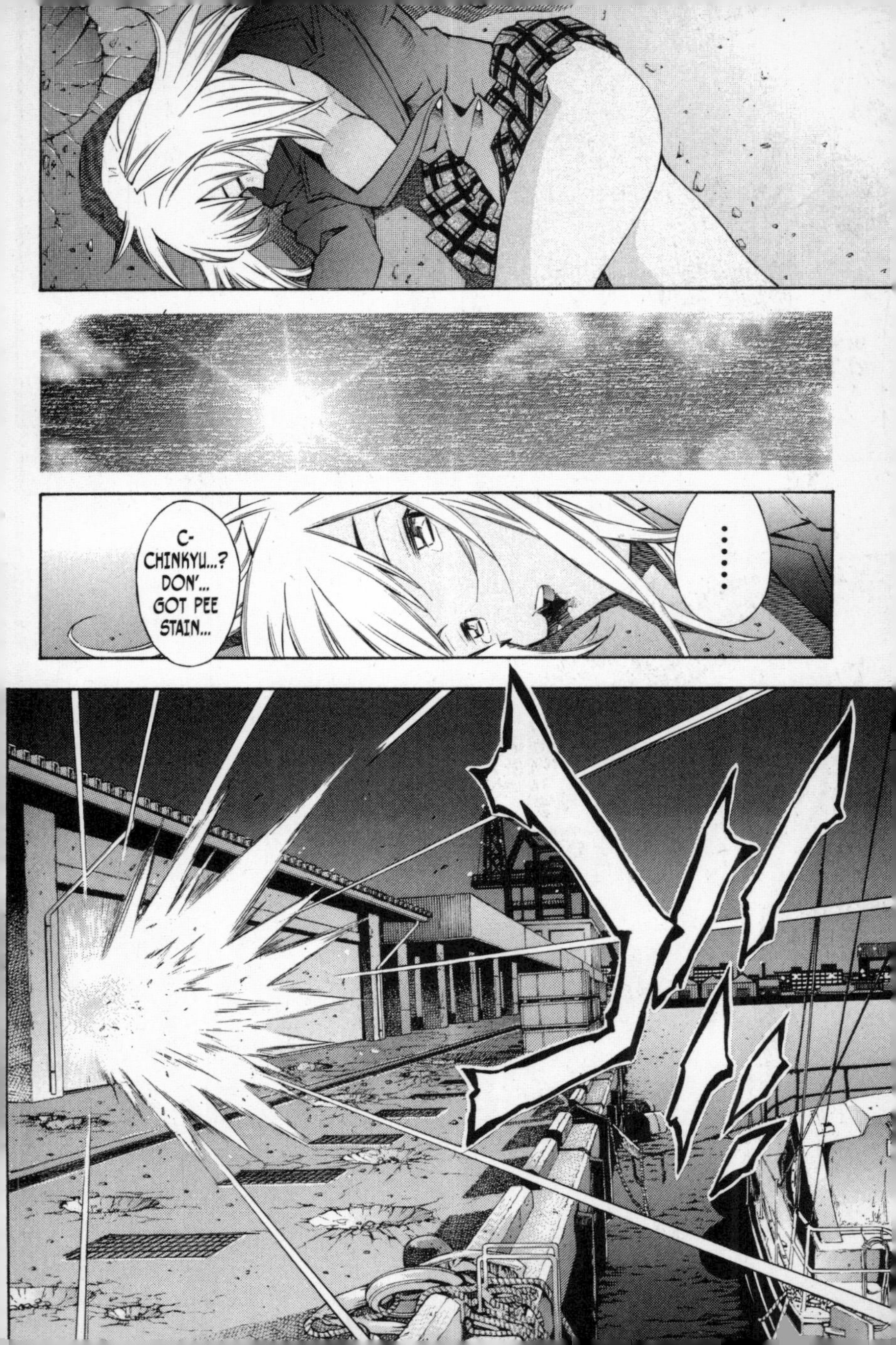
......
C-CHINKYU...? DON'... GOT PEE STAIN...

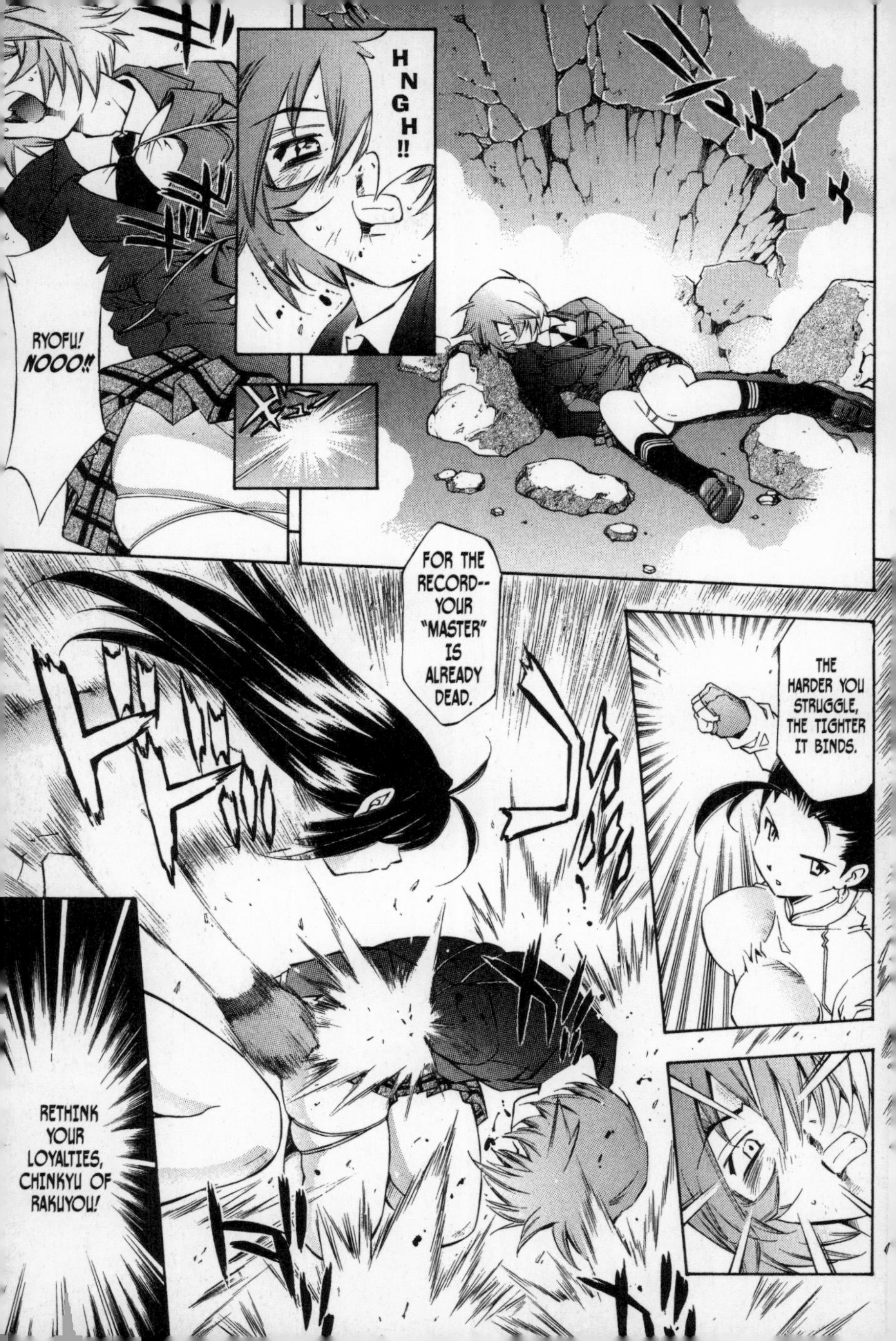
HNGH!!
RYOFU! NOOO!!
THE HARDER YOU STRUGGLE, THE TIGHTER IT BINDS.
FOR THE RECORD-- YOUR "MASTER" IS ALREADY DEAD.
RETHINK YOUR LOYALTIES, CHINKYU OF RAKUYOU!

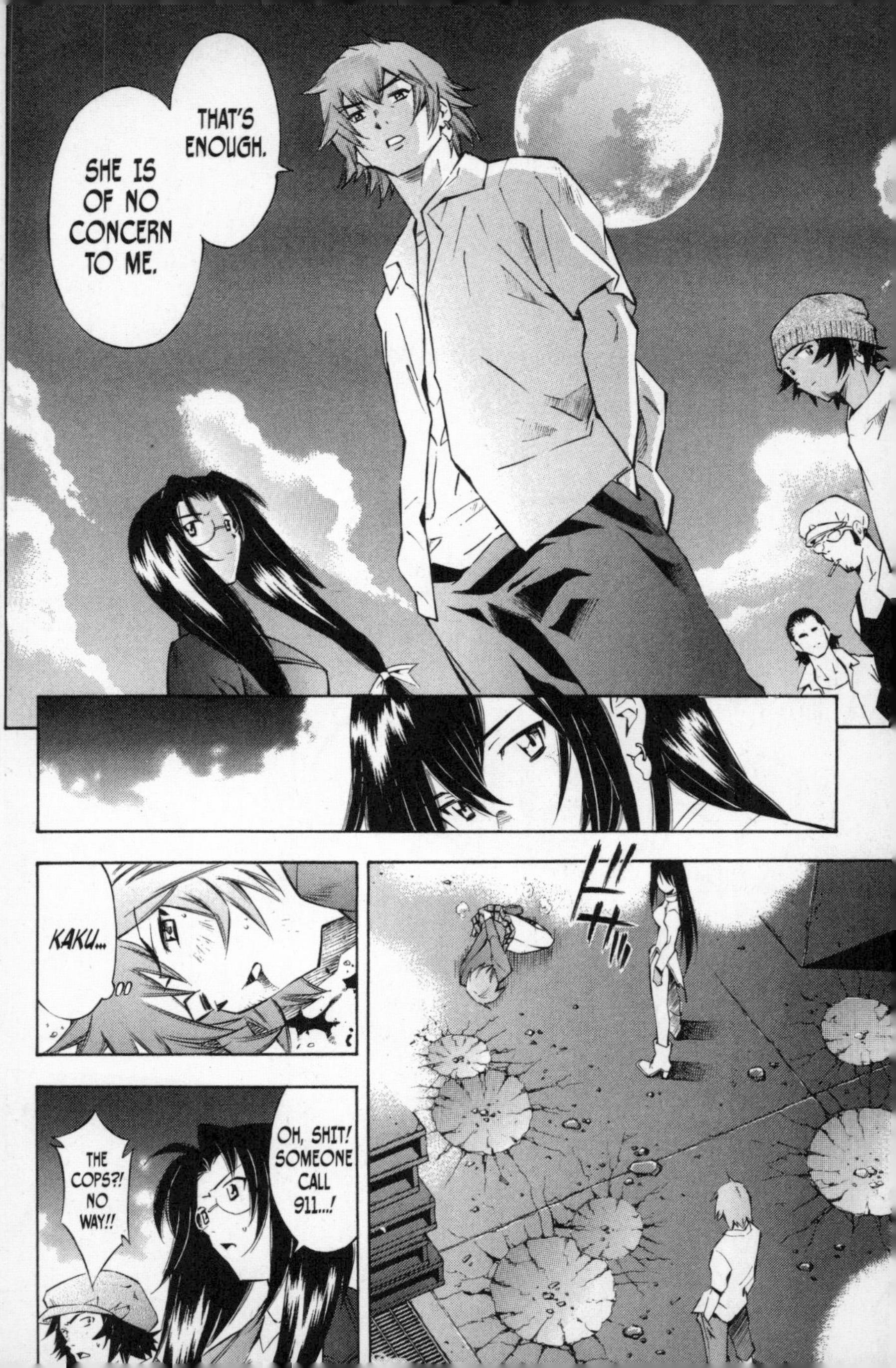
THAT'S ENOUGH.
SHE IS OF NO CONCERN TO ME.
KAKU...
OH, SHIT! SOMEONE CALL 911...!
THE COPS?! NO WAY!!

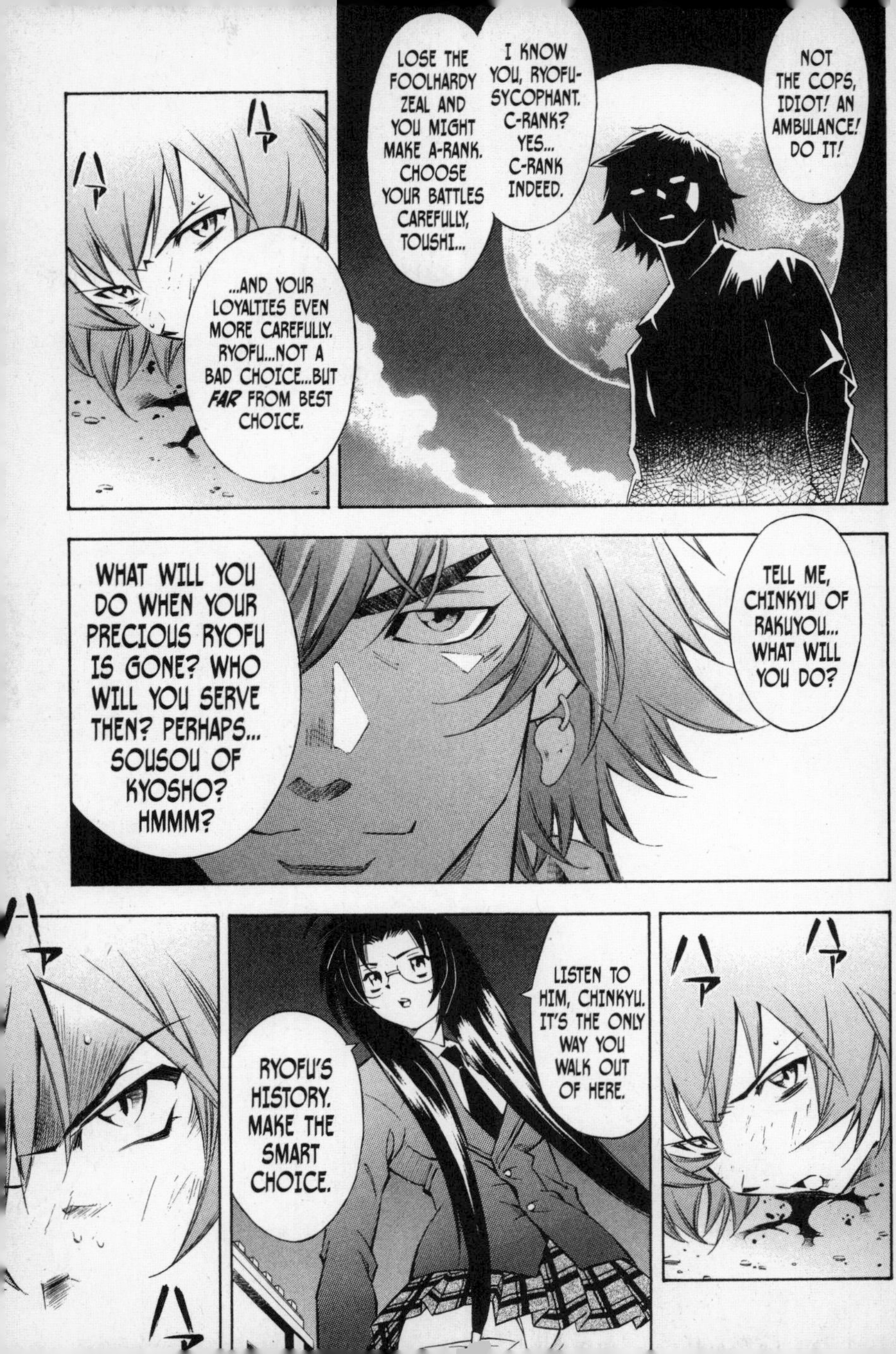
NOT THE COPS, IDIOT! AN AMBULANCE! DO IT!
I KNOW YOU, RYOFU-SYCOPHANT. C-RANK? YES... C-RANK INDEED.
LOSE THE FOOLHARDY ZEAL AND YOU MIGHT MAKE A-RANK. CHOOSE YOUR BATTLES CAREFULLY, TOUSHI...
...AND YOUR LOYALTIES EVEN MORE CAREFULLY. RYOFU...NOT A BAD CHOICE...BUT *FAR* FROM BEST CHOICE.
TELL ME, CHINKYU OF RAKUYOU... WHAT WILL YOU DO?
WHAT WILL YOU DO WHEN YOUR PRECIOUS RYOFU IS GONE? WHO WILL YOU SERVE THEN? PERHAPS... SOUSOU OF KYOSHO? HMMM?
LISTEN TO HIM, CHINKYU. IT'S THE ONLY WAY YOU WALK OUT OF HERE.
RYOFU'S HISTORY. MAKE THE SMART CHOICE.

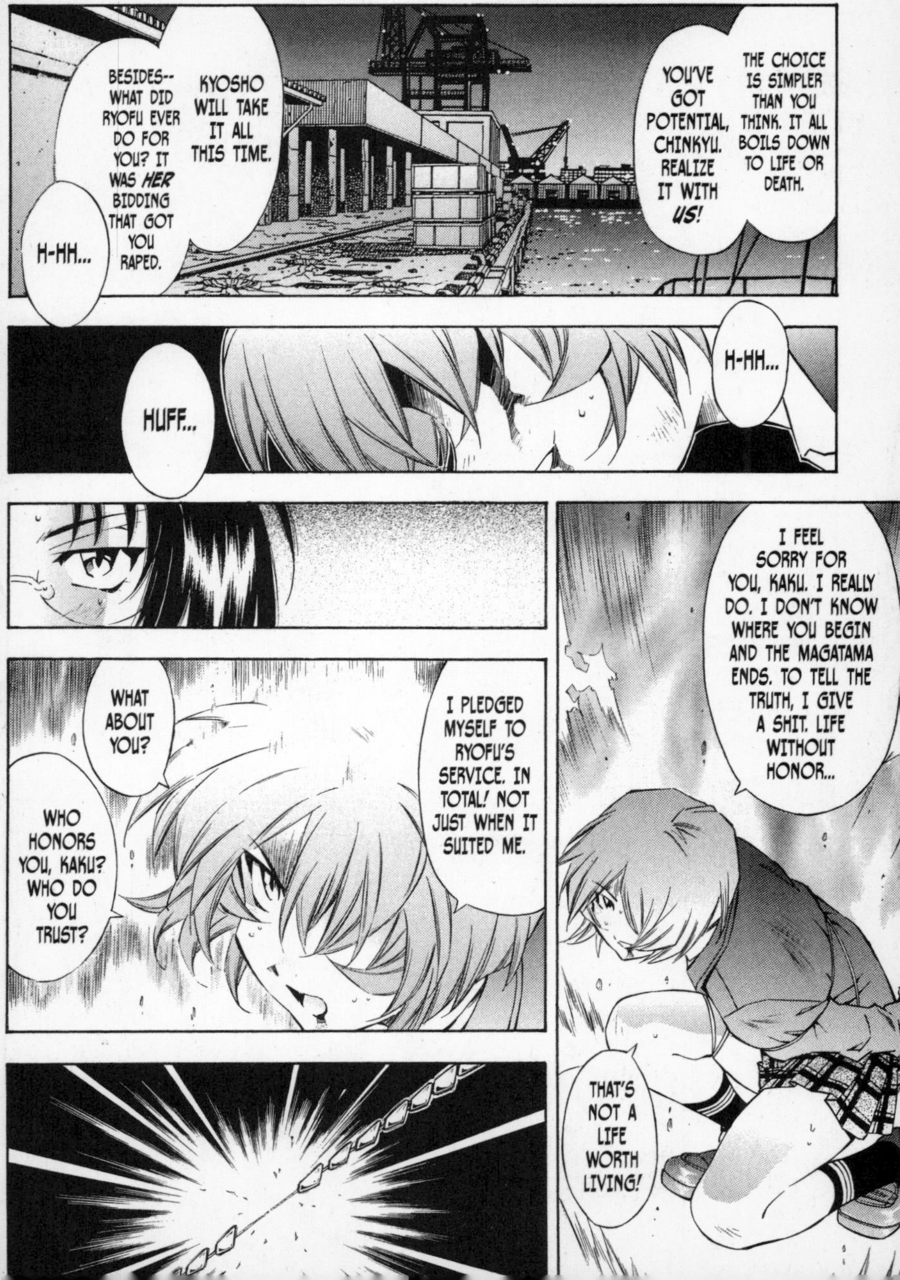
THE CHOICE IS SIMPLER THAN YOU THINK. IT ALL BOILS DOWN TO LIFE OR DEATH.
YOU'VE GOT POTENTIAL, CHINKYU. REALIZE IT WITH *US!*
KYOSHO WILL TAKE IT ALL THIS TIME.
BESIDES-- WHAT DID RYOFU EVER DO FOR YOU? IT WAS *HER* BIDDING THAT GOT YOU RAPED.
H-HH...
H-HH...
HUFF...
I FEEL SORRY FOR YOU, KAKU. I REALLY DO. I DON'T KNOW WHERE YOU BEGIN AND THE MAGATAMA ENDS. TO TELL THE TRUTH, I GIVE A SHIT. LIFE WITHOUT HONOR...
THAT'S NOT A LIFE WORTH LIVING!
I PLEDGED MYSELF TO RYOFU'S SERVICE. IN TOTAL! NOT JUST WHEN IT SUITED ME.
WHAT ABOUT YOU?
WHO HONORS YOU, KAKU? WHO DO YOU TRUST?

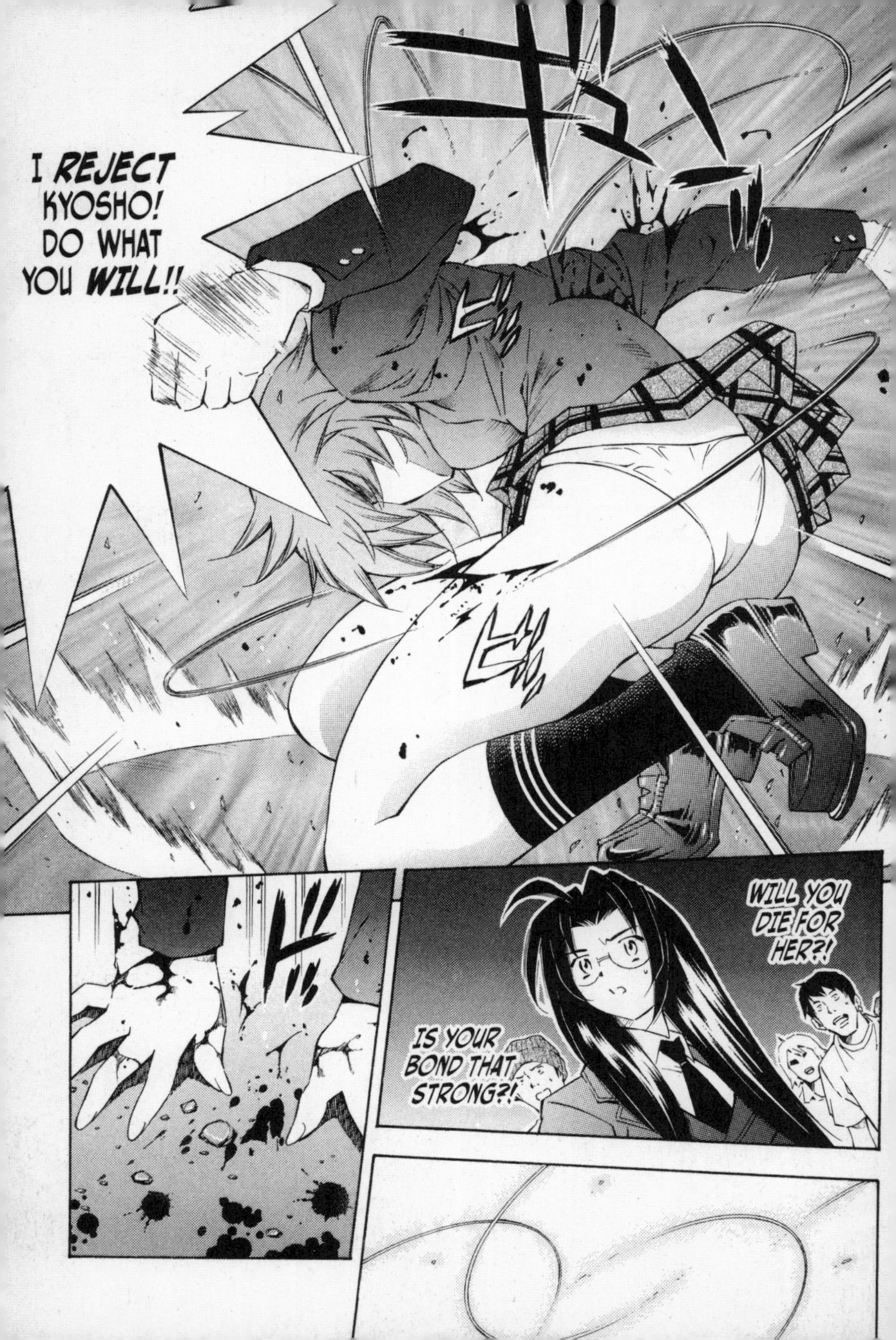
I REJECT KYOSHO! DO WHAT YOU WILL!!
WILL YOU DIE FOR HER?!
IS YOUR BOND THAT STRONG?!

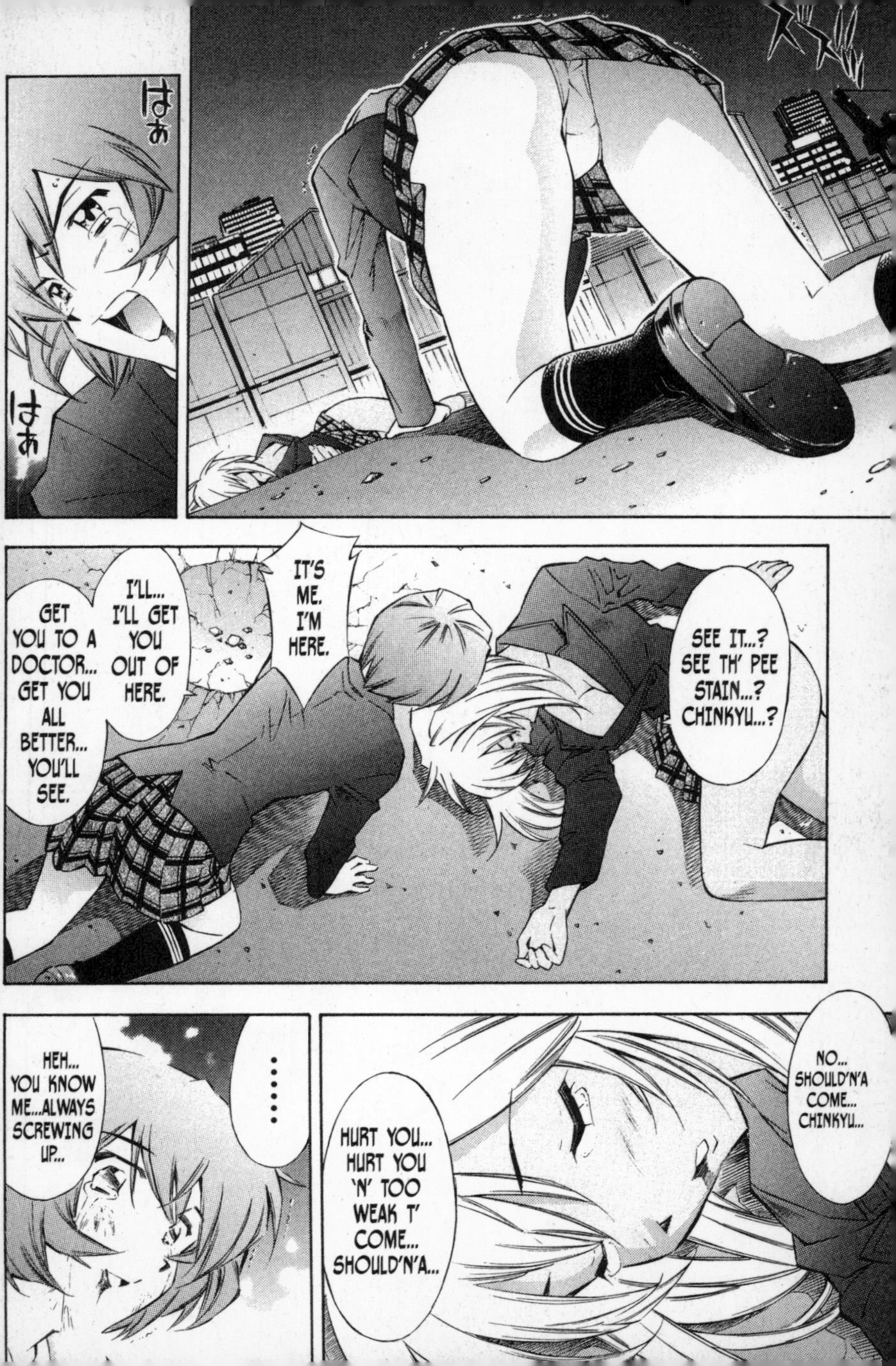
はぁ
はぁ
SEE IT...? SEE TH' PEE STAIN...? CHINKYU...?
IT'S ME. I'M HERE.
I'LL... I'LL GET YOU OUT OF HERE.
GET YOU TO A DOCTOR... GET YOU ALL BETTER... YOU'LL SEE.
NO... SHOULD'N'A COME... CHINKYU...
HURT YOU... HURT YOU 'N' TOO WEAK T' COME... SHOULD'N'A...
......
HEH... YOU KNOW ME...ALWAYS SCREWING UP...

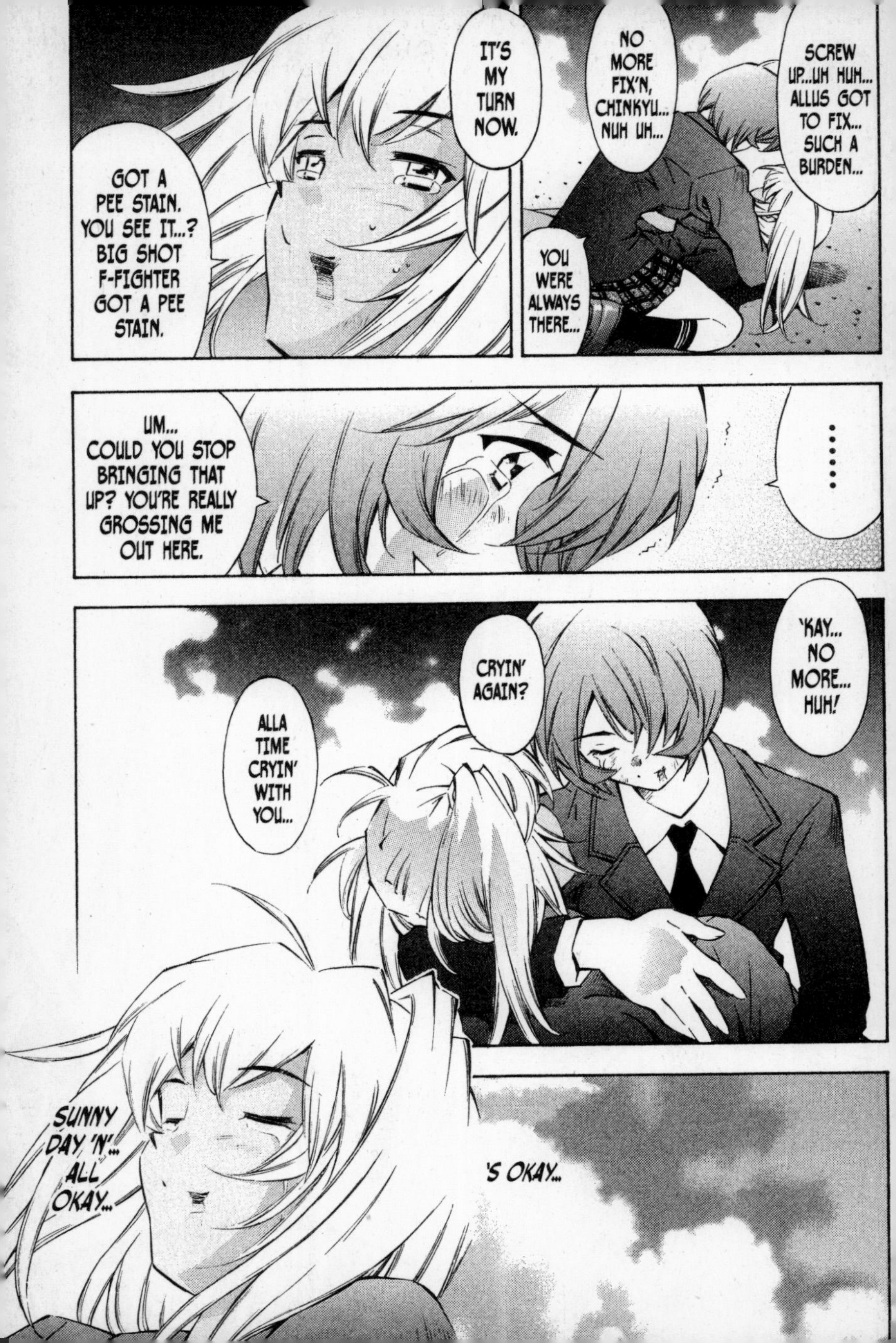
SCREW UP...UH HUH... ALLUS GOT TO FIX... SUCH A BURDEN...
NO MORE FIX'N, CHINKYU... NUH UH...
YOU WERE ALWAYS THERE...
IT'S MY TURN NOW.
GOT A PEE STAIN. YOU SEE IT...? BIG SHOT F-FIGHTER GOT A PEE STAIN.
......
UM... COULD YOU STOP BRINGING THAT UP? YOU'RE REALLY GROSSING ME OUT HERE.
'KAY... NO MORE... HUH!
CRYIN' AGAIN?
ALLA TIME CRYIN' WITH YOU...
'S OKAY...
SUNNY DAY 'N'... ALL OKAY...

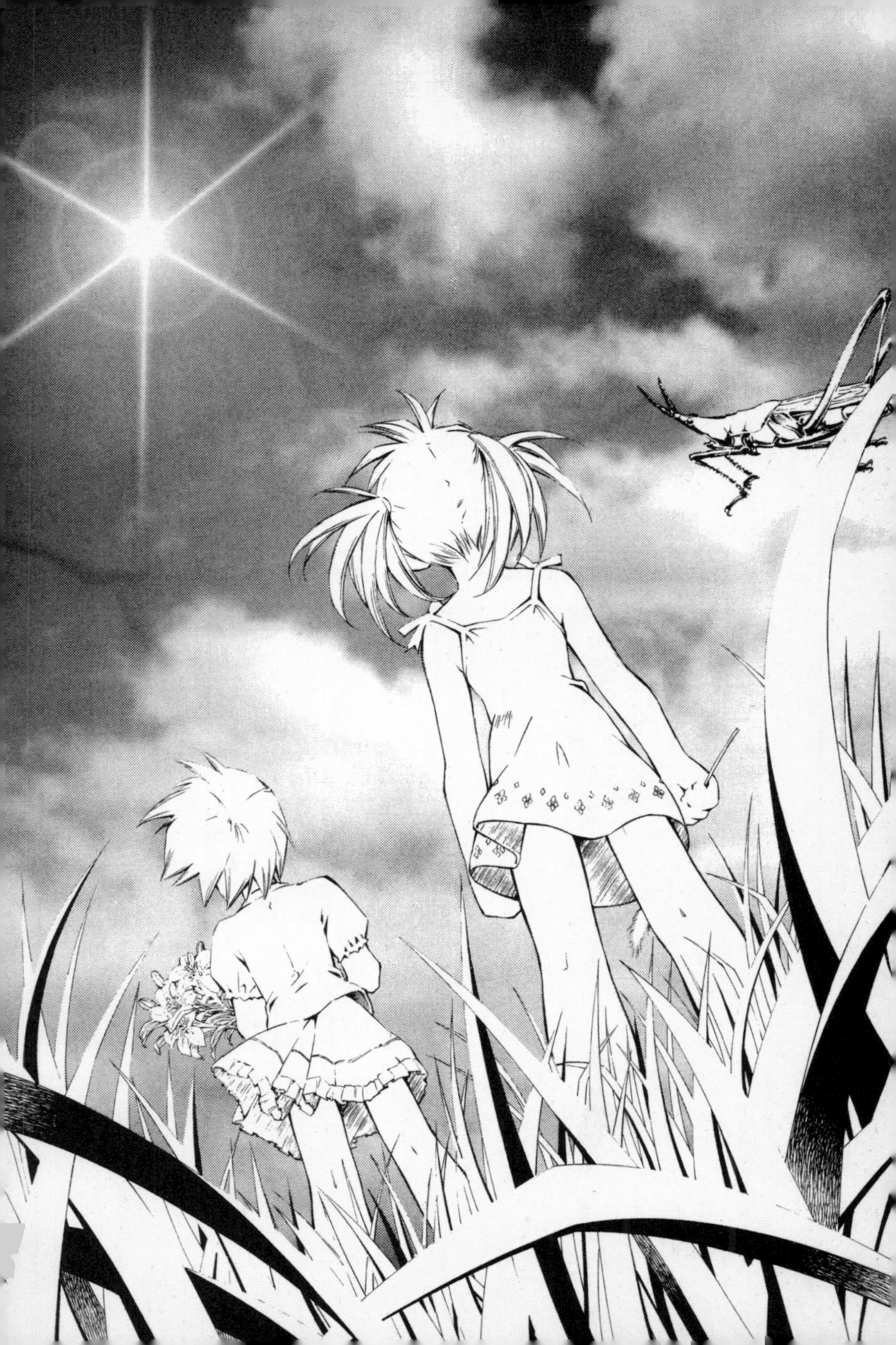

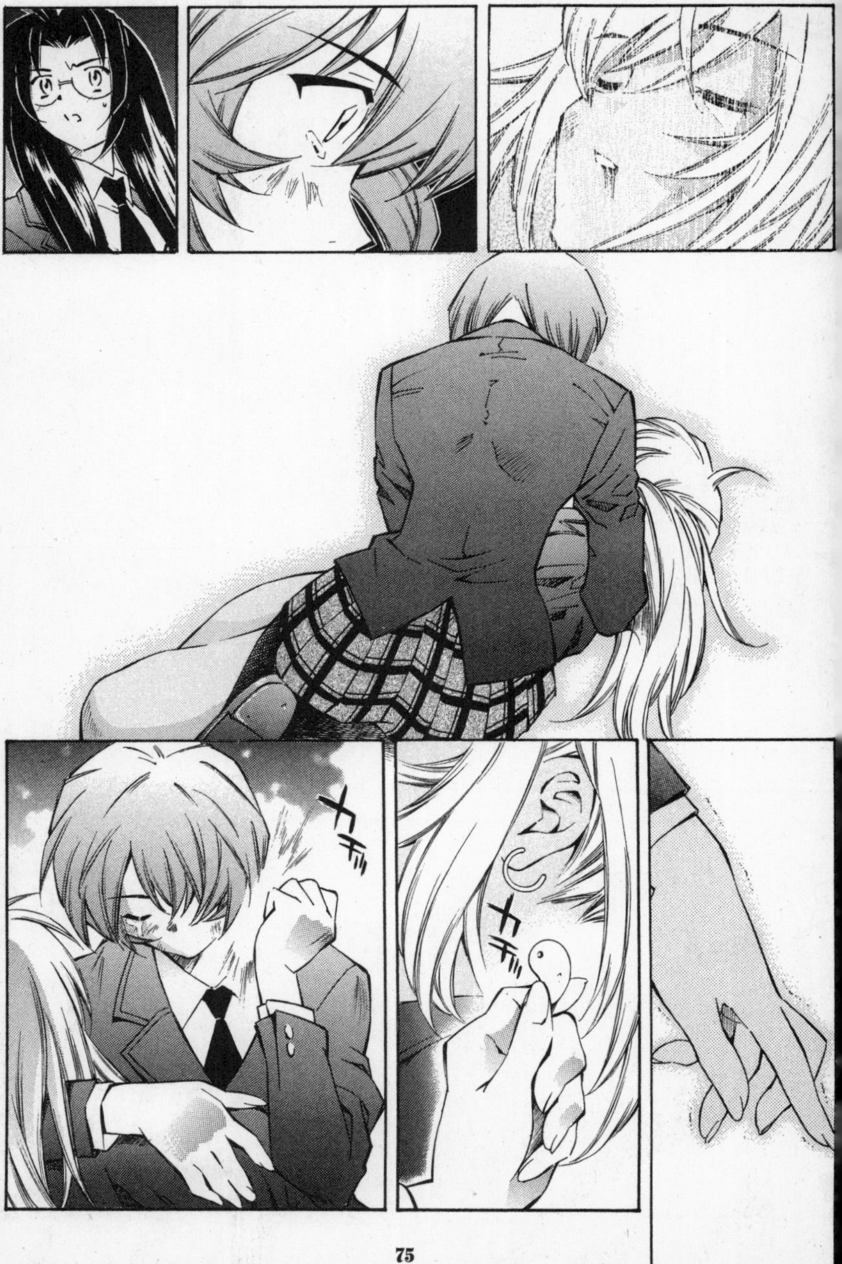
カチッ
カチッ

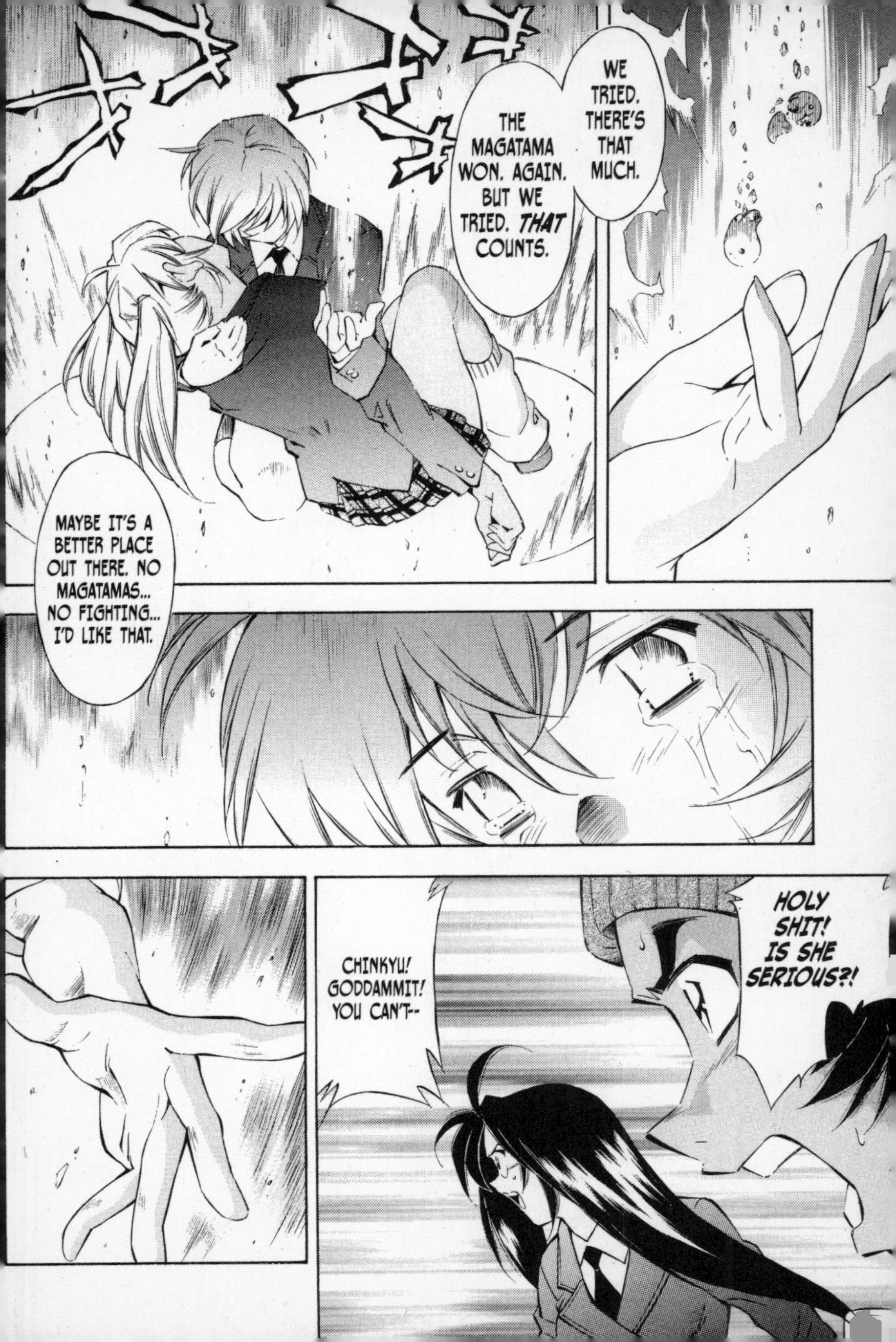
WE TRIED. THERE'S THAT MUCH.
THE MAGATAMA WON. AGAIN. BUT WE TRIED. *THAT* COUNTS.
MAYBE IT'S A BETTER PLACE OUT THERE. NO MAGATAMAS... NO FIGHTING... I'D LIKE THAT.
HOLY SHIT! IS SHE SERIOUS?!
CHINKYU! GODDAMMIT! YOU CAN'T--

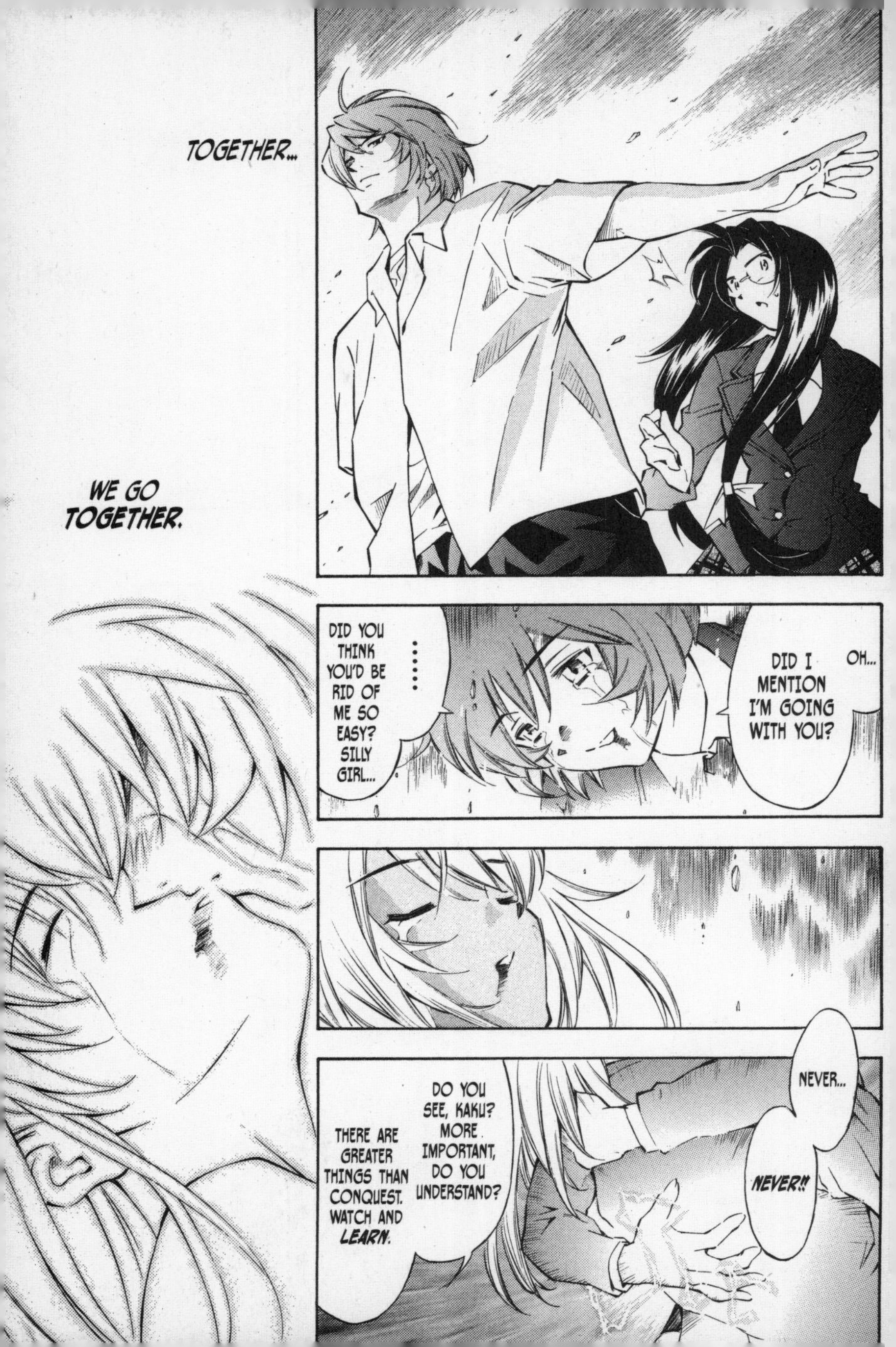
OH...
DID I MENTION I'M GOING WITH YOU?
......
DID YOU THINK YOU'D BE RID OF ME SO EASY? SILLY GIRL...
NEVER...
NEVER!!
DO YOU SEE, KAKU? MORE IMPORTANT, DO YOU UNDERSTAND?
THERE ARE GREATER THINGS THAN CONQUEST. WATCH AND LEARN.
TOGETHER...
WE GO TOGETHER.

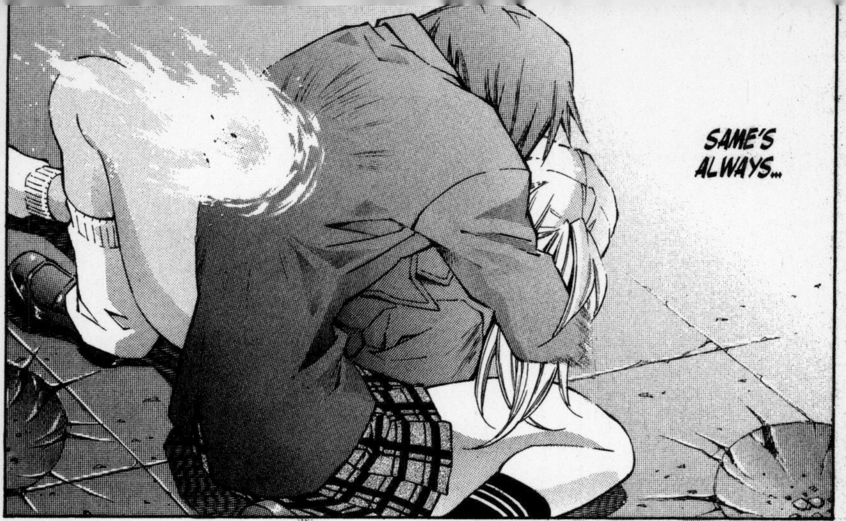
SAME'S ALWAYS...

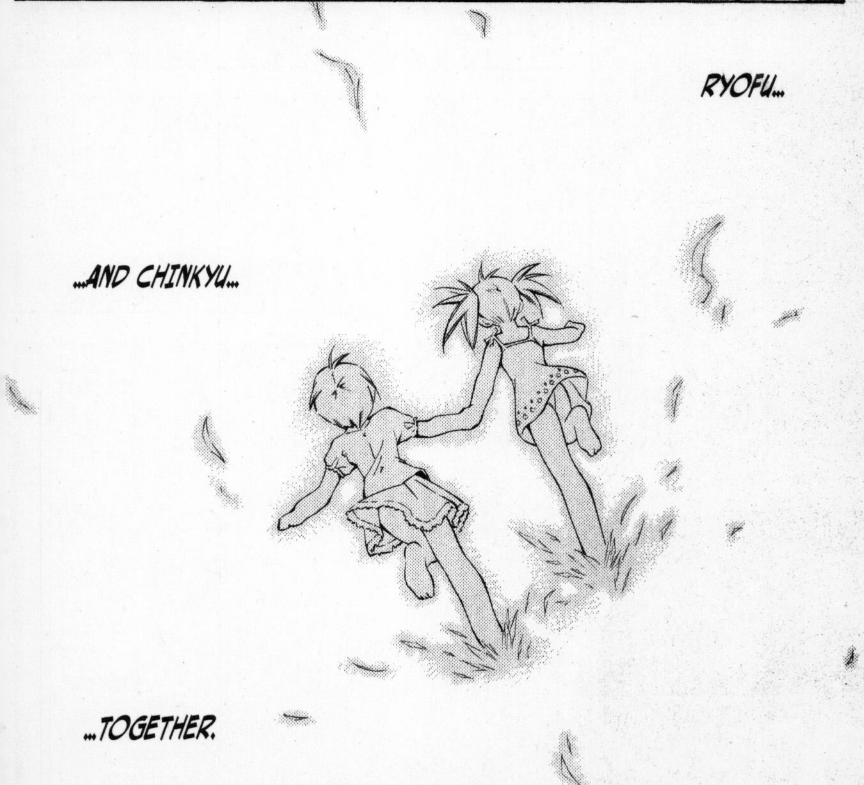
RYOFU...
...AND CHINKYU...
...TOGETHER.

一騎当千

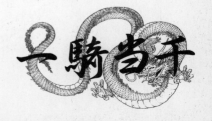

KADA GENKA

A LEGENDARY HEALER/DOCTOR, HE WAS THE FIRST IN HIS FIELD TO UTILIZE GENERAL ANESTHESIA FOR SURGICAL PROCEDURES. KADA'S MEDICAL EXPERTISE ENCOMPASSED BASIC AND COMPOUND MEDICINE, ACUPUNCTURE, MOXIBUSTION, AS WELL AS DANCING AROUND IN A HEADDRESS SHAKING RATTLES WHILE SPEAKING IN TONGUES. ANOTHER FUN FACT IS THAT HE NEVER MADE AN INCORRECT DIAGNOSIS. MANY PEOPLE ACTUALLY CONSIDERED HIS HEALING PROWESS A GIFT FROM THE GODS, WHICH IS HOW HE CAME TO BE KNOWN AS THE GOD DOCTOR. WOW. GET THAT GUY ON ER.

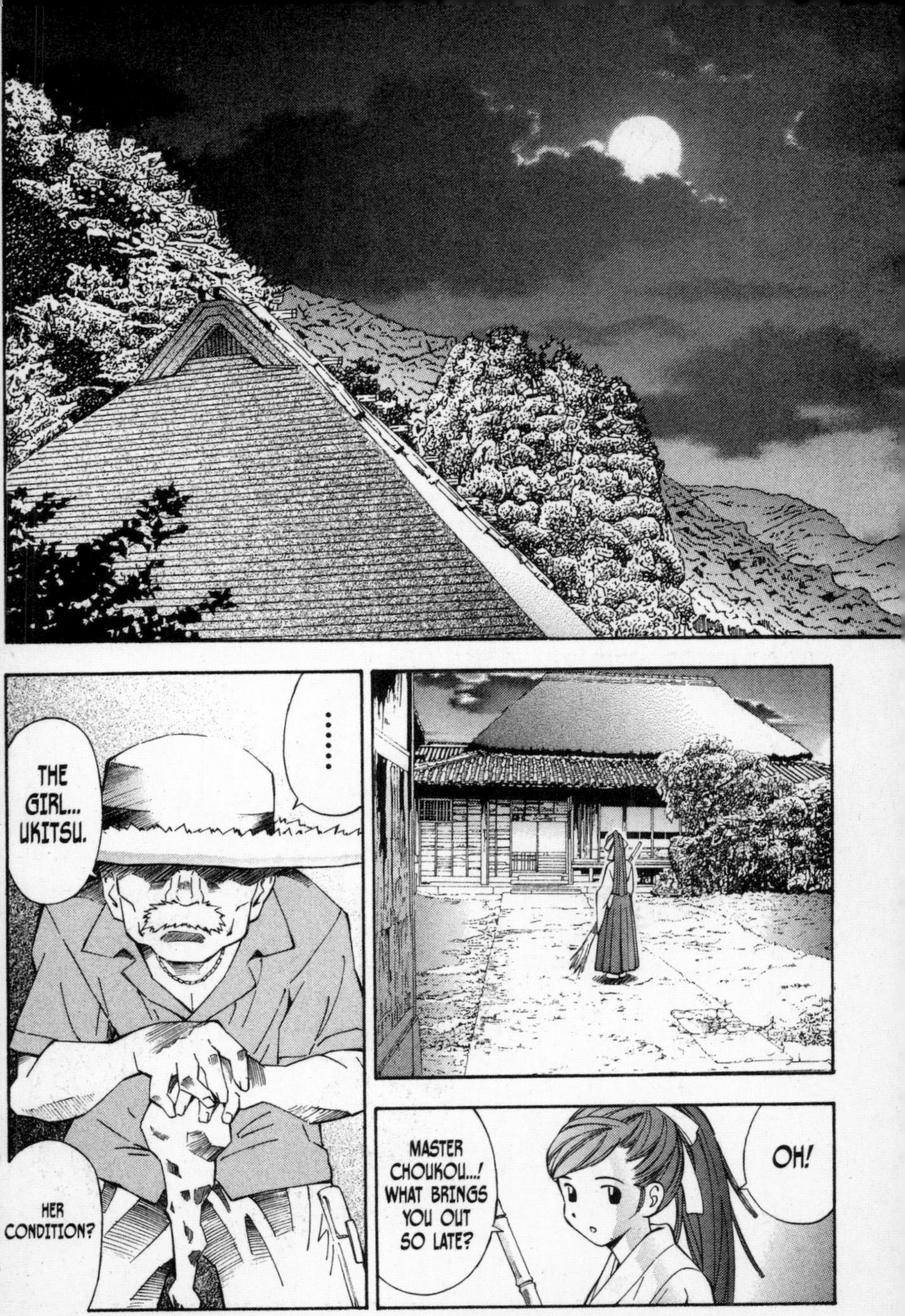
OH!
MASTER CHOUKOU...! WHAT BRINGS YOU OUT SO LATE?
......
THE GIRL... UKITSU.
HER CONDITION?

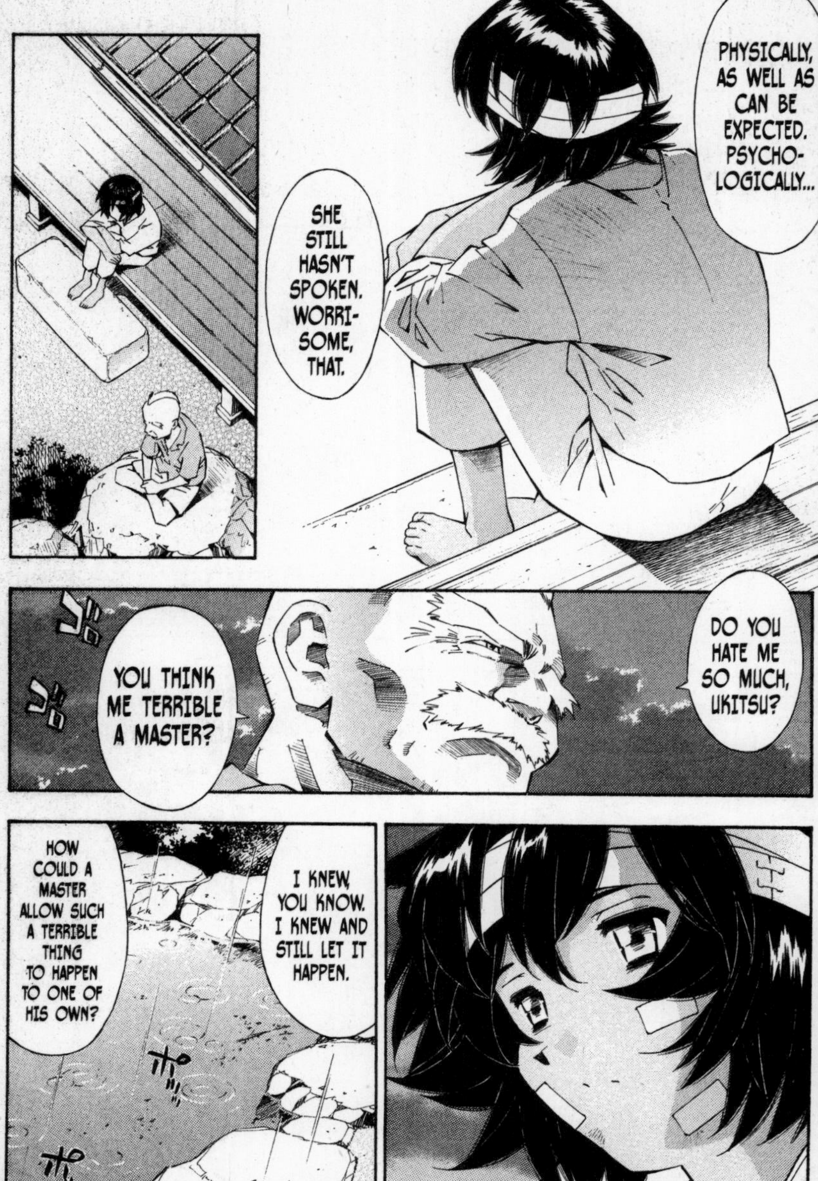
PHYSICALLY, AS WELL AS CAN BE EXPECTED. PSYCHO-LOGICALLY...
SHE STILL HASN'T SPOKEN. WORRI-SOME, THAT.
DO YOU HATE ME SO MUCH, UKITSU?
YOU THINK ME TERRIBLE A MASTER?
I KNEW, YOU KNOW. I KNEW AND STILL LET IT HAPPEN.
HOW COULD A MASTER ALLOW SUCH A TERRIBLE THING TO HAPPEN TO ONE OF HIS OWN?

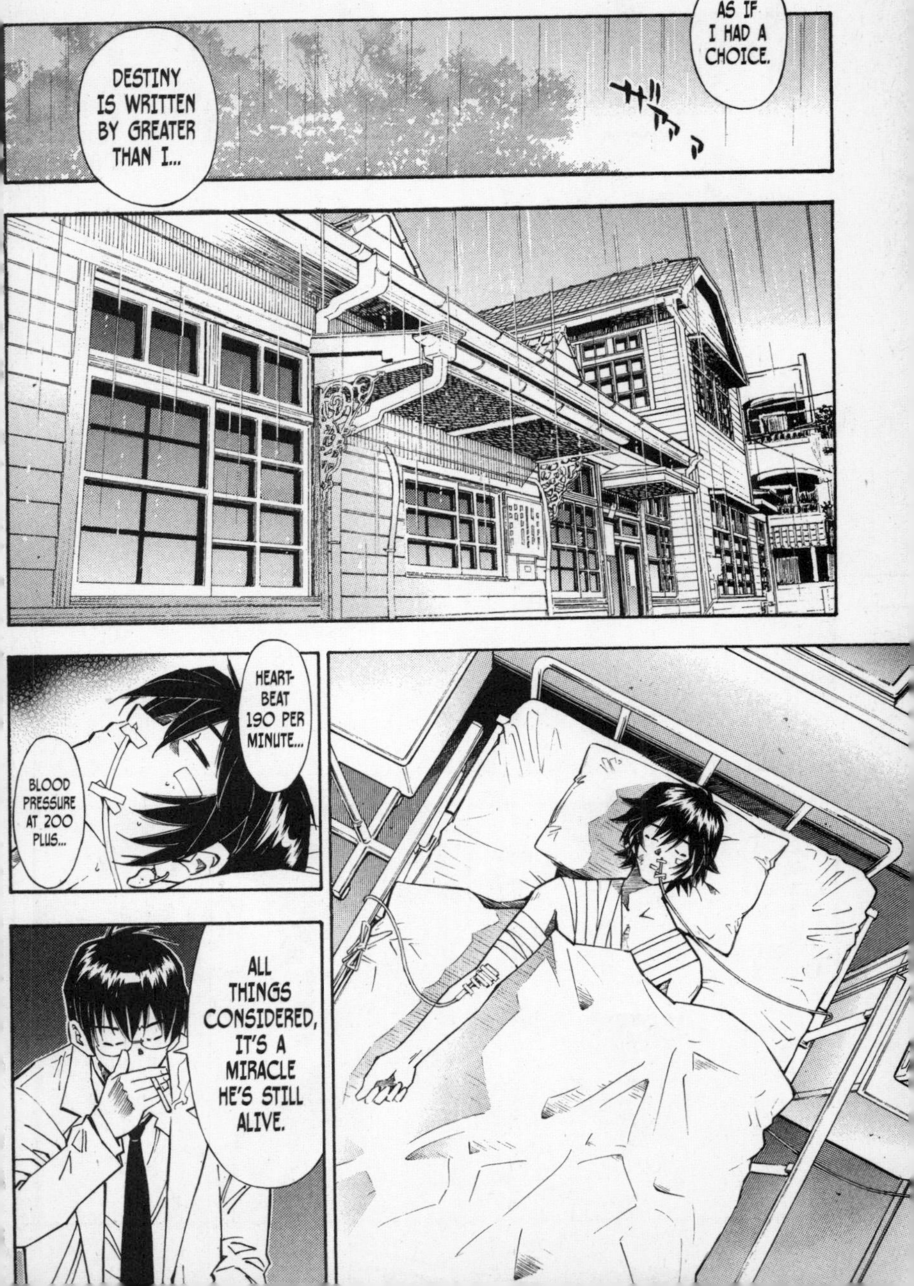
AS IF I HAD A CHOICE.
DESTINY IS WRITTEN BY GREATER THAN I...
HEART-BEAT 190 PER MINUTE...
BLOOD PRESSURE AT 200 PLUS...
ALL THINGS CONSIDERED, IT'S A MIRACLE HE'S STILL ALIVE.

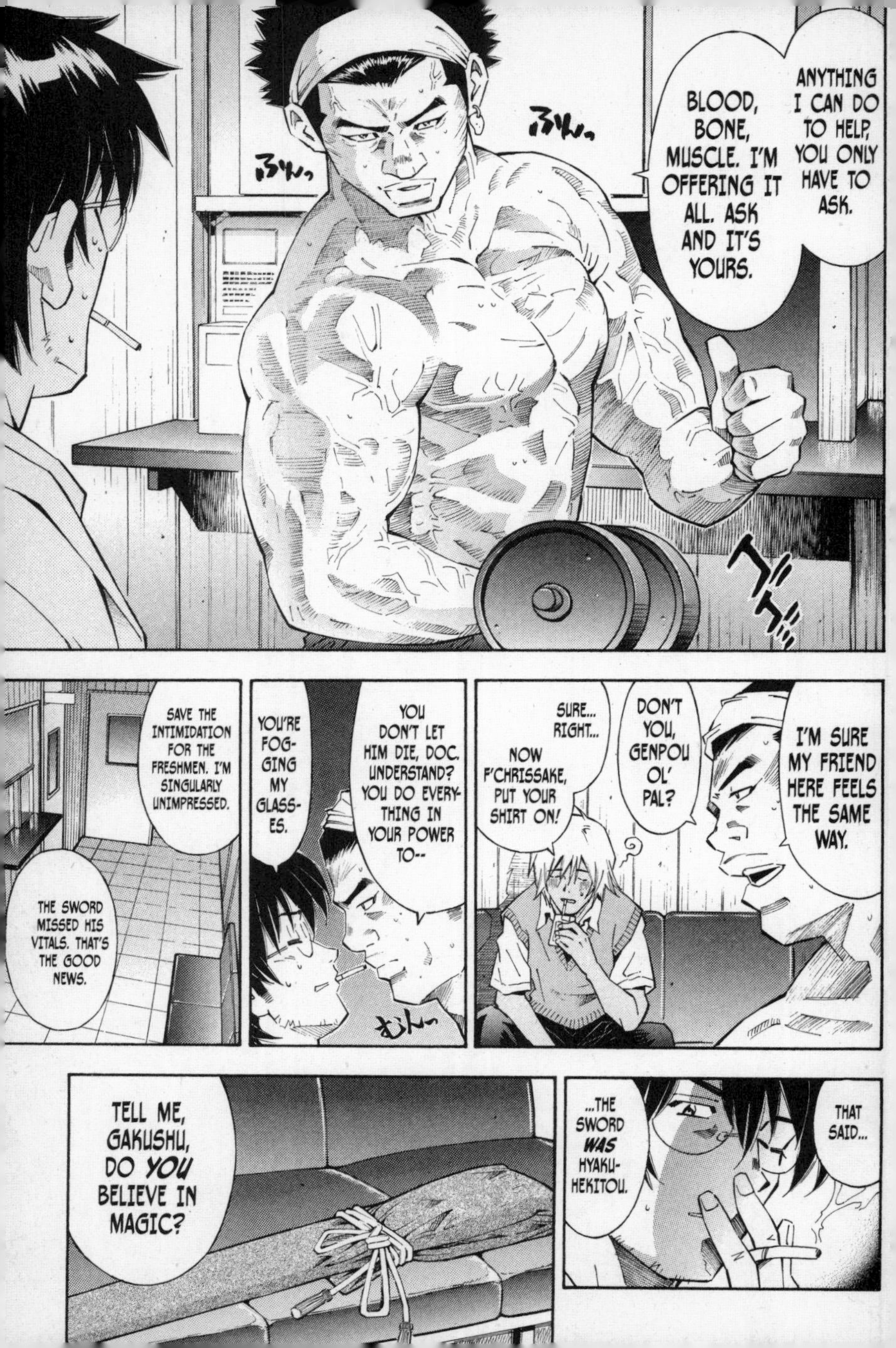
ANYTHING I CAN DO TO HELP, YOU ONLY HAVE TO ASK.
BLOOD, BONE, MUSCLE. I'M OFFERING IT ALL. ASK AND IT'S YOURS.
ふんっ
ふんっ
I'M SURE MY FRIEND HERE FEELS THE SAME WAY.
DON'T YOU, GENPOU OL' PAL?
SURE... RIGHT...
NOW F'CHRISSAKE, PUT YOUR SHIRT ON!
YOU DON'T LET HIM DIE, DOC. UNDERSTAND? YOU DO EVERY-THING IN YOUR POWER TO--
YOU'RE FOG-GING MY GLASS-ES.
SAVE THE INTIMIDATION FOR THE FRESHMEN. I'M SINGULARLY UNIMPRESSED.
THE SWORD MISSED HIS VITALS. THAT'S THE GOOD NEWS.
THAT SAID...
...THE SWORD ***WAS*** HYAKU-HEKITOU.
TELL ME, GAKUSHU, DO ***YOU*** BELIEVE IN MAGIC?

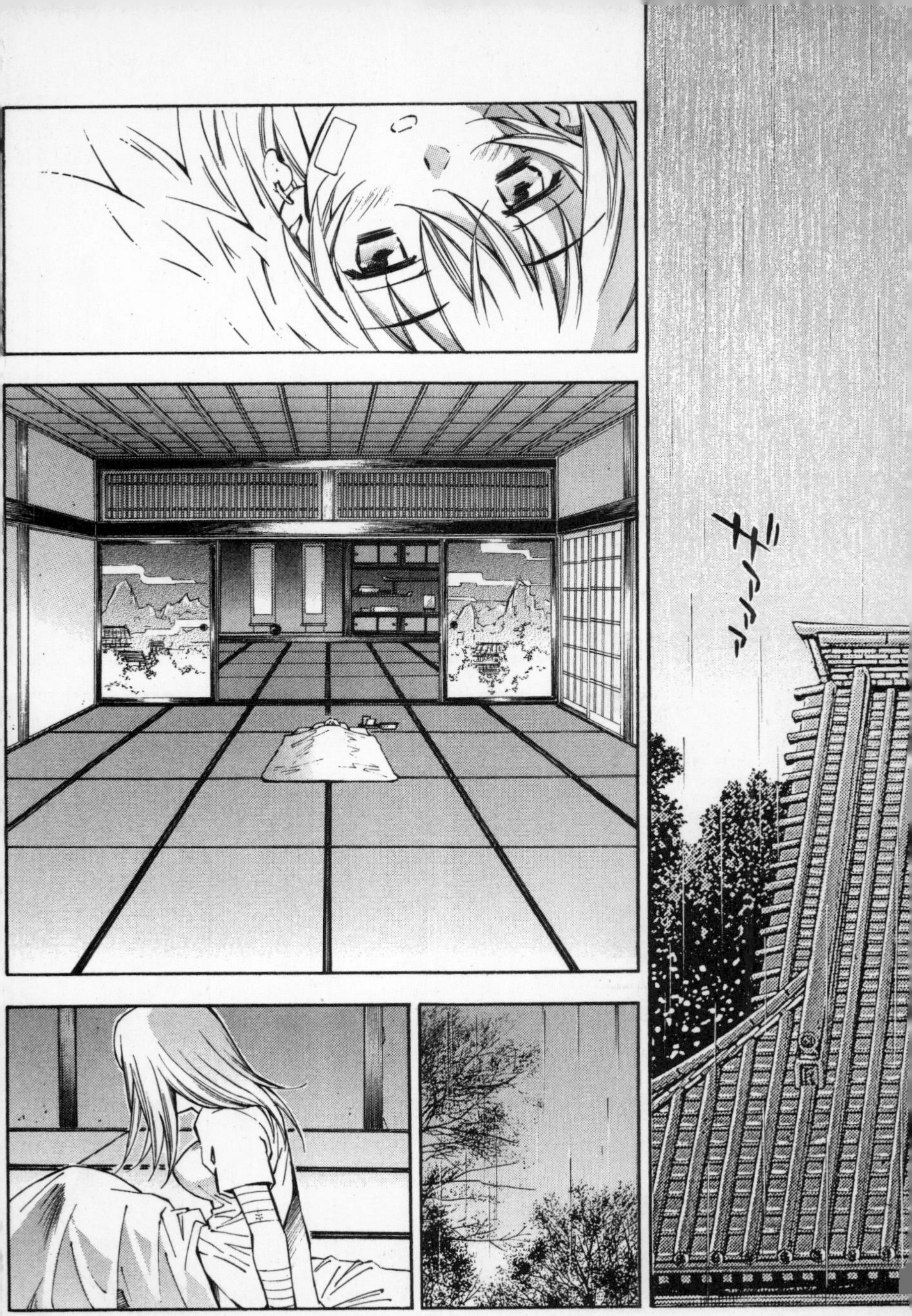
ザァァァ

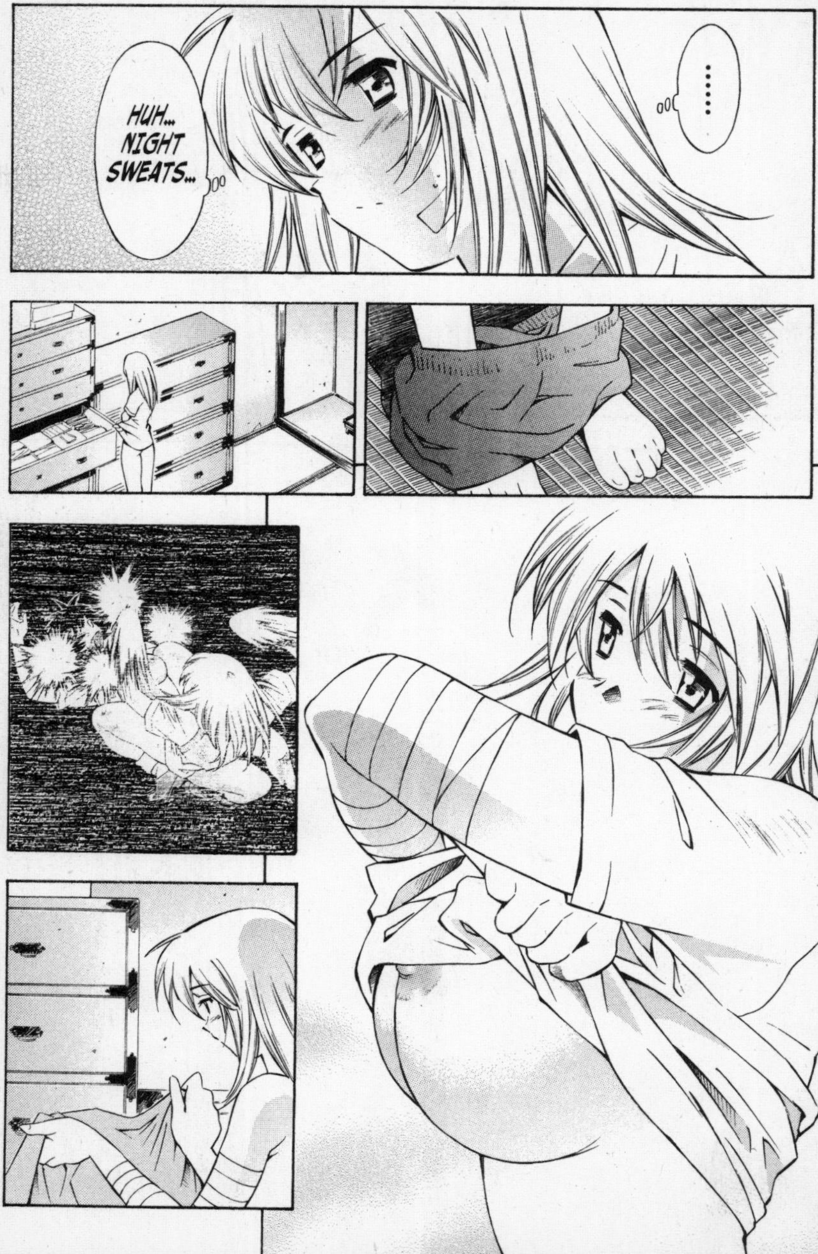
......
HUH... NIGHT SWEATS...

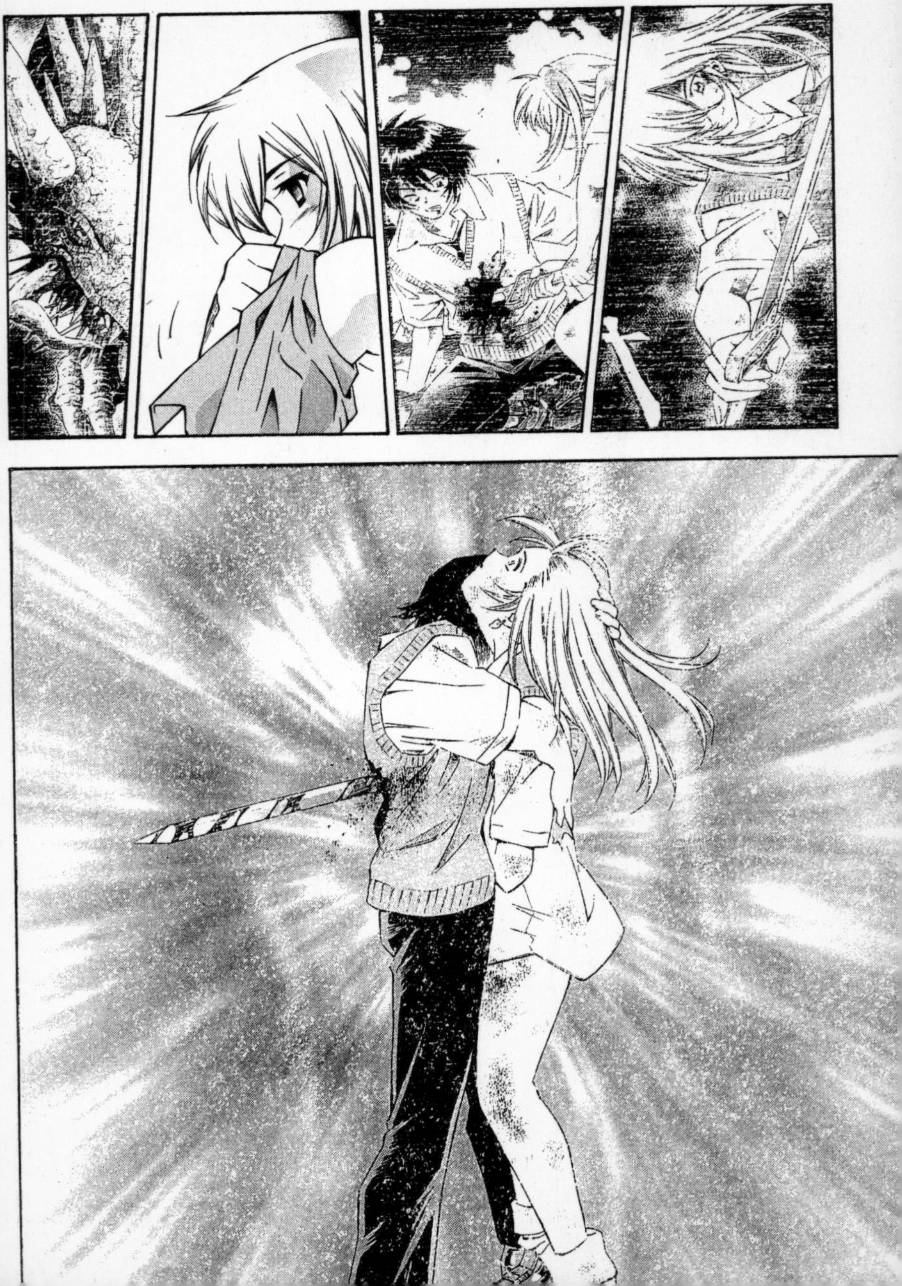

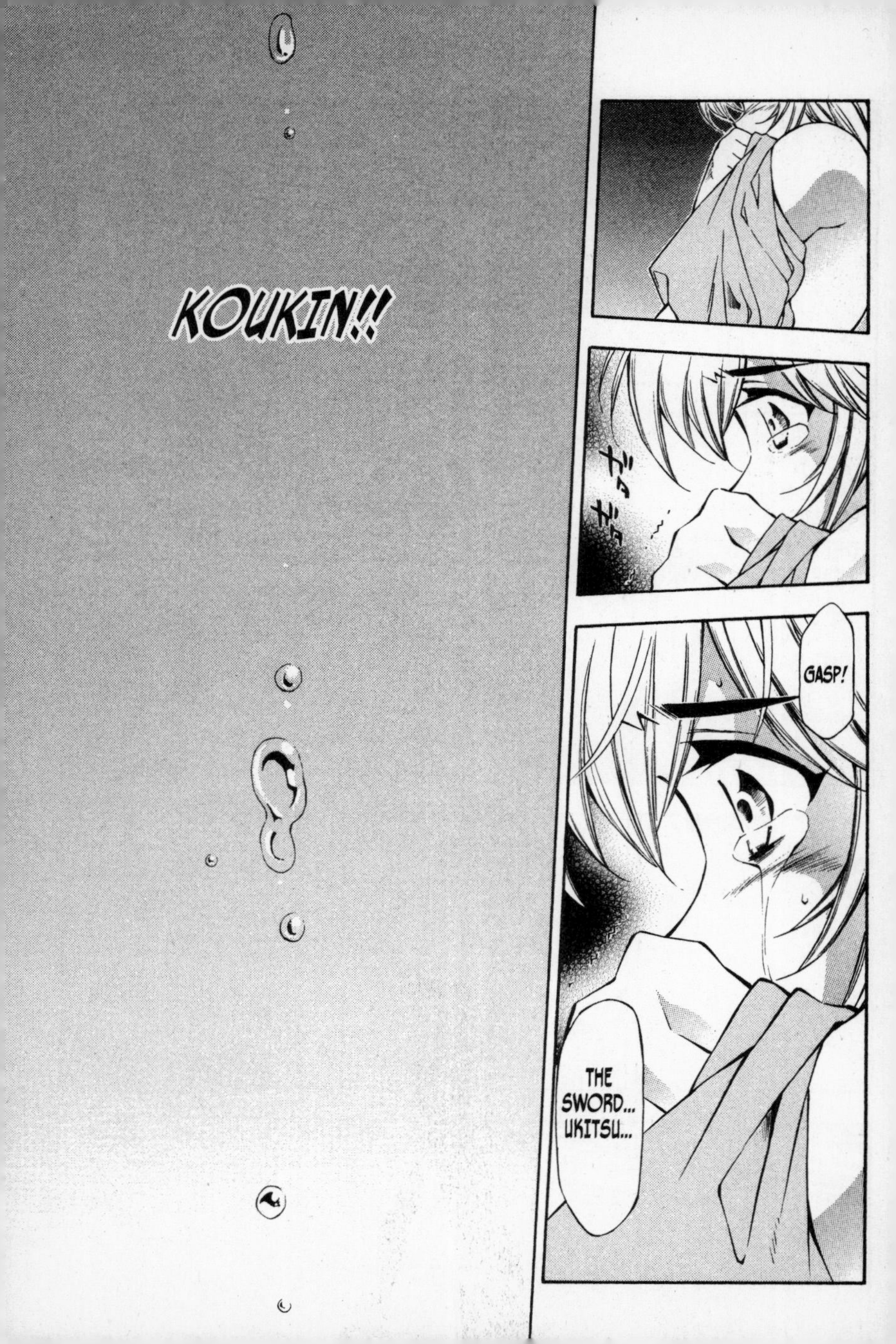
GASP!
THE SWORD... UKITSU...
KOUKIN!!

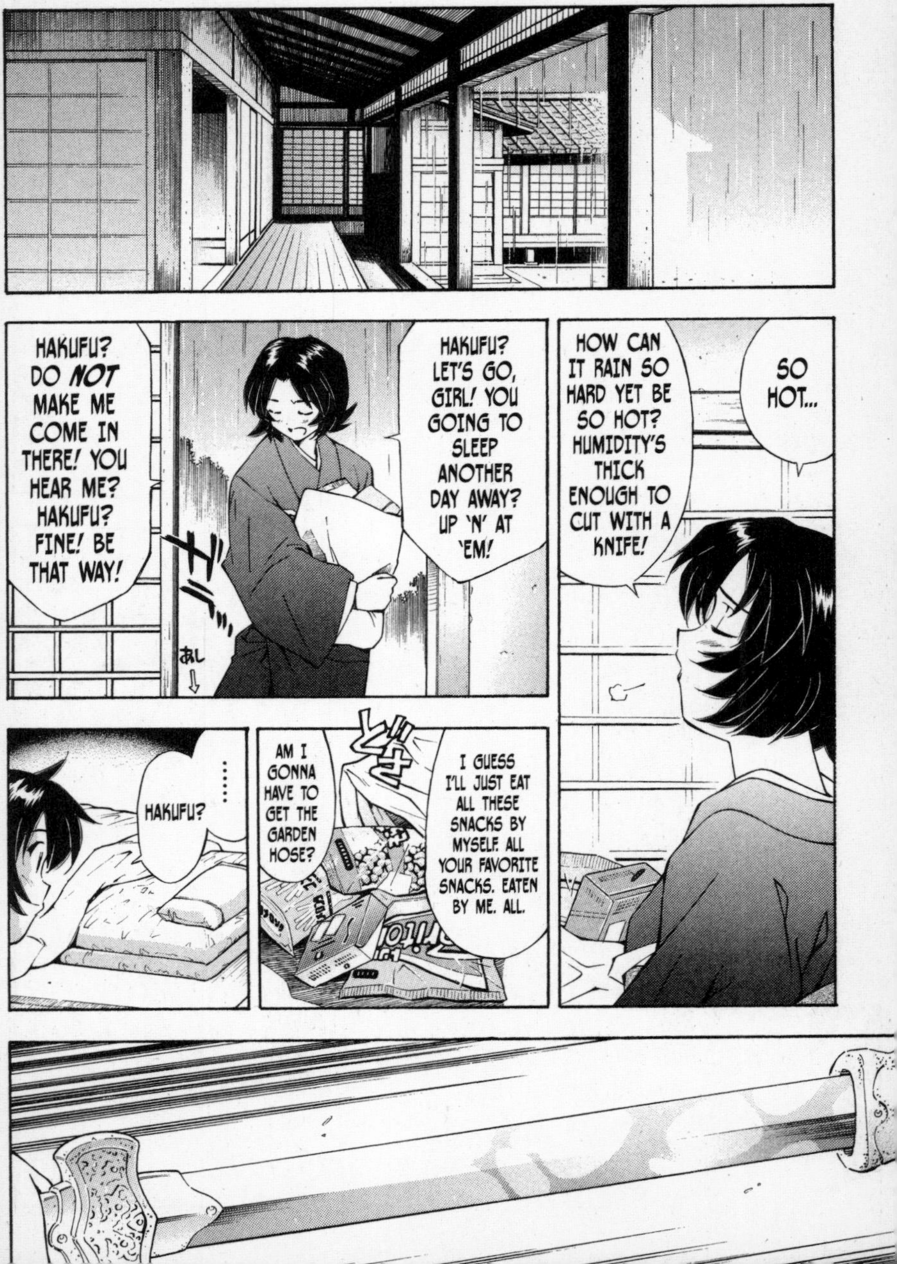
SO HOT...
HOW CAN IT RAIN SO HARD YET BE SO HOT? HUMIDITY'S THICK ENOUGH TO CUT WITH A KNIFE!
HAKUFU? LET'S GO, GIRL! YOU GOING TO SLEEP ANOTHER DAY AWAY? UP 'N' AT 'EM!
HAKUFU? DO *NOT* MAKE ME COME IN THERE! YOU HEAR ME? HAKUFU? FINE! BE THAT WAY!
あし
I GUESS I'LL JUST EAT ALL THESE SNACKS BY MYSELF. ALL YOUR FAVORITE SNACKS. EATEN BY ME. ALL.
AM I GONNA HAVE TO GET THE GARDEN HOSE?
どさ
HAKUFU?
......

DAMN THING GIVES ME THE WILLIES. JUST DON'T *FEEL* RIGHT... Y'KNOW?

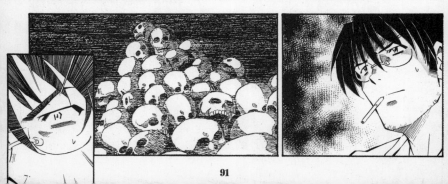

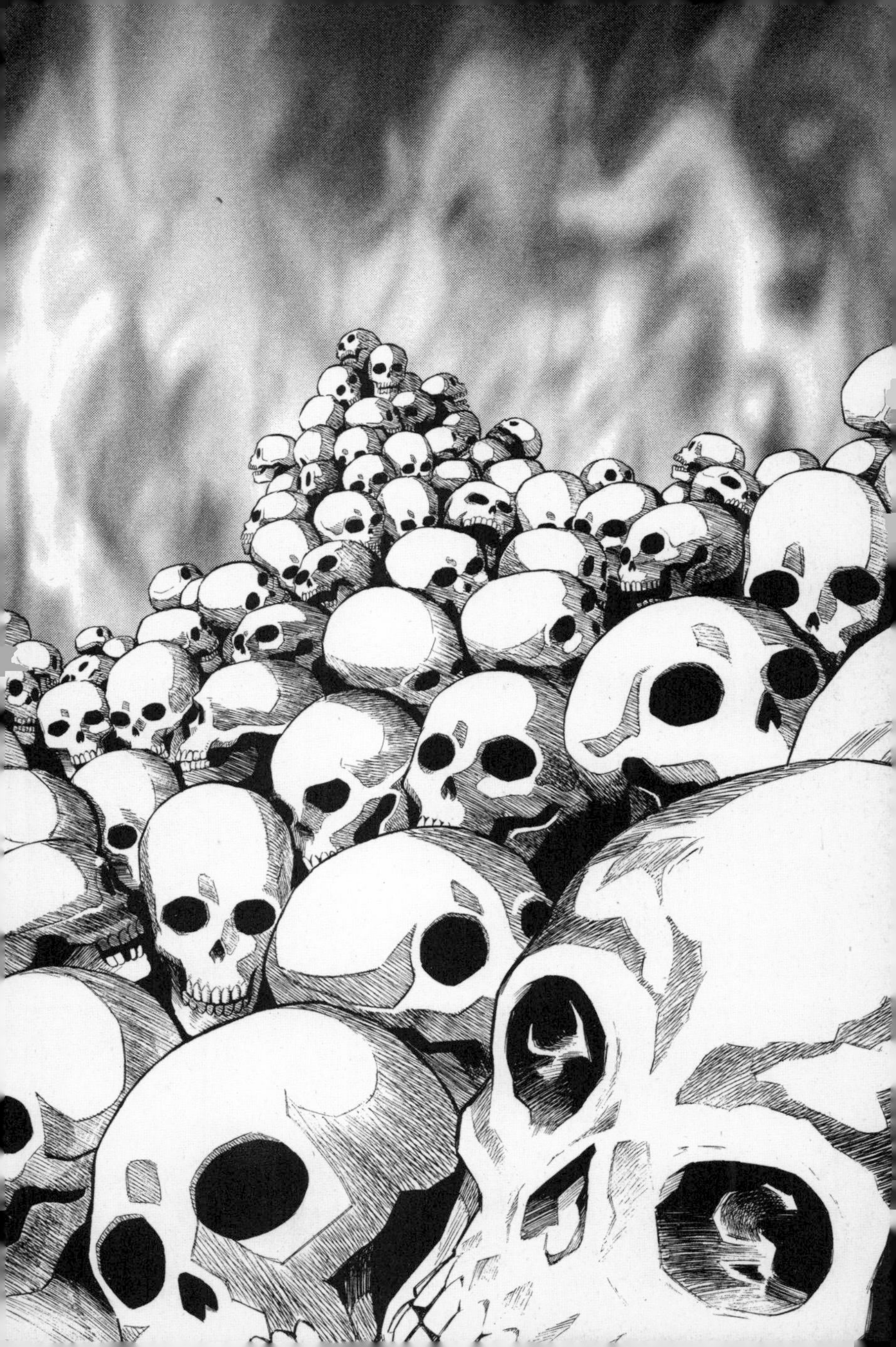

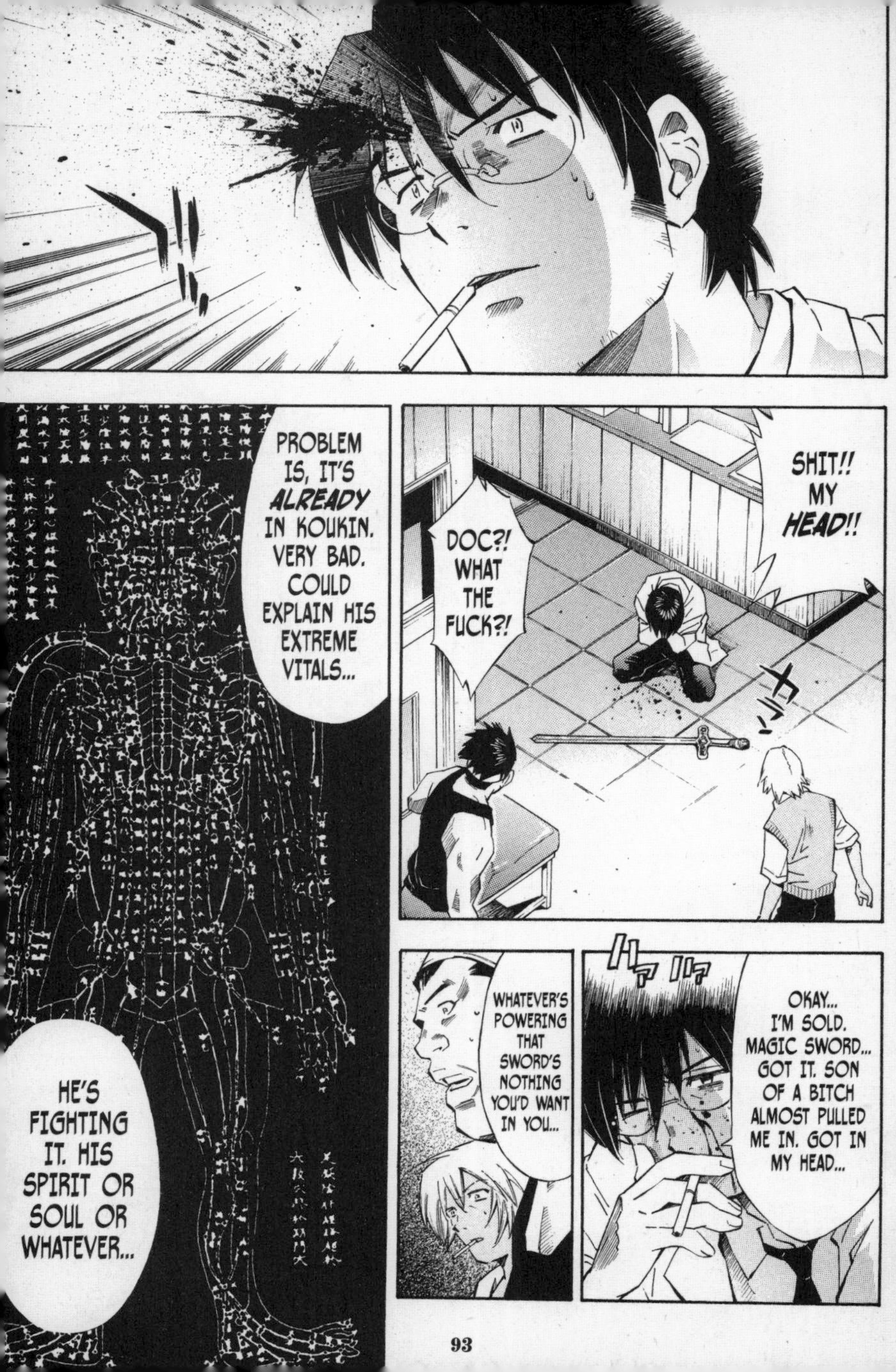
SHIT!! MY *HEAD!!*
DOC?! WHAT THE FUCK?!
OKAY... I'M SOLD. MAGIC SWORD... GOT IT. SON OF A BITCH ALMOST PULLED ME IN. GOT IN MY HEAD...
WHATEVER'S POWERING THAT SWORD'S NOTHING YOU'D WANT IN YOU...
PROBLEM IS, IT'S *ALREADY* IN KOUKIN. VERY BAD. COULD EXPLAIN HIS EXTREME VITALS...
HE'S FIGHTING IT. HIS SPIRIT OR SOUL OR WHATEVER...

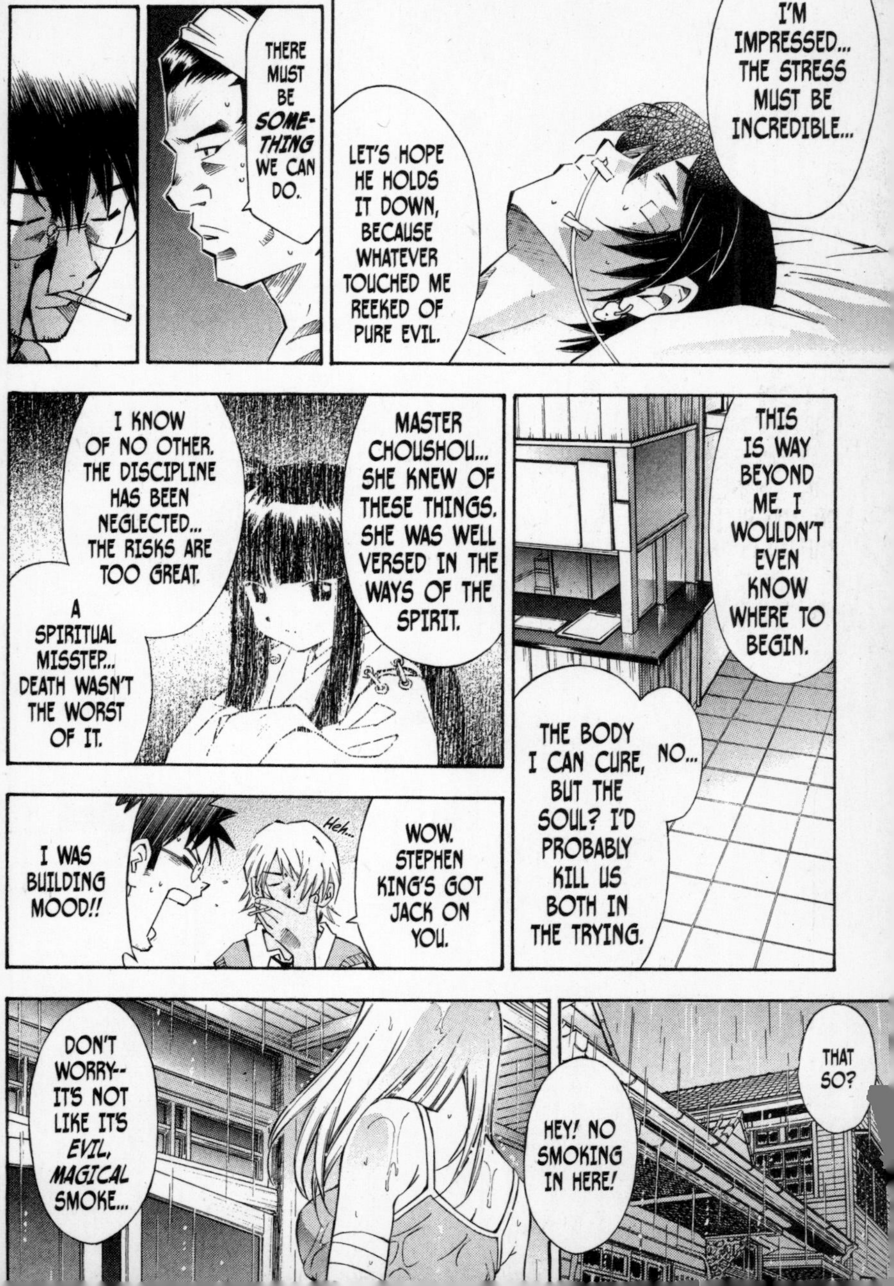
I'M IMPRESSED... THE STRESS MUST BE INCREDIBLE...
LET'S HOPE HE HOLDS IT DOWN, BECAUSE WHATEVER TOUCHED ME REEKED OF PURE EVIL.
THERE MUST BE *SOMETHING* WE CAN DO.
THIS IS WAY BEYOND ME. I WOULDN'T EVEN KNOW WHERE TO BEGIN.
NO...
THE BODY I CAN CURE, BUT THE SOUL? I'D PROBABLY KILL US BOTH IN THE TRYING.
MASTER CHOUSHOU... SHE KNEW OF THESE THINGS. SHE WAS WELL VERSED IN THE WAYS OF THE SPIRIT.
I KNOW OF NO OTHER. THE DISCIPLINE HAS BEEN NEGLECTED... THE RISKS ARE TOO GREAT.
A SPIRITUAL MISSTEP... DEATH WASN'T THE WORST OF IT.
WOW. STEPHEN KING'S GOT JACK ON YOU.
Heh...
I WAS BUILDING MOOD!!
THAT SO?
HEY! NO SMOKING IN HERE!
DON'T WORRY-- IT'S NOT LIKE IT'S *EVIL, MAGICAL* SMOKE...

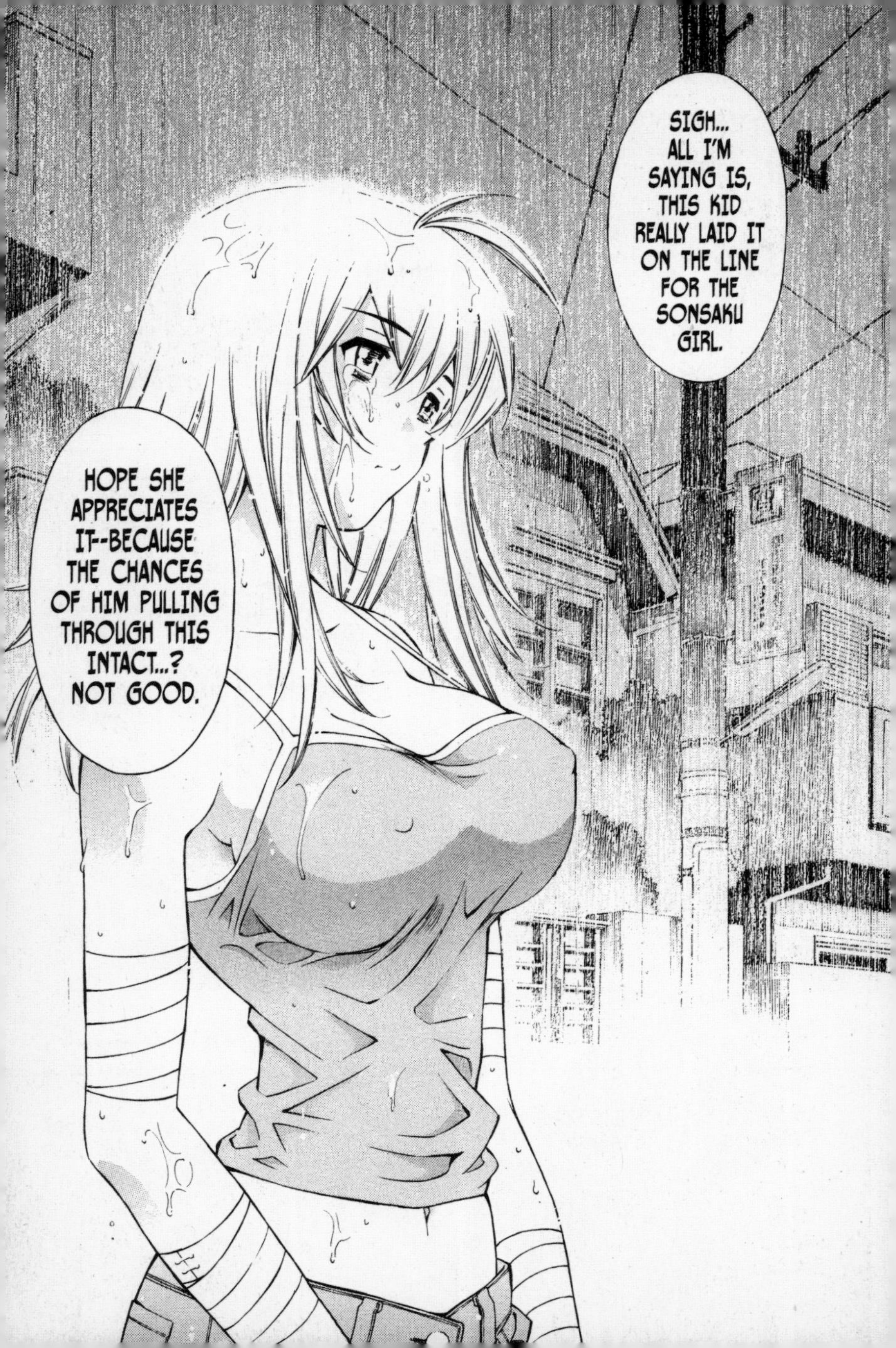
SIGH... ALL I'M SAYING IS, THIS KID REALLY LAID IT ON THE LINE FOR THE SONSAKU GIRL.
HOPE SHE APPRECIATES IT--BECAUSE THE CHANCES OF HIM PULLING THROUGH THIS INTACT...? NOT GOOD.

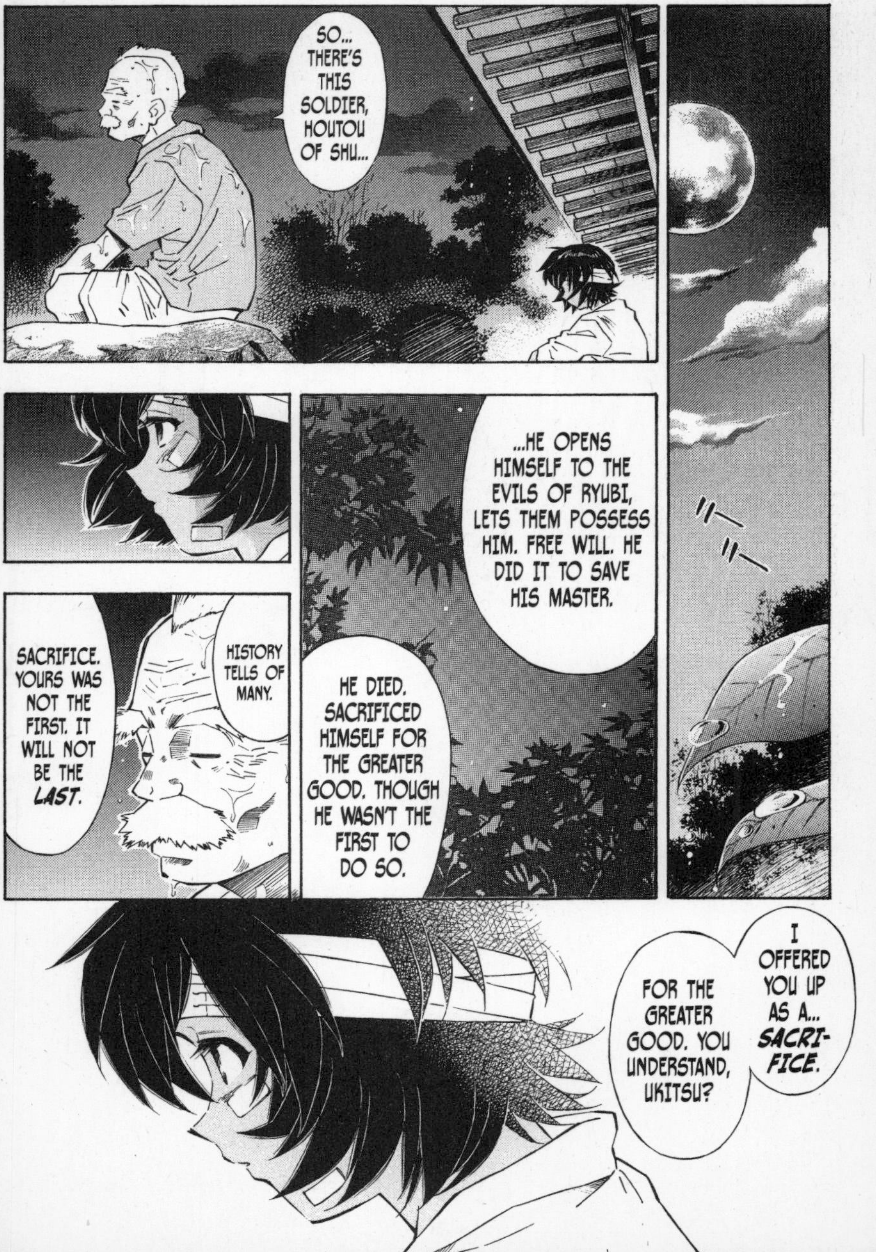
SO... THERE'S THIS SOLDIER, HOUTOU OF SHU...
...HE OPENS HIMSELF TO THE EVILS OF RYUBI, LETS THEM POSSESS HIM. FREE WILL. HE DID IT TO SAVE HIS MASTER.
HE DIED. SACRIFICED HIMSELF FOR THE GREATER GOOD. THOUGH HE WASN'T THE FIRST TO DO SO.
HISTORY TELLS OF MANY.
SACRIFICE. YOURS WAS NOT THE FIRST. IT WILL NOT BE THE ***LAST***.
I OFFERED YOU UP AS A... ***SACRI-FICE***.
FOR THE GREATER GOOD. YOU UNDERSTAND, UKITSU?

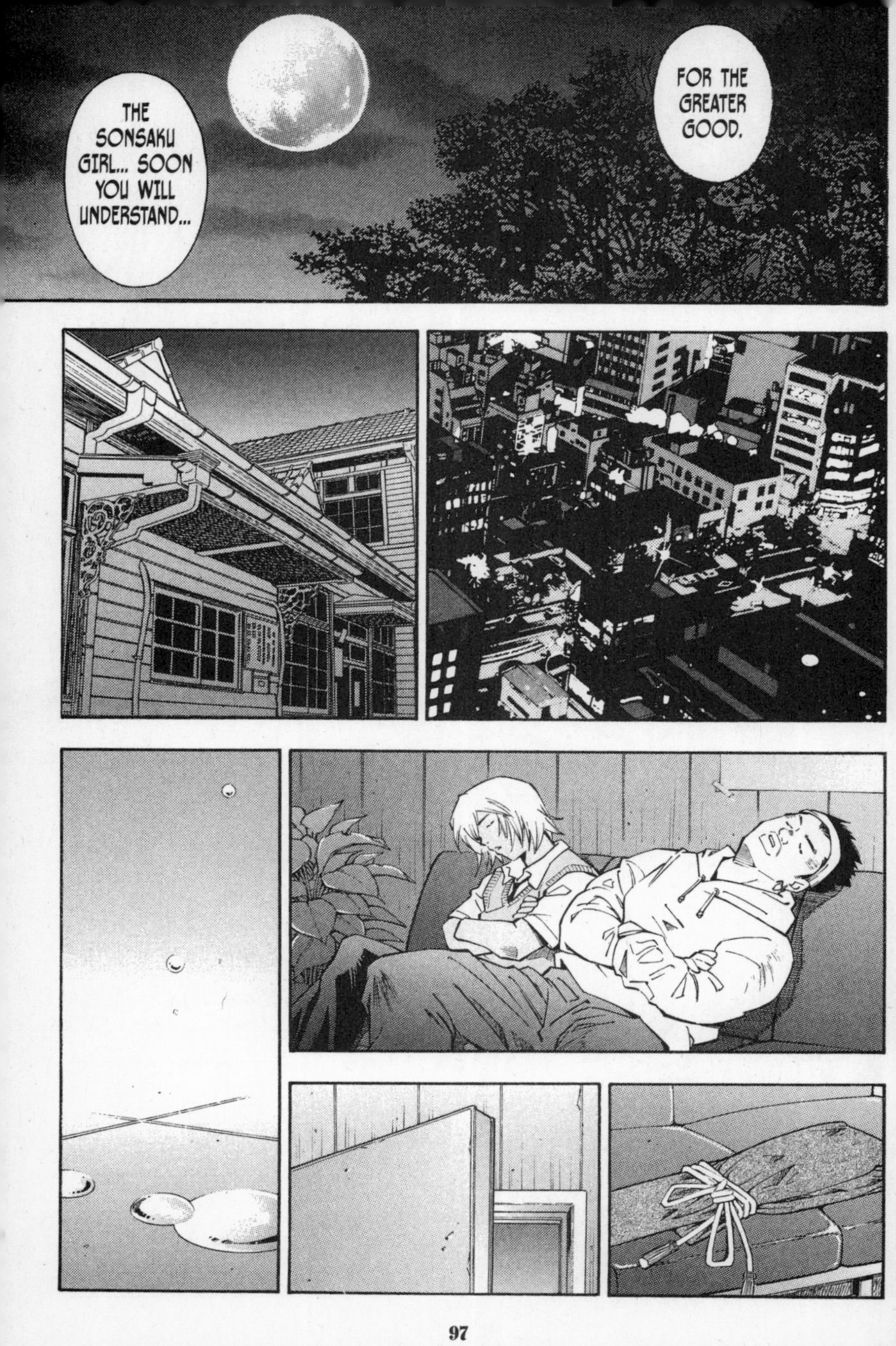
FOR THE GREATER GOOD.
THE SONSAKU GIRL... SOON YOU WILL UNDERSTAND...

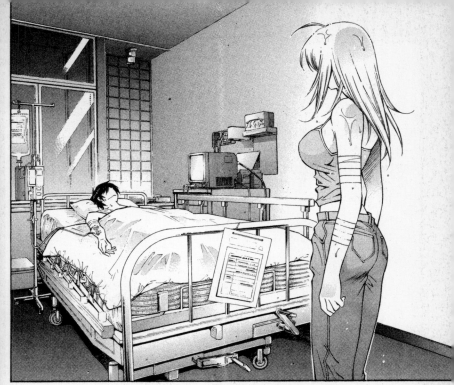

I NEED YOU TOO MUCH.

I'M SCARED AND I NEED YOU TO BE WITH ME...

DON'T DIE...

YOU *CAN'T* DIE...

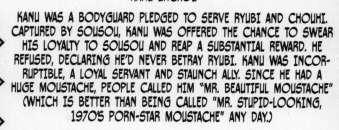

KANU UNCHOU

KANU WAS A BODYGUARD PLEDGED TO SERVE RYUBI AND CHOUHI. CAPTURED BY SOUSOU, KANU WAS OFFERED THE CHANCE TO SWEAR HIS LOYALTY TO SOUSOU AND REAP A SUBSTANTIAL REWARD. HE REFUSED, DECLARING HE'D NEVER BETRAY RYUBI. KANU WAS INCORRUPTIBLE, A LOYAL SERVANT AND STAUNCH ALLY. SINCE HE HAD A HUGE MOUSTACHE, PEOPLE CALLED HIM "MR. BEAUTIFUL MOUSTACHE" (WHICH IS BETTER THAN BEING CALLED "MR. STUPID-LOOKING, 1970'S PORN-STAR MOUSTACHE" ANY DAY.)

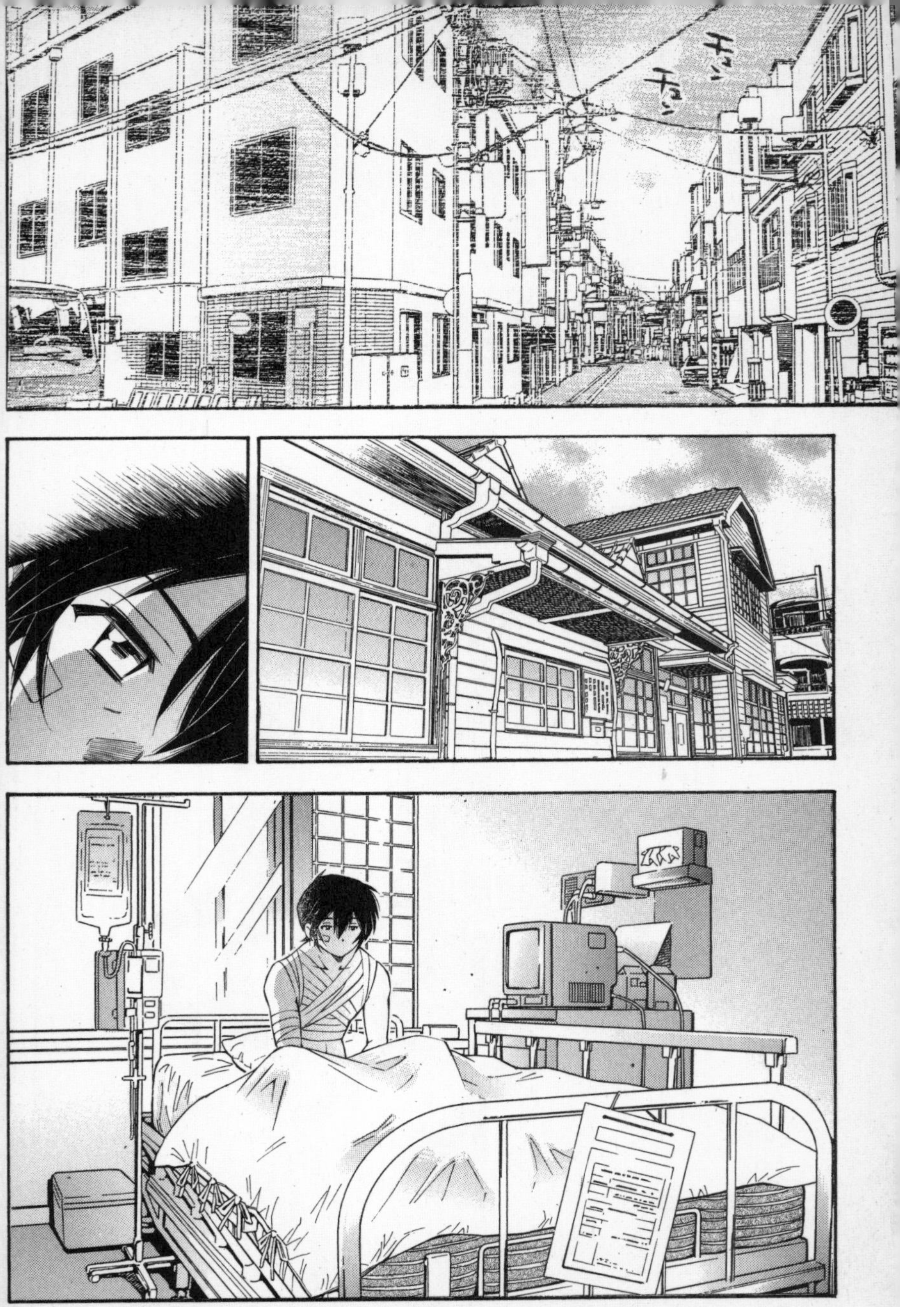
チュン
チュン

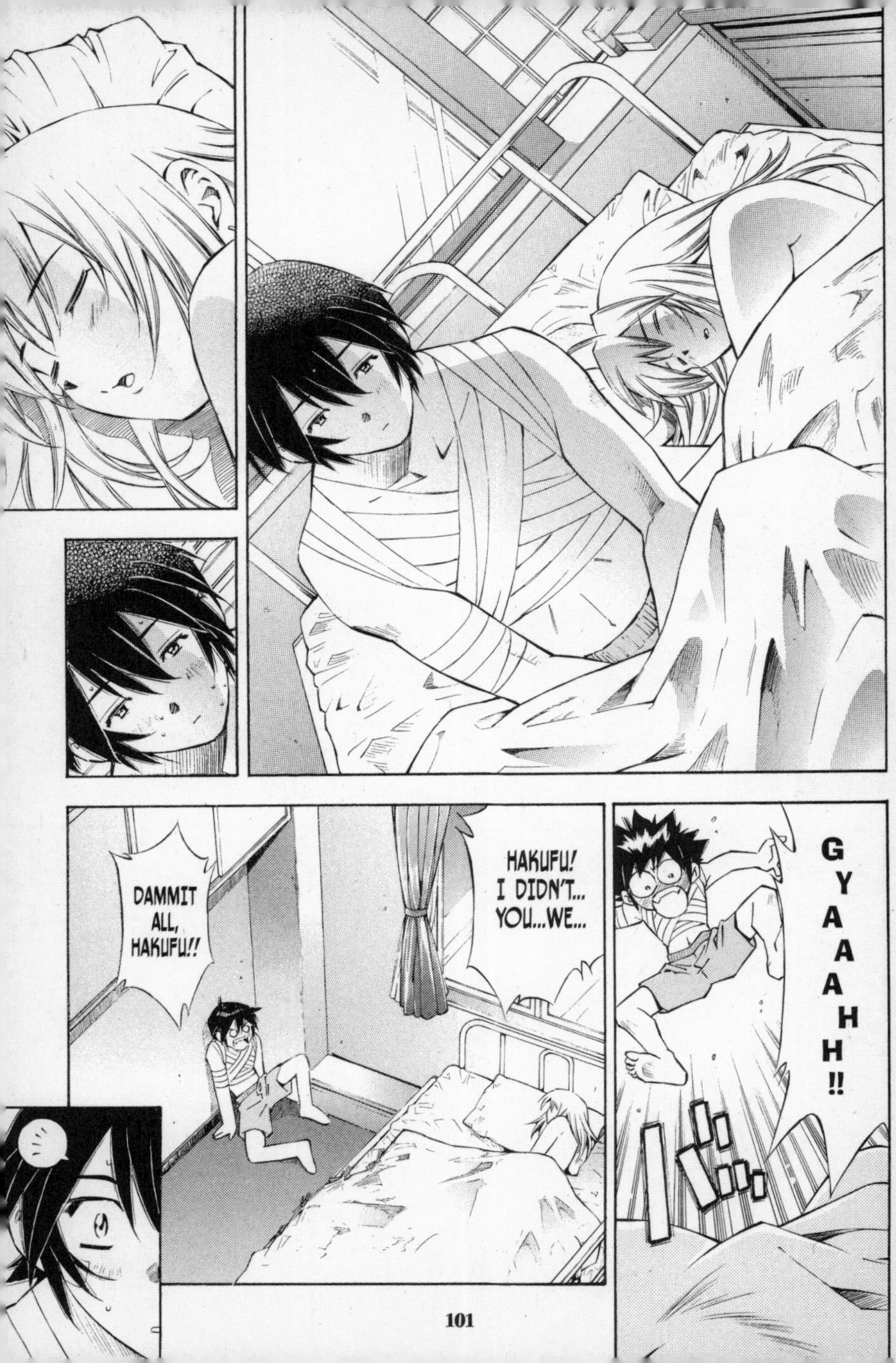
GYAAAHH!!
HAKUFU! I DIDN'T... YOU...WE...
DAMMIT ALL, HAKUFU!!
...

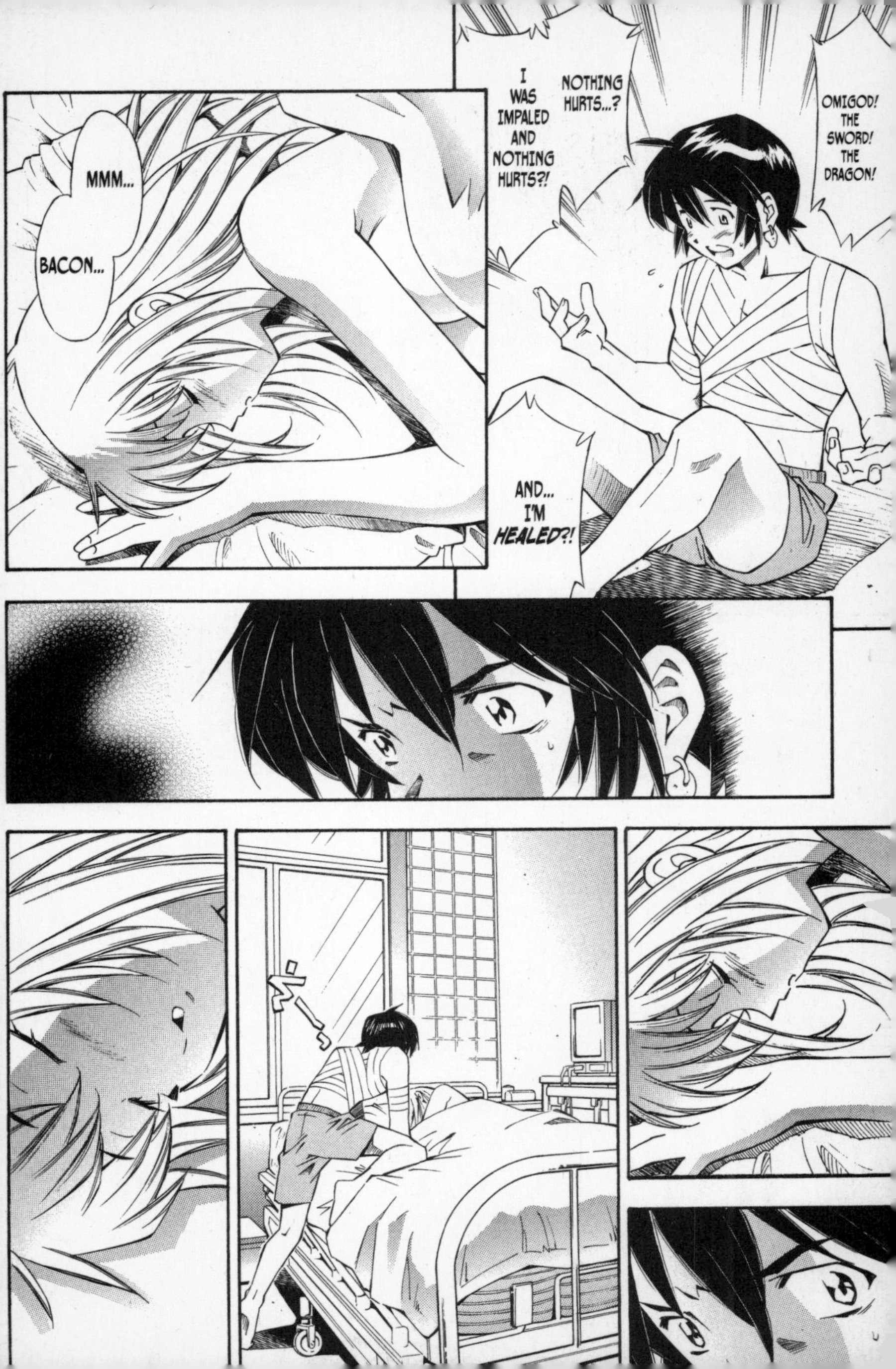
OMIGOD! THE SWORD! THE DRAGON!
NOTHING HURTS...?
I WAS IMPALED AND NOTHING HURTS?!
AND... I'M *HEALED*?!
MMM...
BACON...

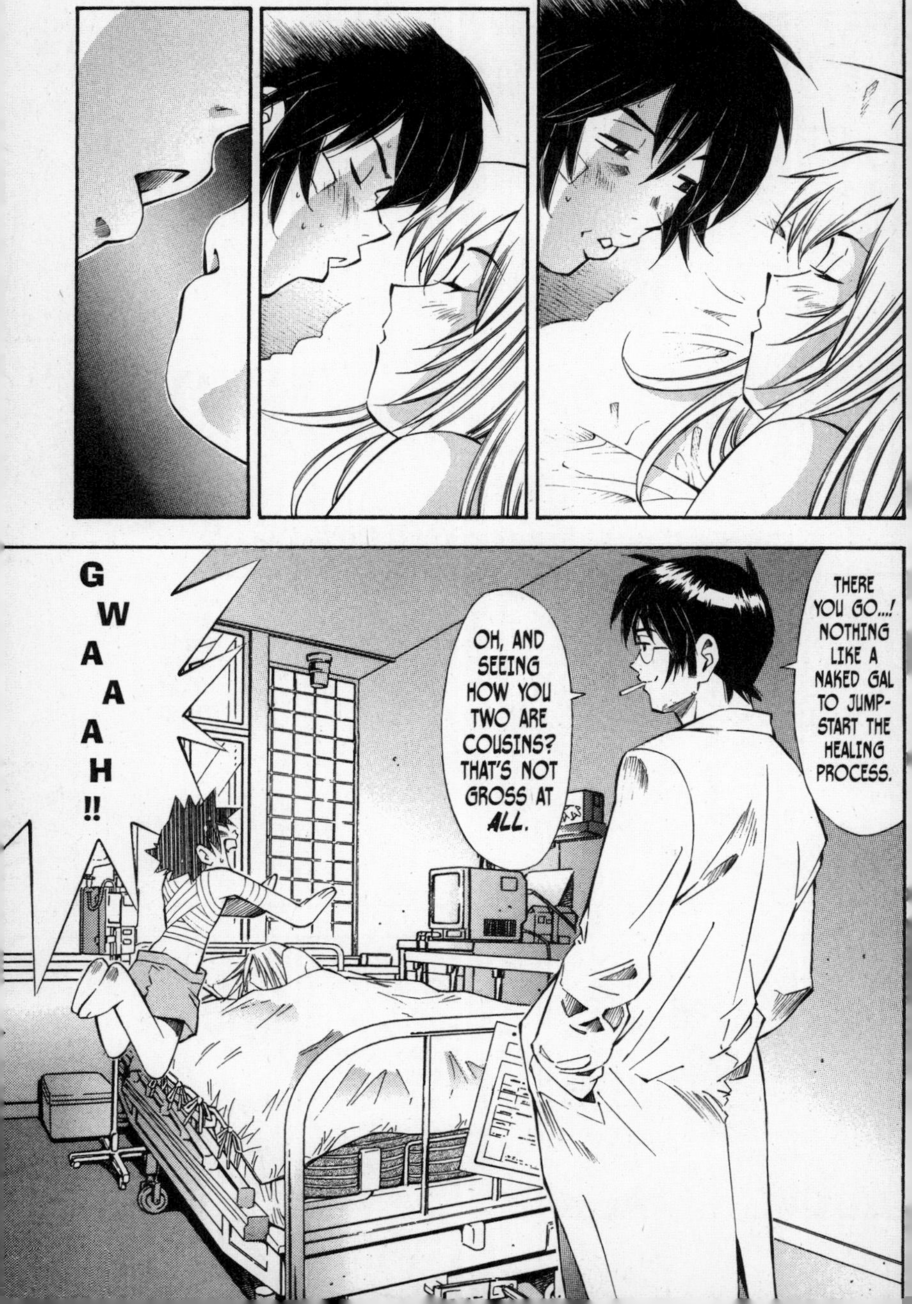
THERE YOU GO...! NOTHING LIKE A NAKED GAL TO JUMP-START THE HEALING PROCESS.
OH, AND SEEING HOW YOU TWO ARE COUSINS? THAT'S NOT GROSS AT *ALL*.
GWAAAH!!

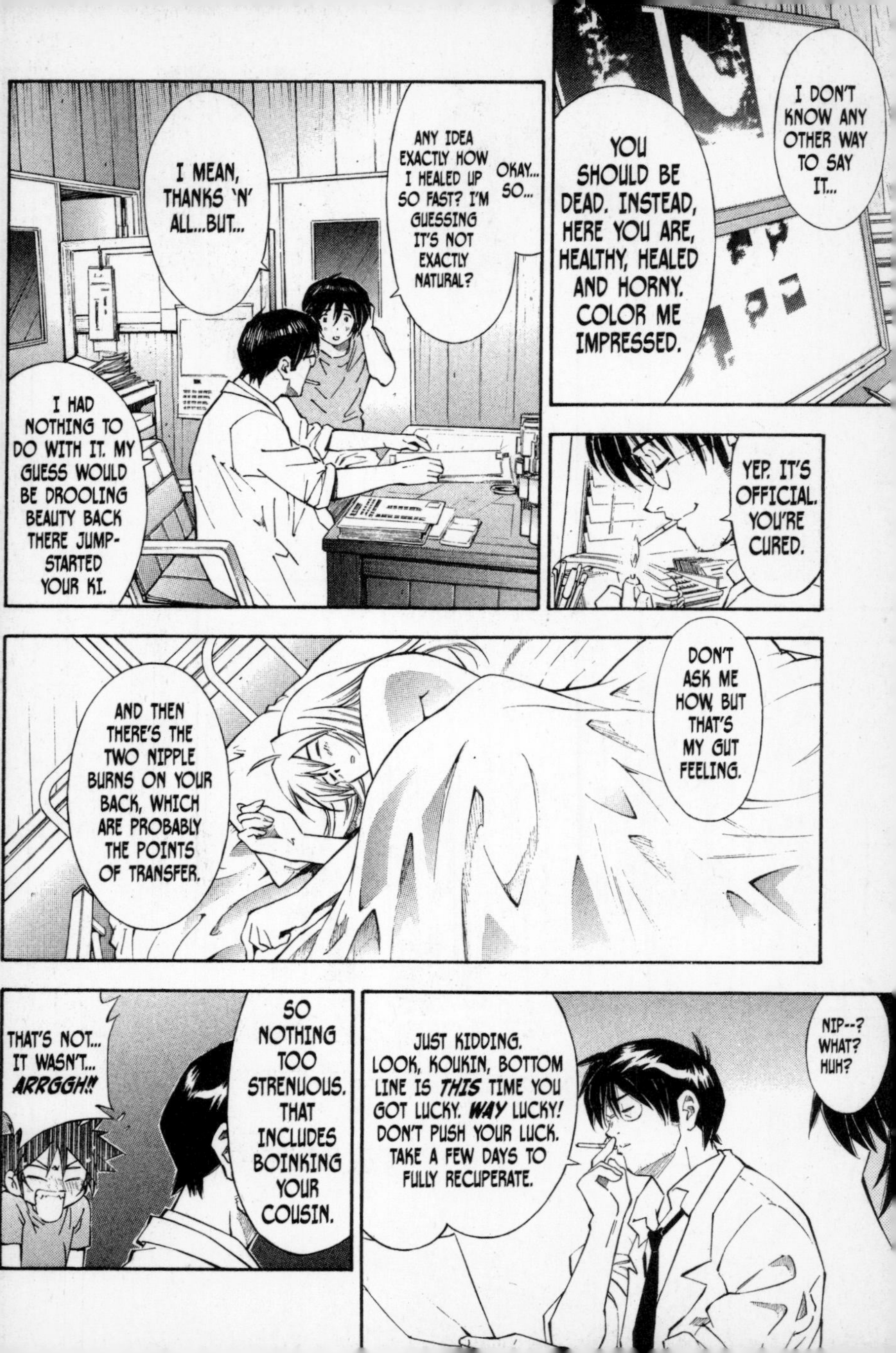
I DON'T KNOW ANY OTHER WAY TO SAY IT...
YOU SHOULD BE DEAD. INSTEAD, HERE YOU ARE, HEALTHY, HEALED AND HORNY. COLOR ME IMPRESSED.
YEP. IT'S OFFICIAL. YOU'RE CURED.
OKAY... SO...
ANY IDEA EXACTLY HOW I HEALED UP SO FAST? I'M GUESSING IT'S NOT EXACTLY NATURAL?
I MEAN, THANKS 'N' ALL...BUT...
I HAD NOTHING TO DO WITH IT. MY GUESS WOULD BE DROOLING BEAUTY BACK THERE JUMP-STARTED YOUR KI.
DON'T ASK ME HOW, BUT THAT'S MY GUT FEELING.
AND THEN THERE'S THE TWO NIPPLE BURNS ON YOUR BACK, WHICH ARE PROBABLY THE POINTS OF TRANSFER.
NIP--? WHAT? HUH?
JUST KIDDING. LOOK, KOUKIN, BOTTOM LINE IS *THIS* TIME YOU GOT LUCKY. *WAY* LUCKY! DON'T PUSH YOUR LUCK. TAKE A FEW DAYS TO FULLY RECUPERATE.
SO NOTHING TOO STRENUOUS. THAT INCLUDES BOINKING YOUR COUSIN.
THAT'S NOT... IT WASN'T... *ARRGGH!!*

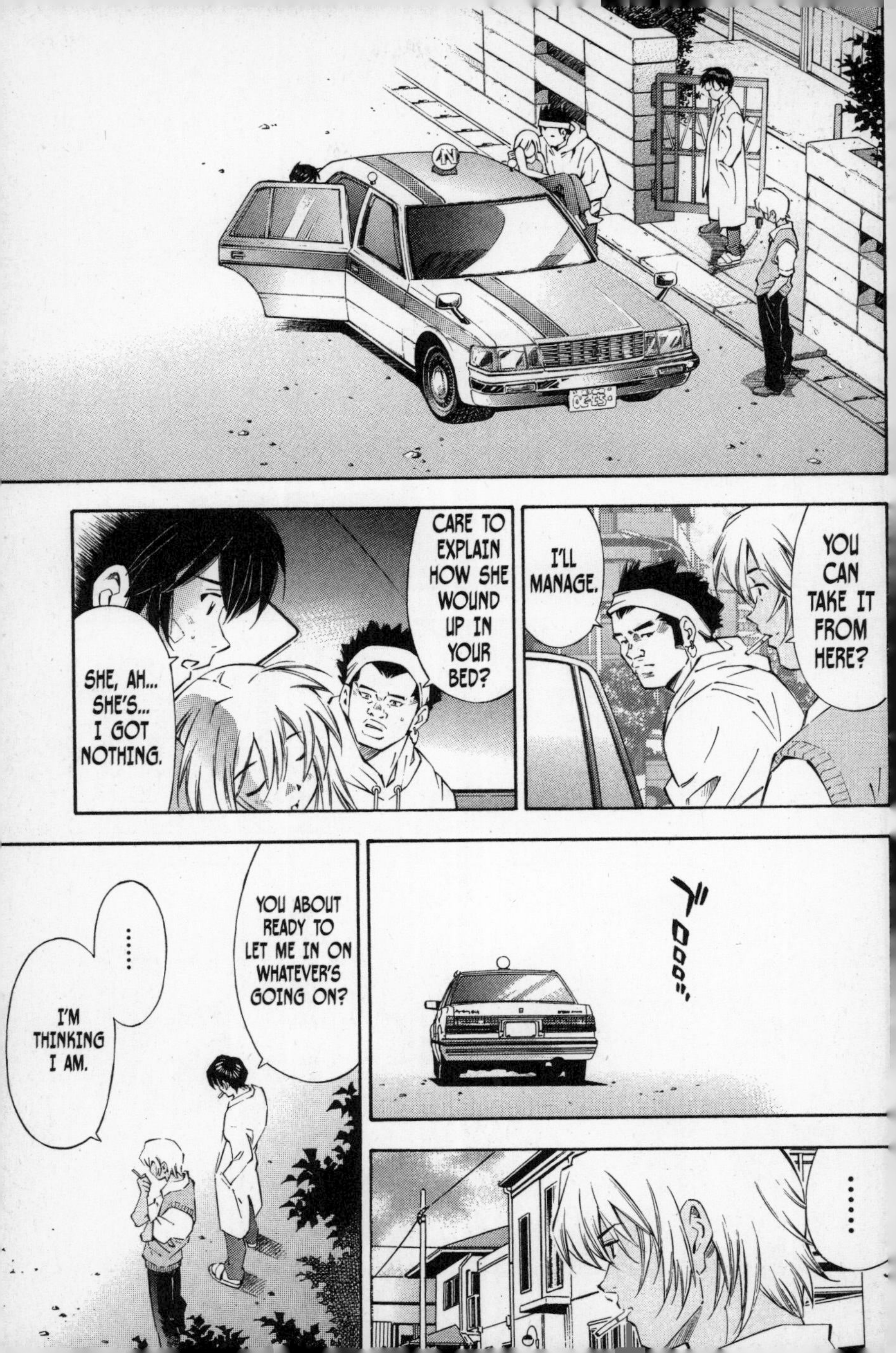
YOU CAN TAKE IT FROM HERE?
I'LL MANAGE.
CARE TO EXPLAIN HOW SHE WOUND UP IN YOUR BED?
SHE, AH... SHE'S... I GOT NOTHING.
ドロロロ
......
YOU ABOUT READY TO LET ME IN ON WHATEVER'S GOING ON?
......
I'M THINKING I AM.

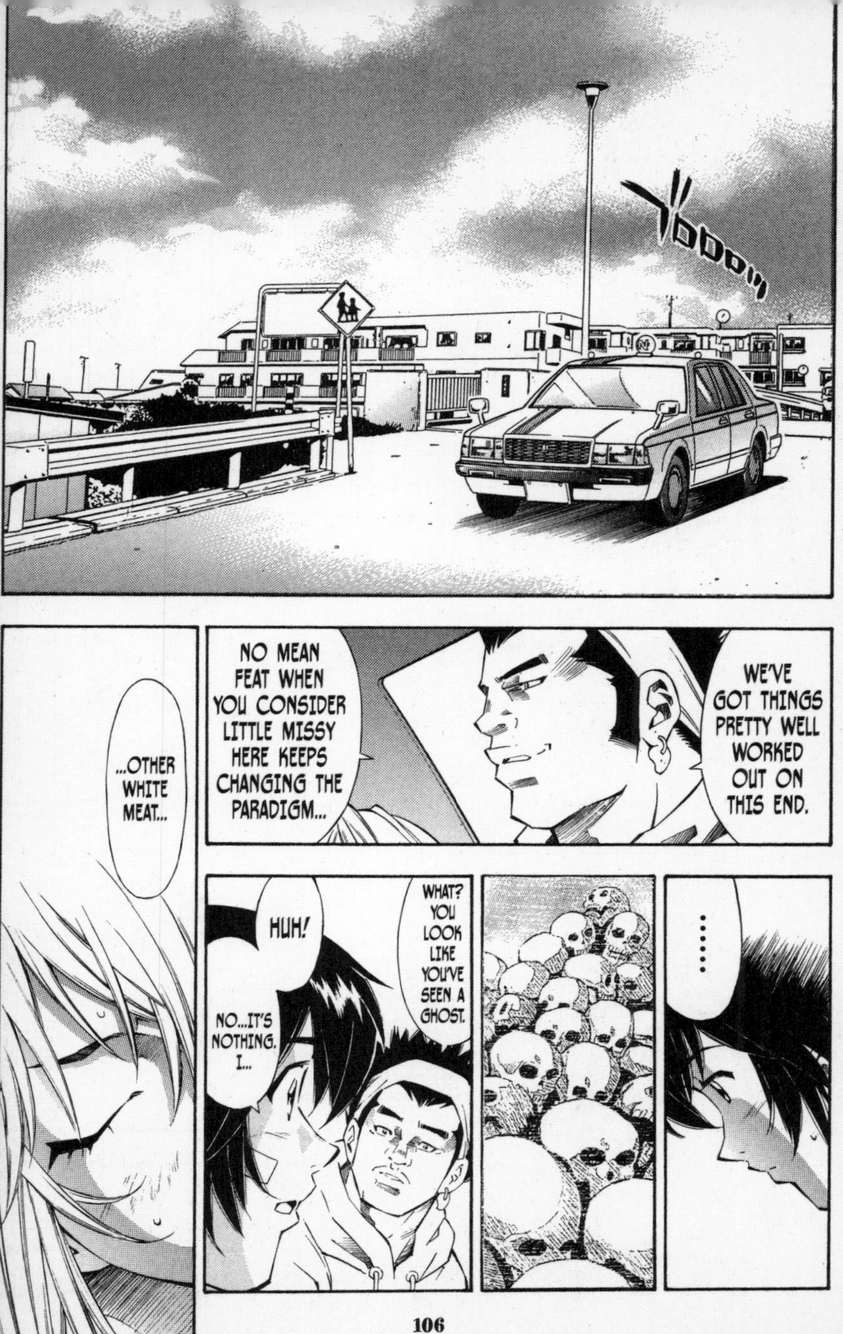
WE'VE GOT THINGS PRETTY WELL WORKED OUT ON THIS END.
NO MEAN FEAT WHEN YOU CONSIDER LITTLE MISSY HERE KEEPS CHANGING THE PARADIGM...
......
WHAT? YOU LOOK LIKE YOU'VE SEEN A GHOST.
HUH!
NO...IT'S NOTHING. I...
...OTHER WHITE MEAT...

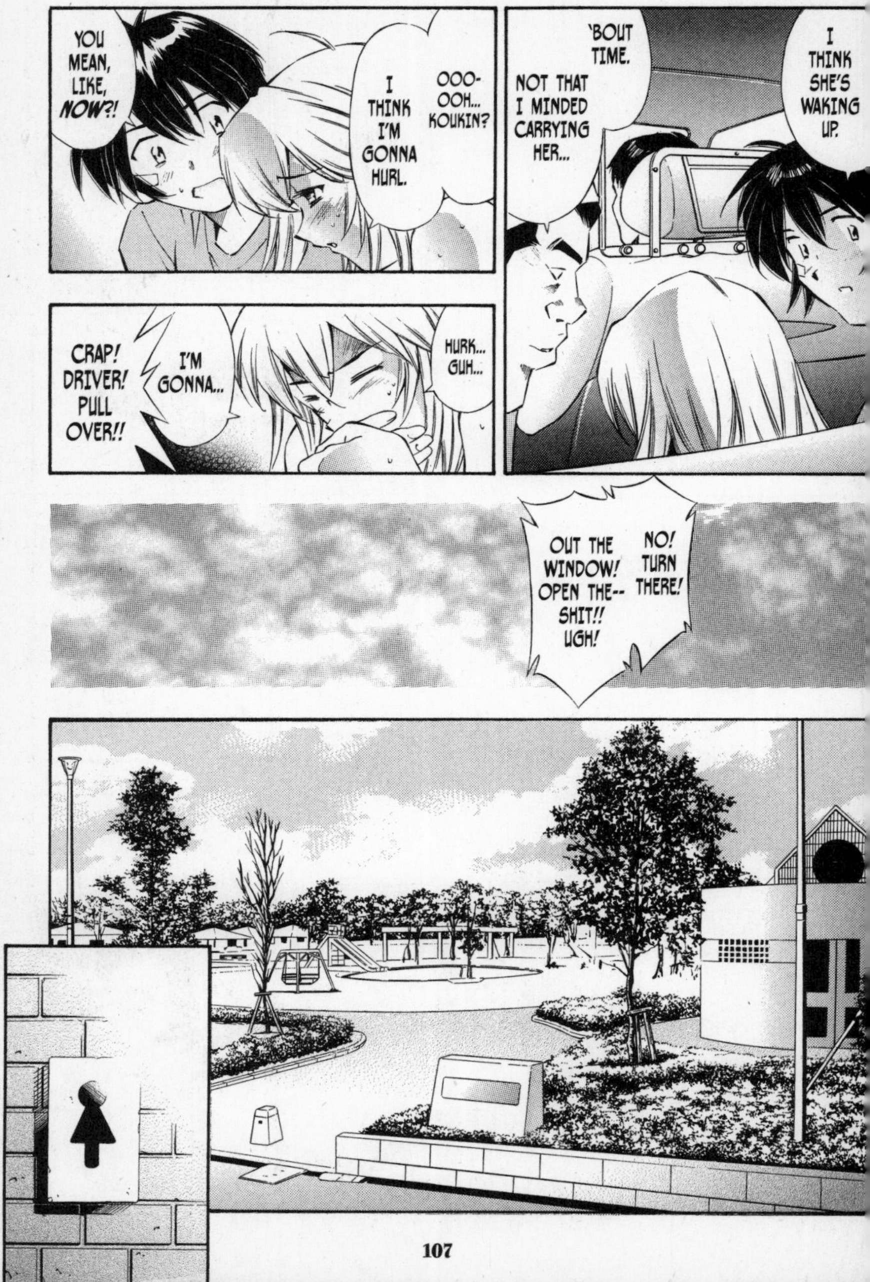
I THINK SHE'S WAKING UP.
'BOUT TIME. NOT THAT I MINDED CARRYING HER...
OOO-OOH... KOUKIN?
I THINK I'M GONNA HURL.
YOU MEAN, LIKE, *NOW*?!
HURK... GUH...
I'M GONNA...
CRAP! DRIVER! PULL OVER!!
NO! TURN THERE!
OUT THE WINDOW! OPEN THE-- SHIT!! UGH!

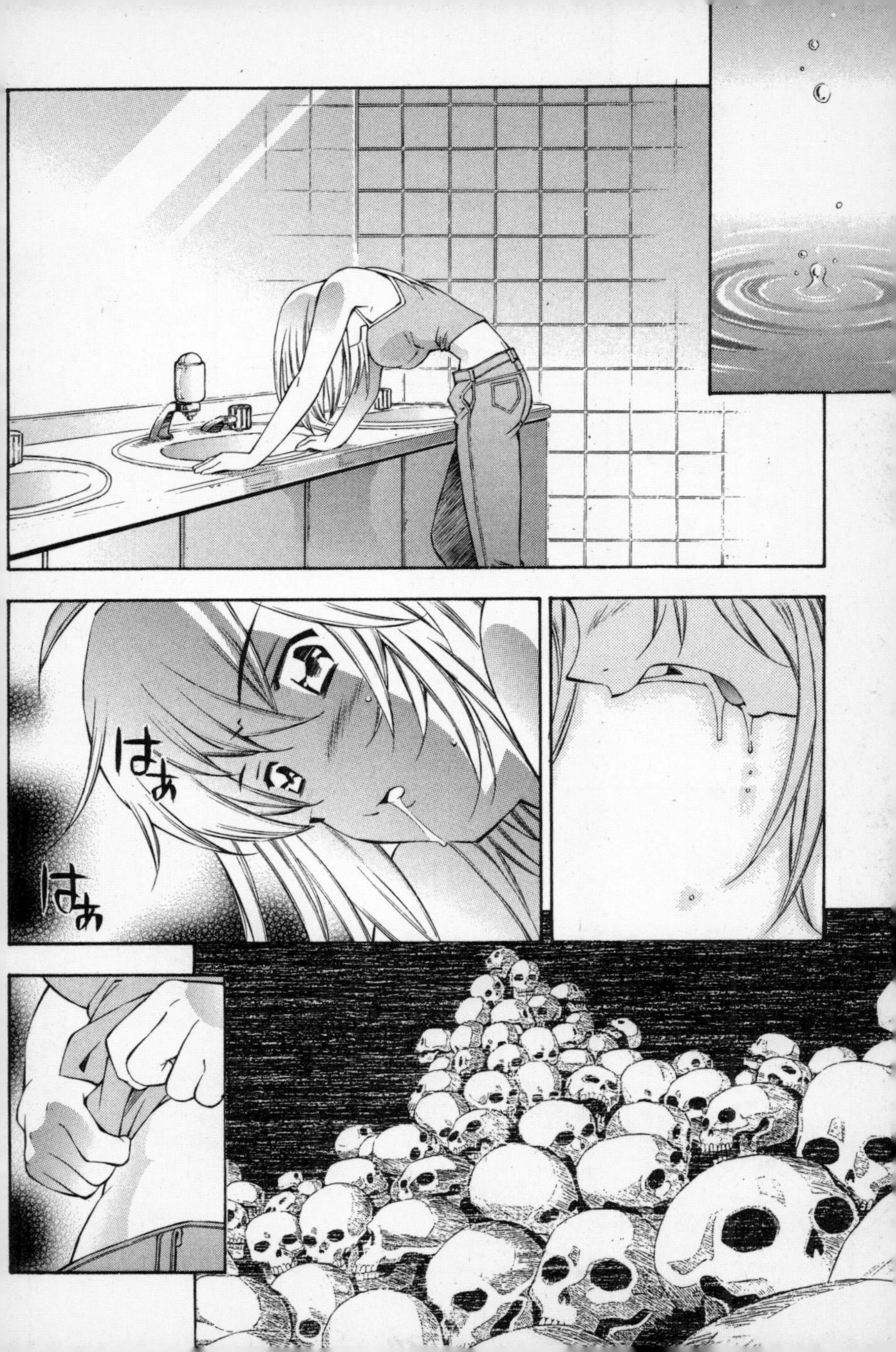
はぁ
はぁ

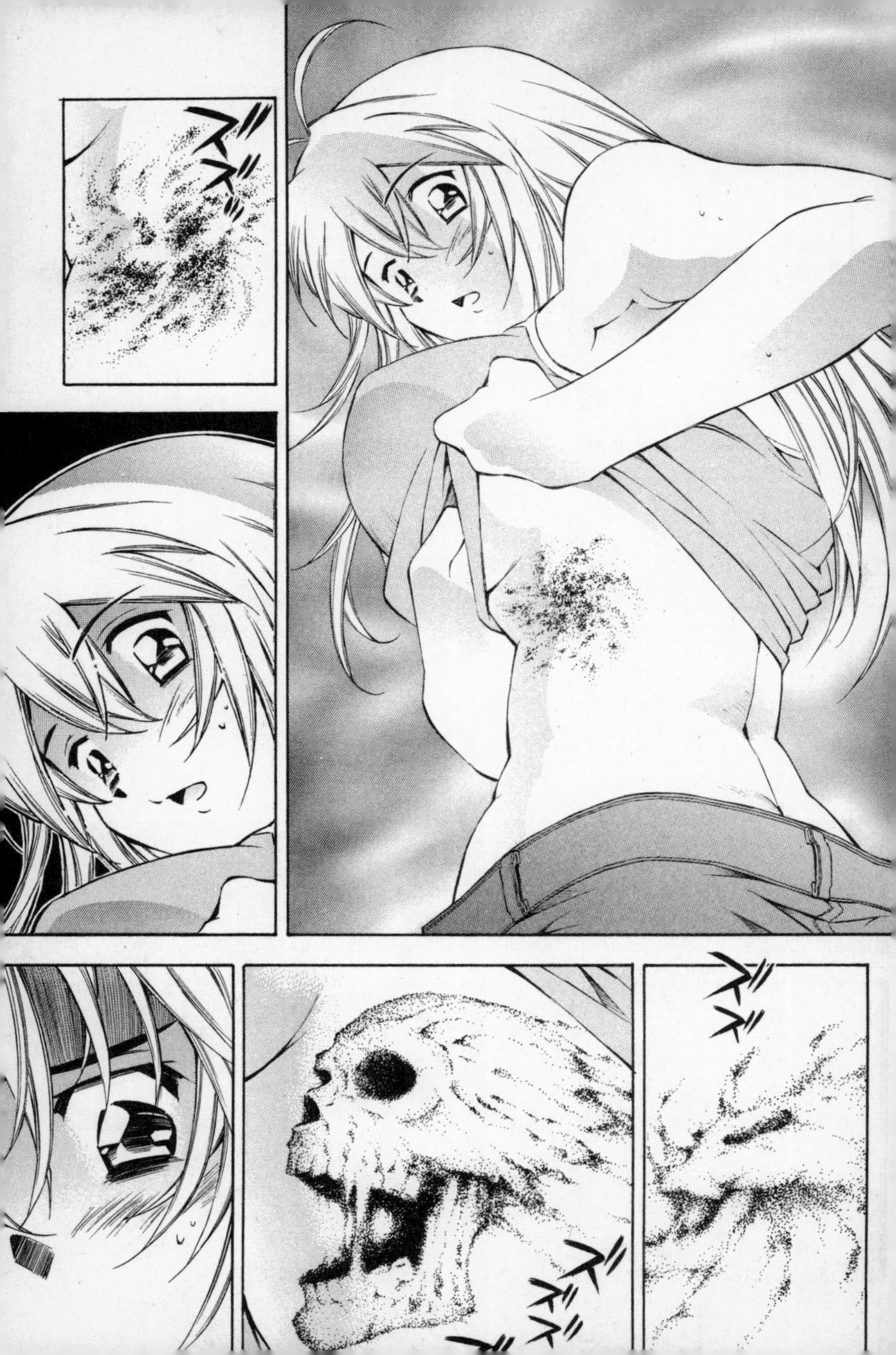
ズズズ
ズズ
ズズズ

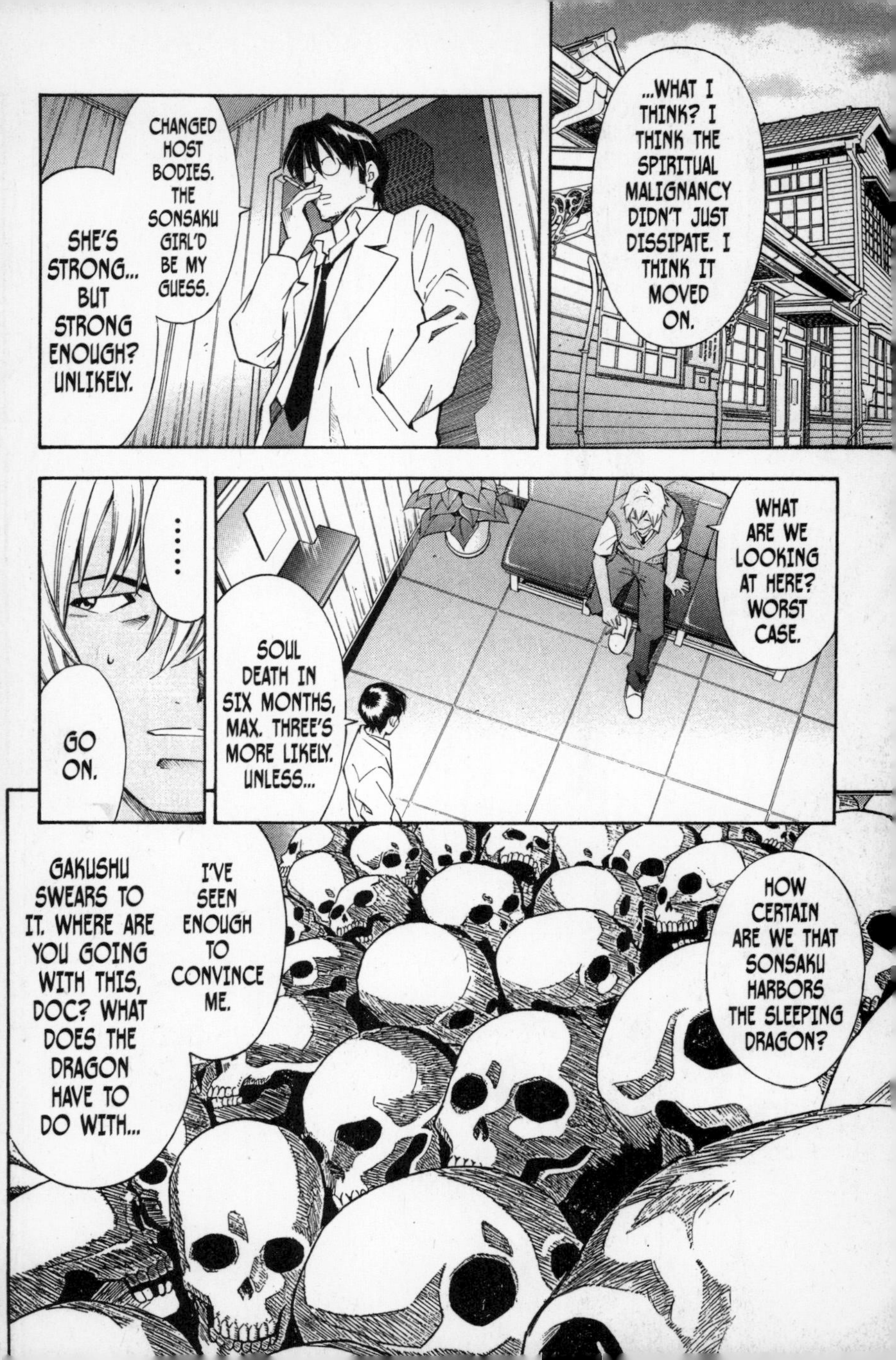
...WHAT I THINK? I THINK THE SPIRITUAL MALIGNANCY DIDN'T JUST DISSIPATE. I THINK IT MOVED ON.
CHANGED HOST BODIES. THE SONSAKU GIRL'D BE MY GUESS.
SHE'S STRONG... BUT STRONG ENOUGH? UNLIKELY.
WHAT ARE WE LOOKING AT HERE? WORST CASE.
SOUL DEATH IN SIX MONTHS, MAX. THREE'S MORE LIKELY. UNLESS...
......
GO ON.
HOW CERTAIN ARE WE THAT SONSAKU HARBORS THE SLEEPING DRAGON?
I'VE SEEN ENOUGH TO CONVINCE ME.
GAKUSHU SWEARS TO IT. WHERE ARE YOU GOING WITH THIS, DOC? WHAT DOES THE DRAGON HAVE TO DO WITH...

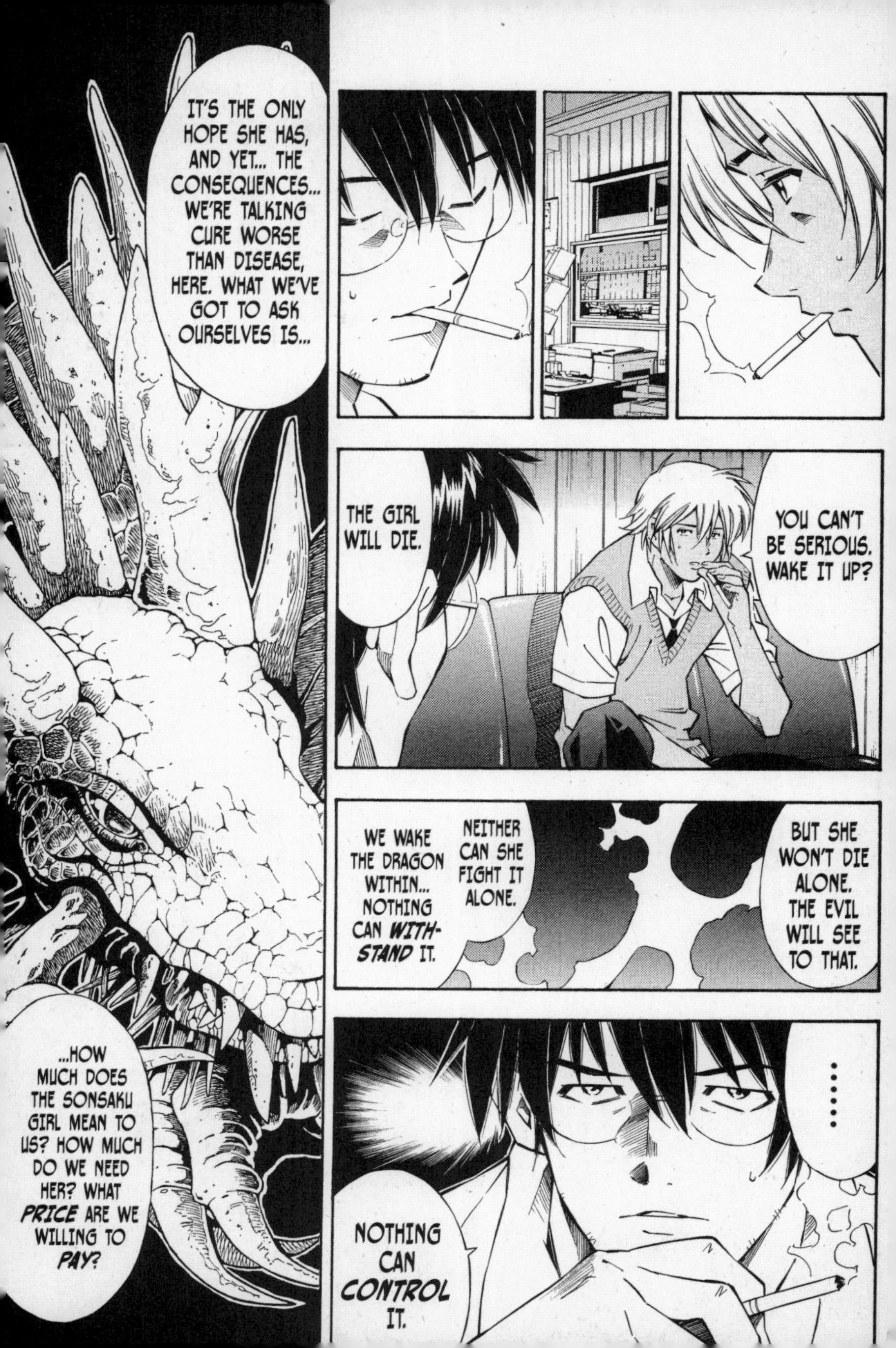
YOU CAN'T BE SERIOUS. WAKE IT UP?
THE GIRL WILL DIE.
BUT SHE WON'T DIE ALONE. THE EVIL WILL SEE TO THAT.
NEITHER CAN SHE FIGHT IT ALONE.
WE WAKE THE DRAGON WITHIN... NOTHING CAN *WITHSTAND* IT.
......
NOTHING CAN *CONTROL* IT.
IT'S THE ONLY HOPE SHE HAS, AND YET... THE CONSEQUENCES... WE'RE TALKING CURE WORSE THAN DISEASE, HERE. WHAT WE'VE GOT TO ASK OURSELVES IS...
...HOW MUCH DOES THE SONSAKU GIRL MEAN TO US? HOW MUCH DO WE NEED HER? WHAT *PRICE* ARE WE WILLING TO *PAY*?

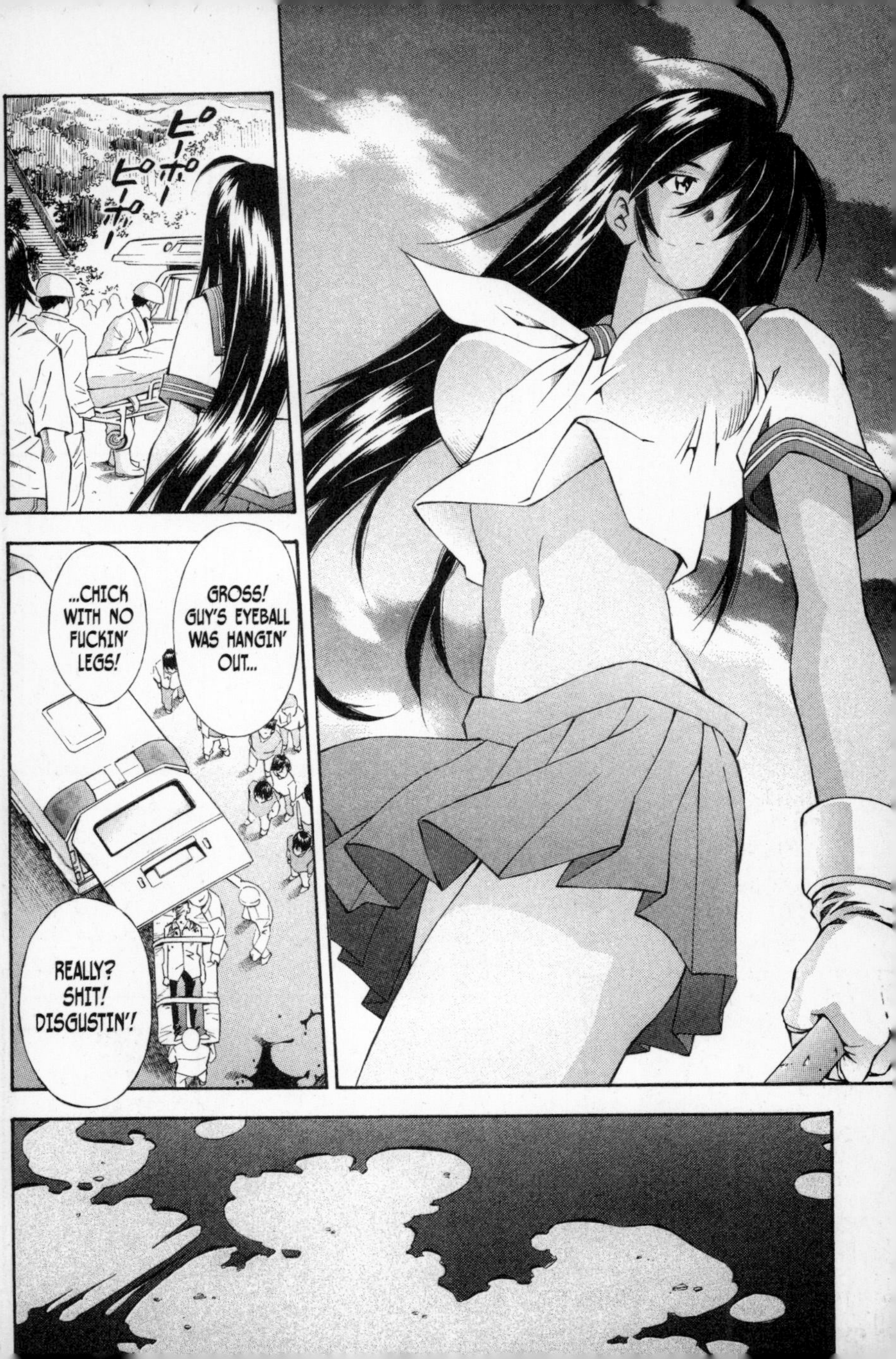
ピーポーピーポー
GROSS! GUY'S EYEBALL WAS HANGIN' OUT...
...CHICK WITH NO FUCKIN' LEGS!
REALLY? SHIT! DISGUSTIN'!

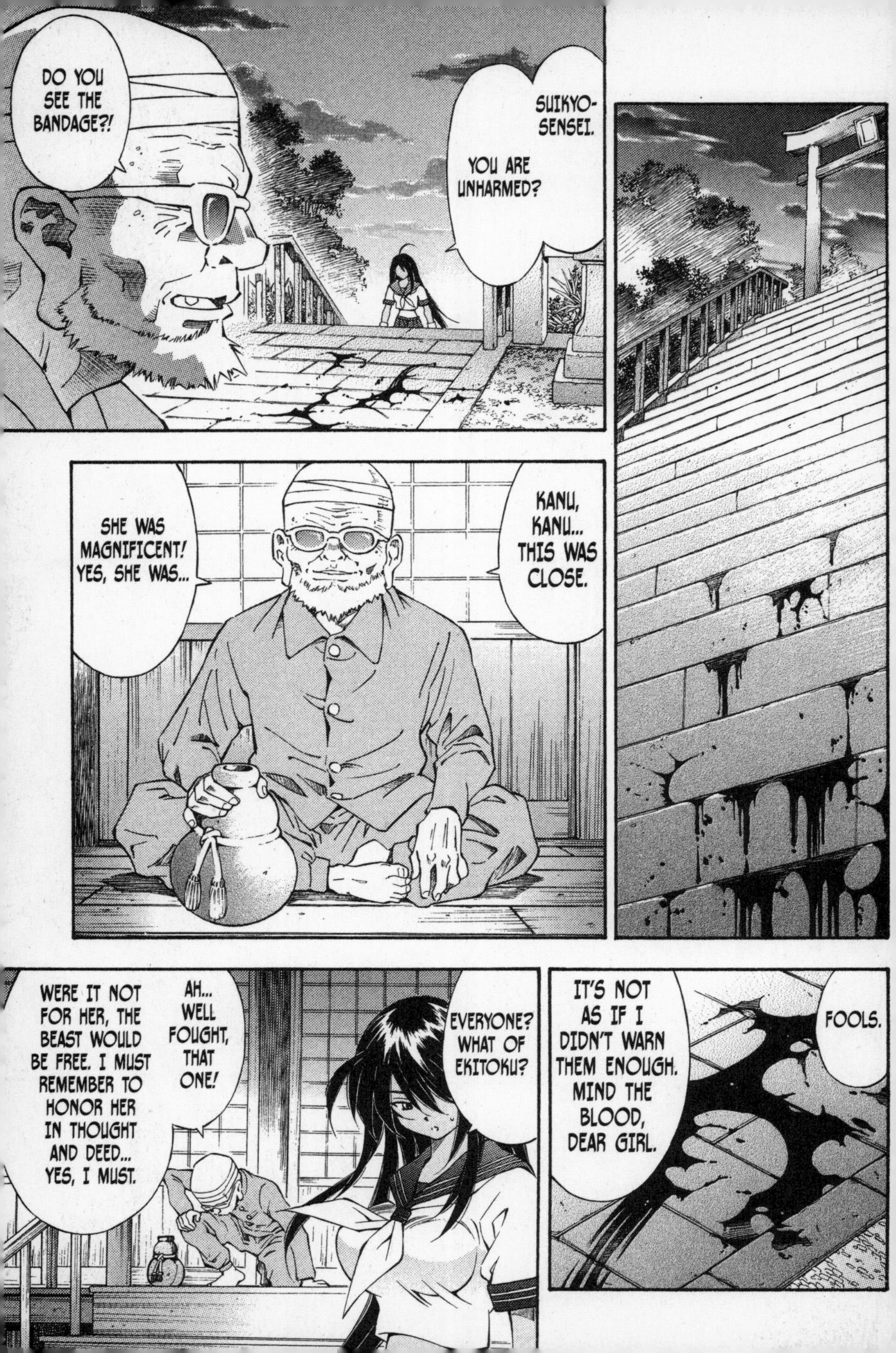
SUIKYO-SENSEI.
YOU ARE UNHARMED?
DO YOU SEE THE BANDAGE?!
KANU, KANU... THIS WAS CLOSE.
SHE WAS MAGNIFICENT! YES, SHE WAS...
FOOLS.
IT'S NOT AS IF I DIDN'T WARN THEM ENOUGH. MIND THE BLOOD, DEAR GIRL.
EVERYONE? WHAT OF EKITOKU?
AH... WELL FOUGHT, THAT ONE!
WERE IT NOT FOR HER, THE BEAST WOULD BE FREE. I MUST REMEMBER TO HONOR HER IN THOUGHT AND DEED... YES, I MUST.

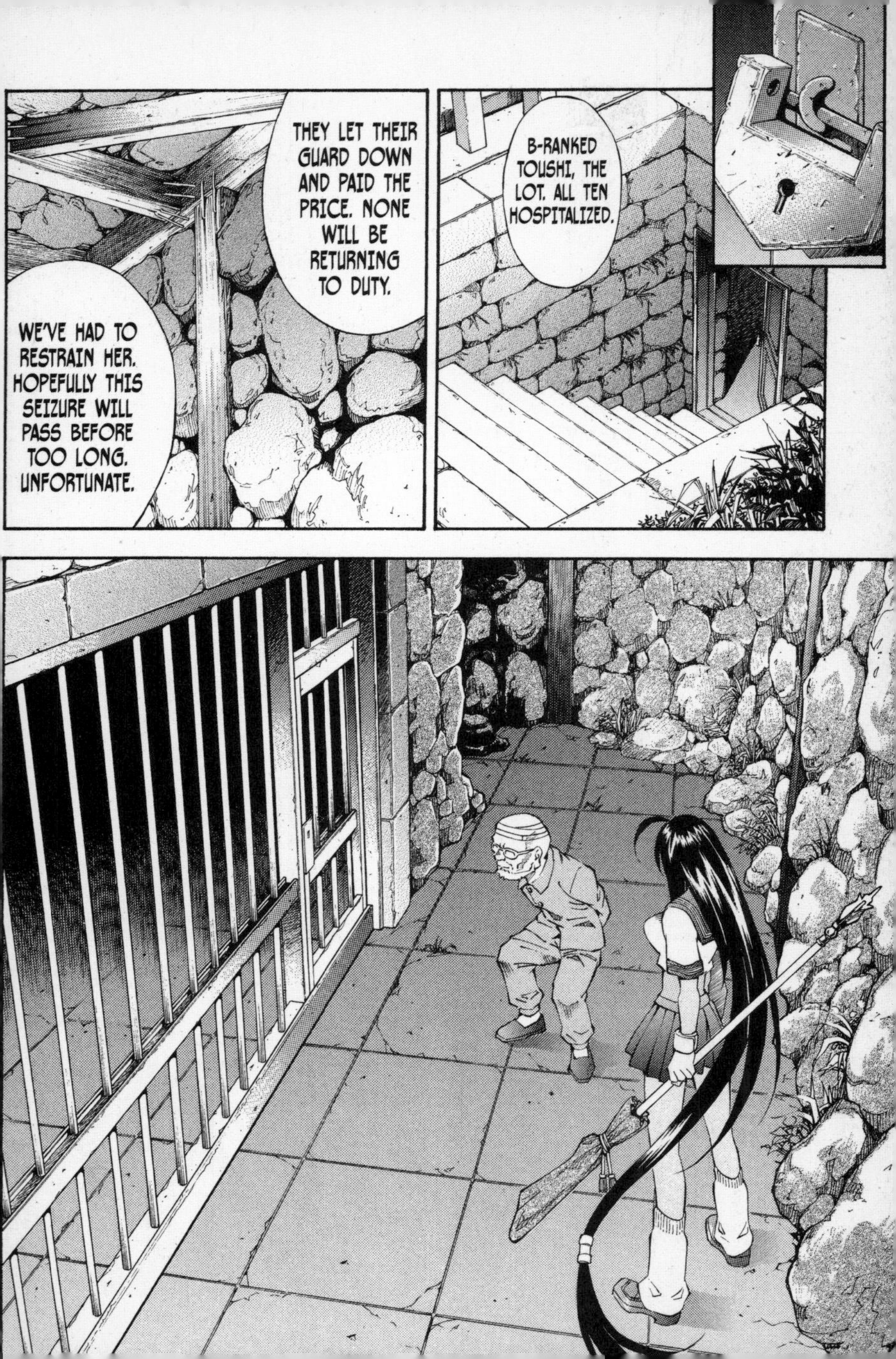
B-RANKED TOUSHI, THE LOT. ALL TEN HOSPITALIZED.
THEY LET THEIR GUARD DOWN AND PAID THE PRICE. NONE WILL BE RETURNING TO DUTY.
WE'VE HAD TO RESTRAIN HER. HOPEFULLY THIS SEIZURE WILL PASS BEFORE TOO LONG. UNFORTUNATE.

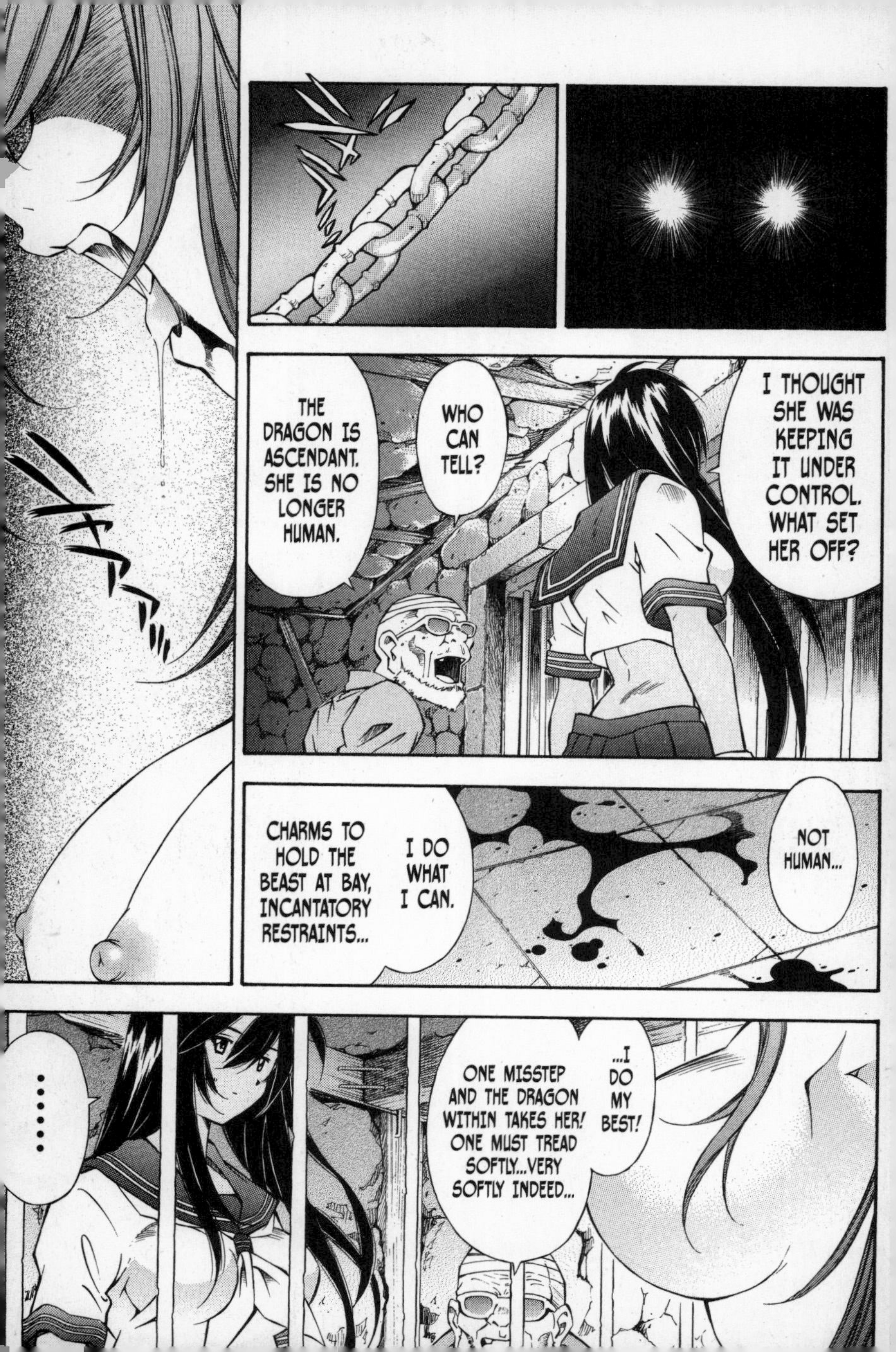
I THOUGHT SHE WAS KEEPING IT UNDER CONTROL. WHAT SET HER OFF?
WHO CAN TELL?
THE DRAGON IS ASCENDANT. SHE IS NO LONGER HUMAN.
NOT HUMAN...
I DO WHAT I CAN.
CHARMS TO HOLD THE BEAST AT BAY, INCANTATORY RESTRAINTS...
...I DO MY BEST!
ONE MISSTEP AND THE DRAGON WITHIN TAKES HER! ONE MUST TREAD SOFTLY...VERY SOFTLY INDEED...
......

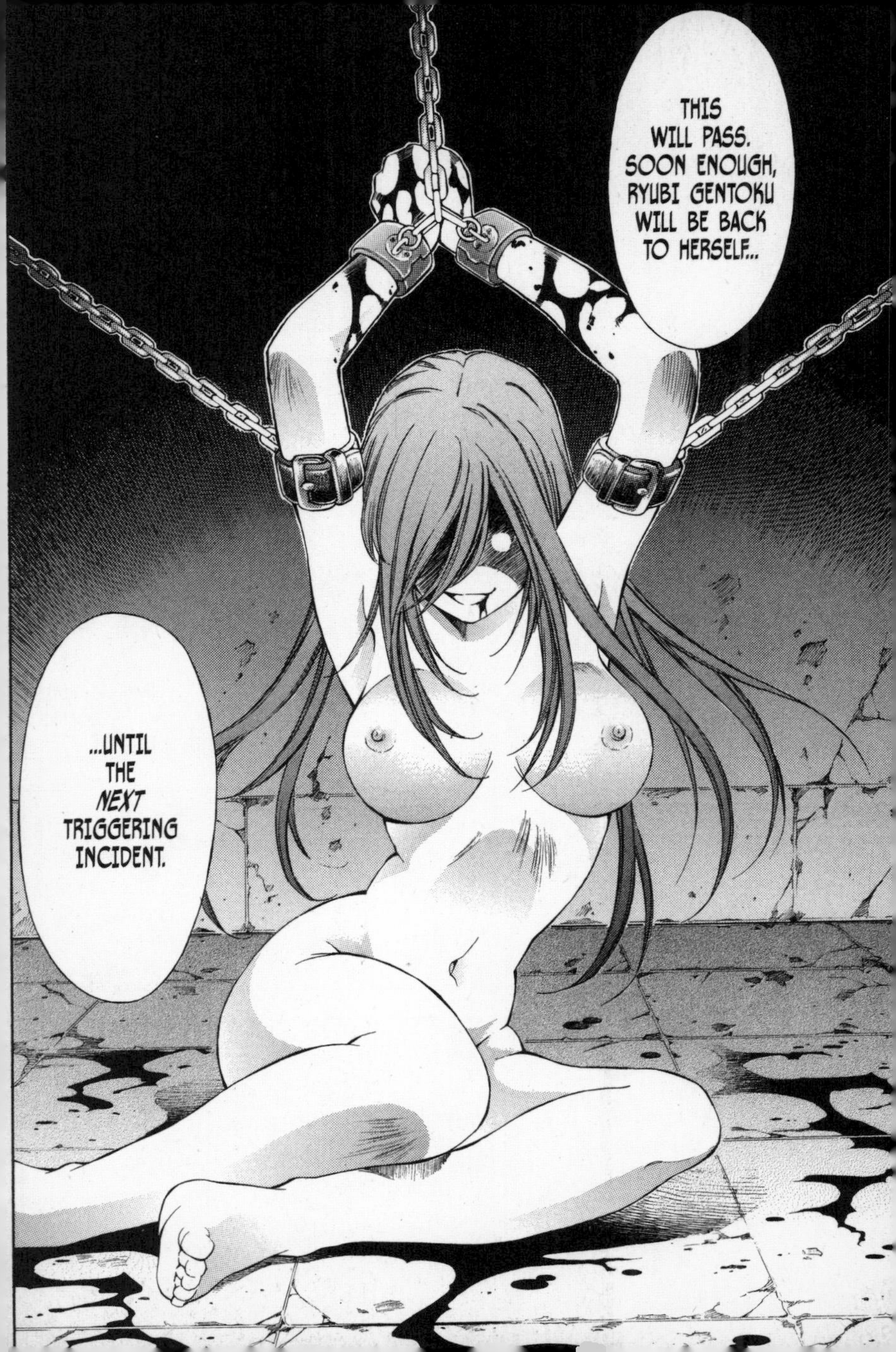
THIS WILL PASS. SOON ENOUGH, RYUBI GENTOKU WILL BE BACK TO HERSELF...
...UNTIL THE *NEXT* TRIGGERING INCIDENT.

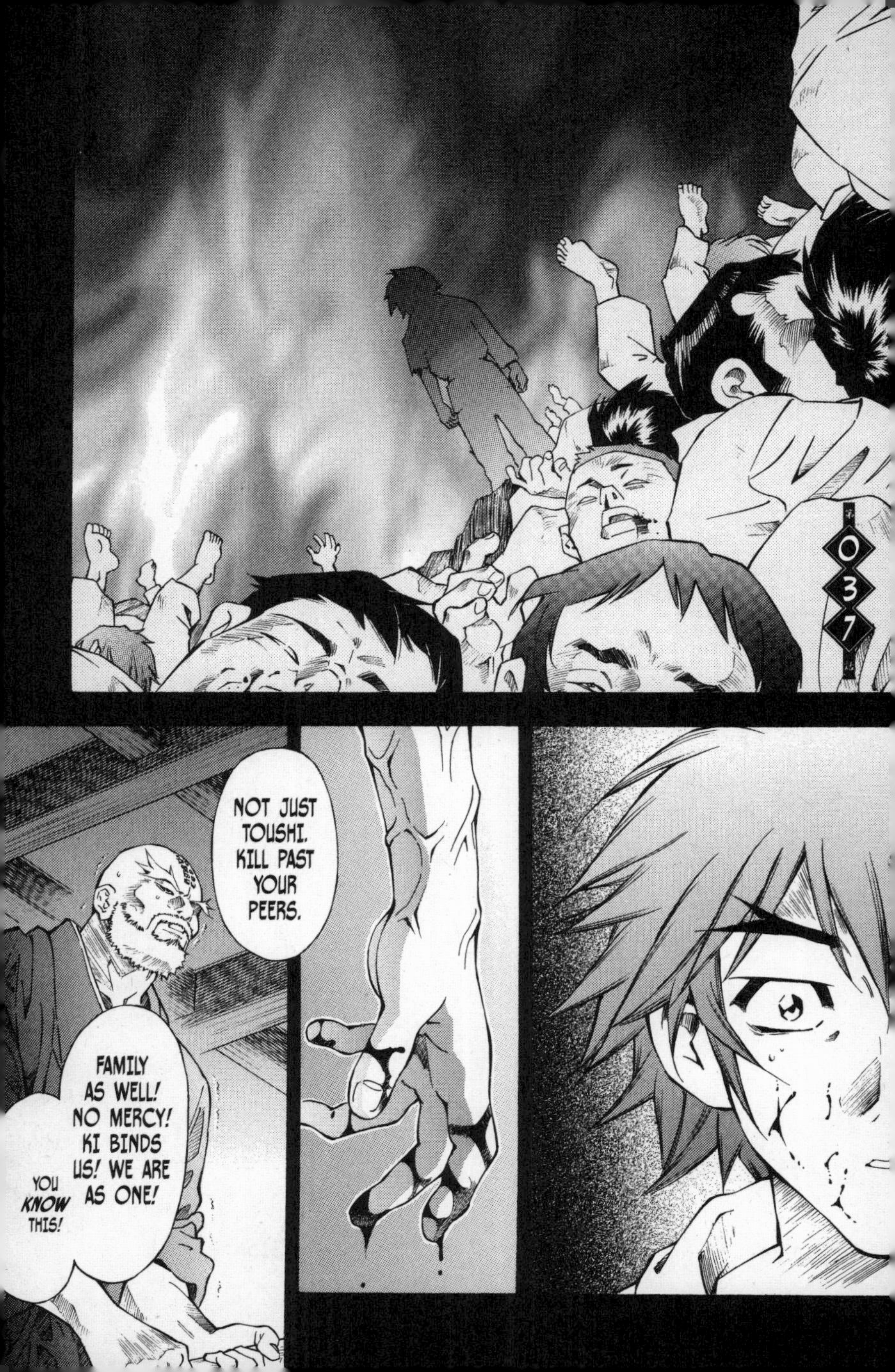
037
NOT JUST TOUSHI. KILL PAST YOUR PEERS.
FAMILY AS WELL! NO MERCY! KI BINDS US! WE ARE AS ONE!
YOU *KNOW* THIS!

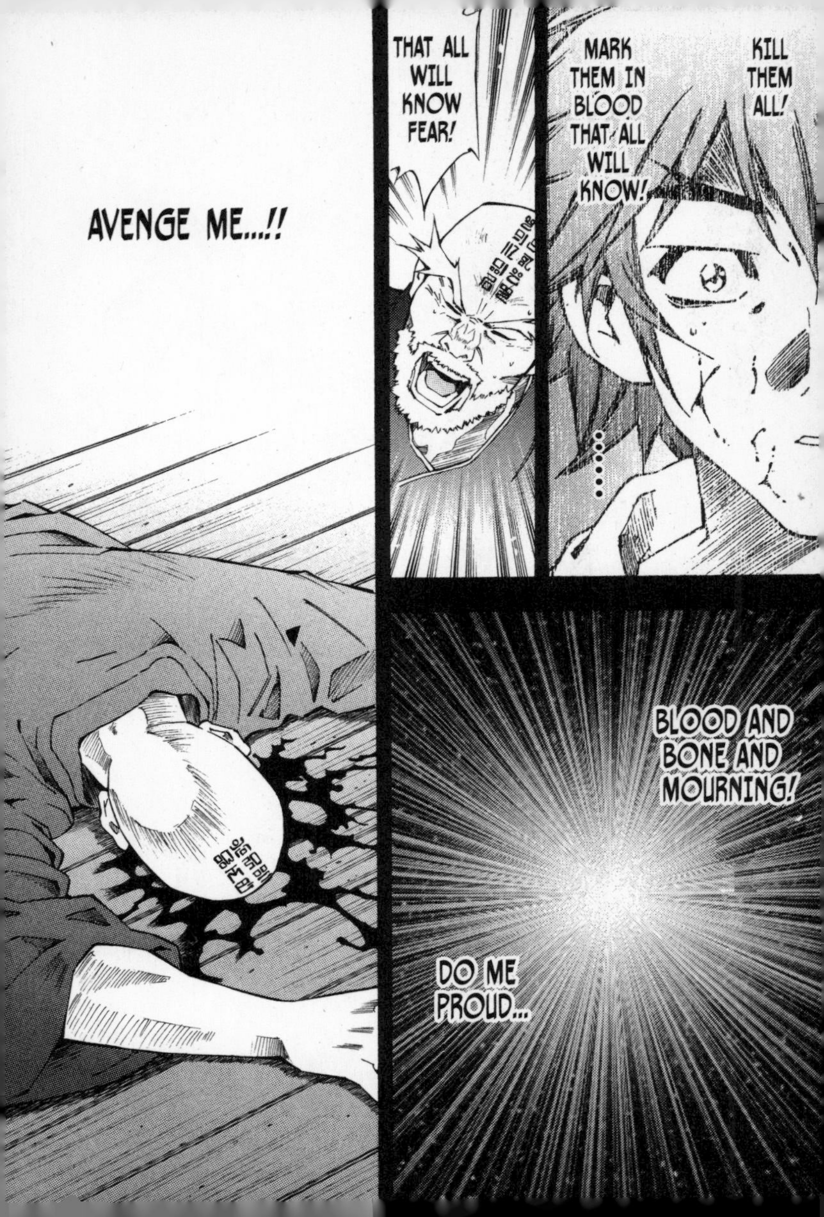
KILL THEM ALL!
MARK THEM IN BLOOD THAT ALL WILL KNOW!
......
THAT ALL WILL KNOW FEAR!
BLOOD AND BONE AND MOURNING!
DO ME PROUD...
AVENGE ME...!!

KAKOUTON GENJOU

KAKOUTON WAS A GREAT WARRIOR WHO FOUGHT ALONGSIDE SOUSOU AND HELPED HIM TO RAISE AN ARMY. SHORT-TEMPERED AND GREATLY FEARED, KAKOUTON ONCE KILLED A MAN OVER AN INSULT DIRECTED AT SOUSOU (KAKOUTON WAS FOURTEEN YEARS OLD AT THE TIME). LEGEND HAS IT THAT WHEN HIS EYE WAS PIERCED BY AN ARROW, HE PLUCKED THE EYEBALL OUT WITH THE ARROW AND ATE IT. OH, YEAH...? BUT WHERE'S THE CREME FILLING?!

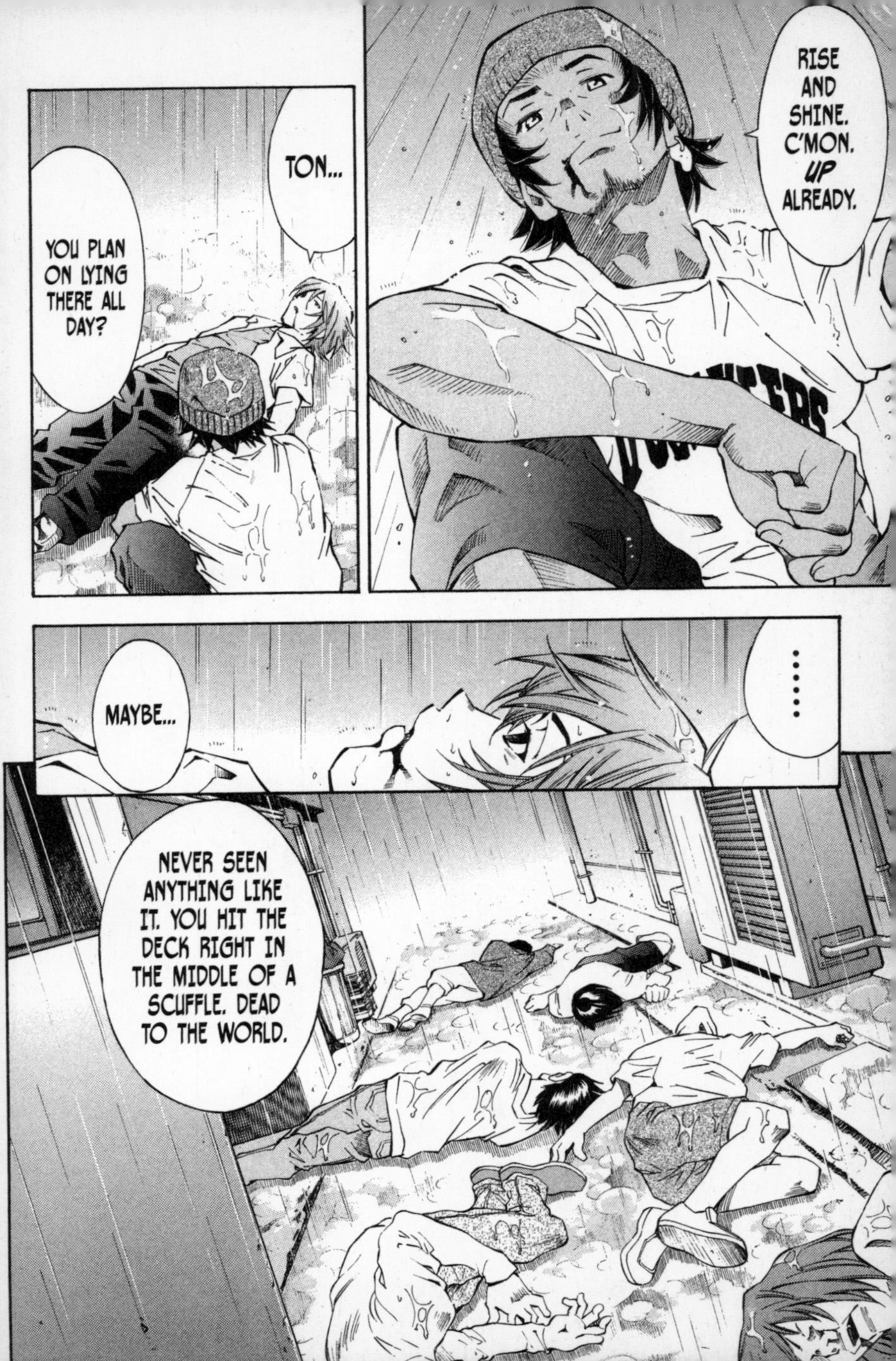
RISE AND SHINE. C'MON. *UP* ALREADY.
TON...
YOU PLAN ON LYING THERE ALL DAY?
......
MAYBE...
NEVER SEEN ANYTHING LIKE IT. YOU HIT THE DECK RIGHT IN THE MIDDLE OF A SCUFFLE. DEAD TO THE WORLD.

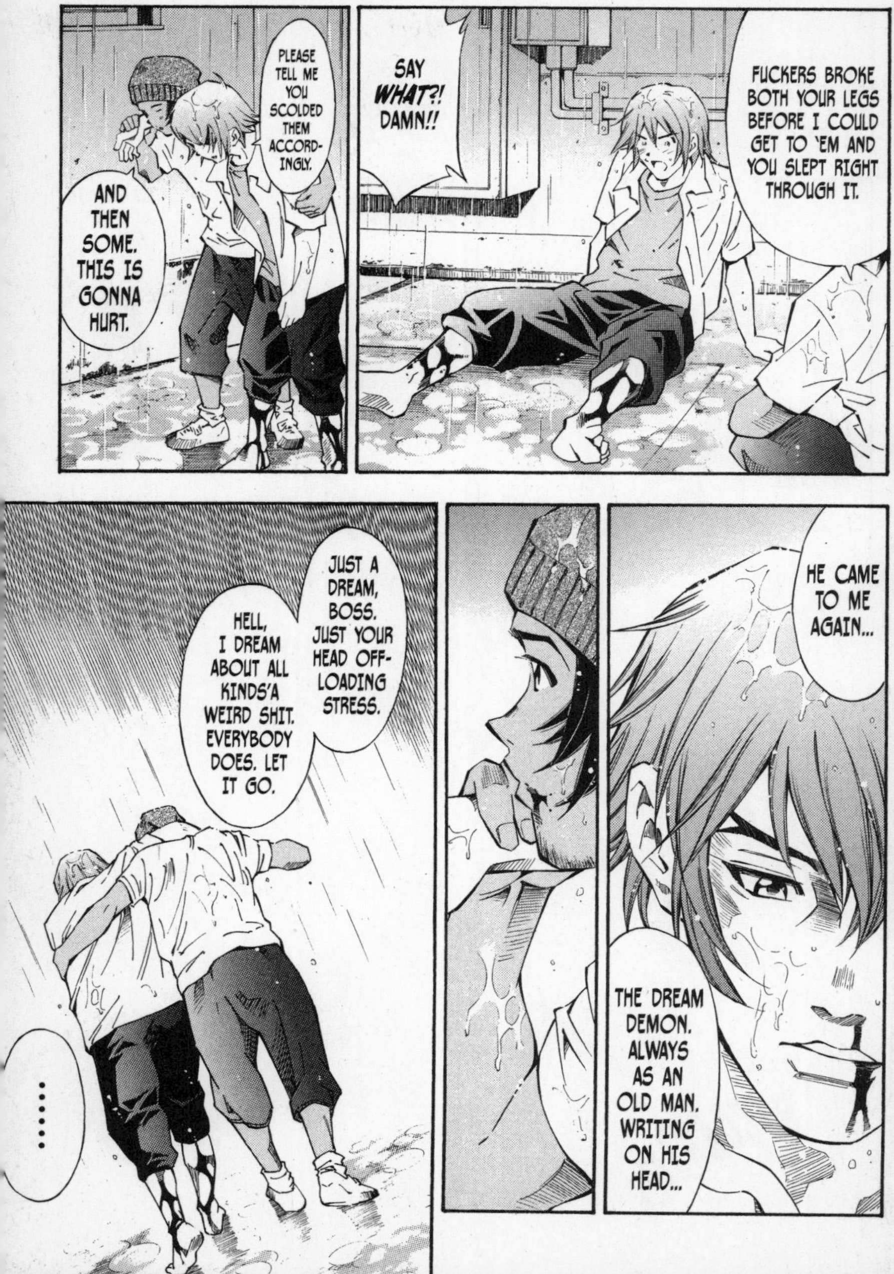
FUCKERS BROKE BOTH YOUR LEGS BEFORE I COULD GET TO 'EM AND YOU SLEPT RIGHT THROUGH IT.
SAY WHAT?! DAMN!!
PLEASE TELL ME YOU SCOLDED THEM ACCORDINGLY.
AND THEN SOME. THIS IS GONNA HURT.
HE CAME TO ME AGAIN...
THE DREAM DEMON. ALWAYS AS AN OLD MAN. WRITING ON HIS HEAD...
JUST A DREAM, BOSS. JUST YOUR HEAD OFF-LOADING STRESS.
HELL, I DREAM ABOUT ALL KINDS'A WEIRD SHIT. EVERYBODY DOES. LET IT GO.
......

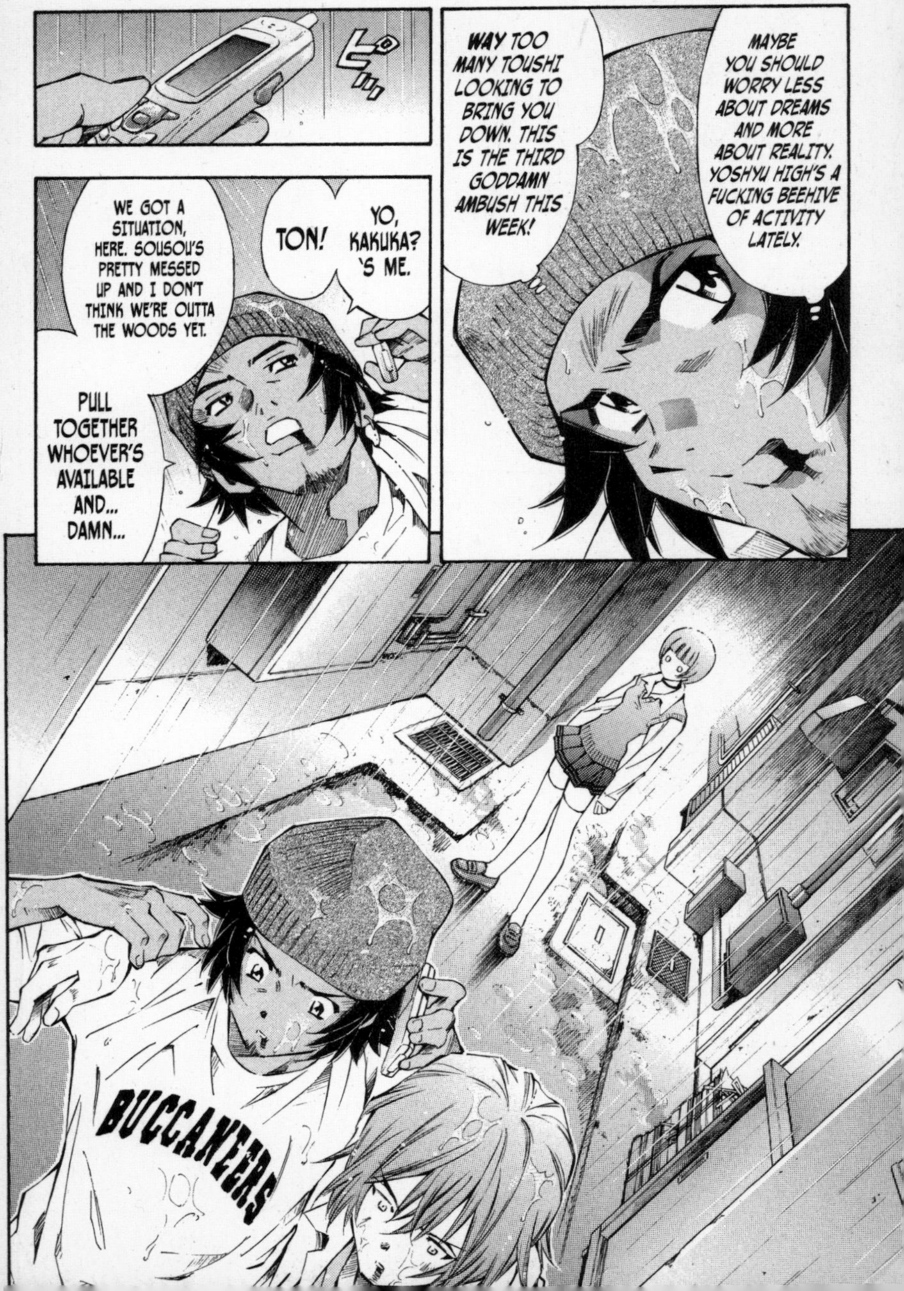
MAYBE YOU SHOULD WORRY LESS ABOUT DREAMS AND MORE ABOUT REALITY. YOSHYU HIGH'S A FUCKING BEEHIVE OF ACTIVITY LATELY.
WAY TOO MANY TOUSHI LOOKING TO BRING YOU DOWN. THIS IS THE THIRD GODDAMN AMBUSH THIS WEEK!
YO, KAKUKA? 'S ME.
TON!
WE GOT A SITUATION, HERE. SOUSOU'S PRETTY MESSED UP AND I DON'T THINK WE'RE OUTTA THE WOODS YET.
PULL TOGETHER WHOEVER'S AVAILABLE AND... DAMN...
BUCCANEERS

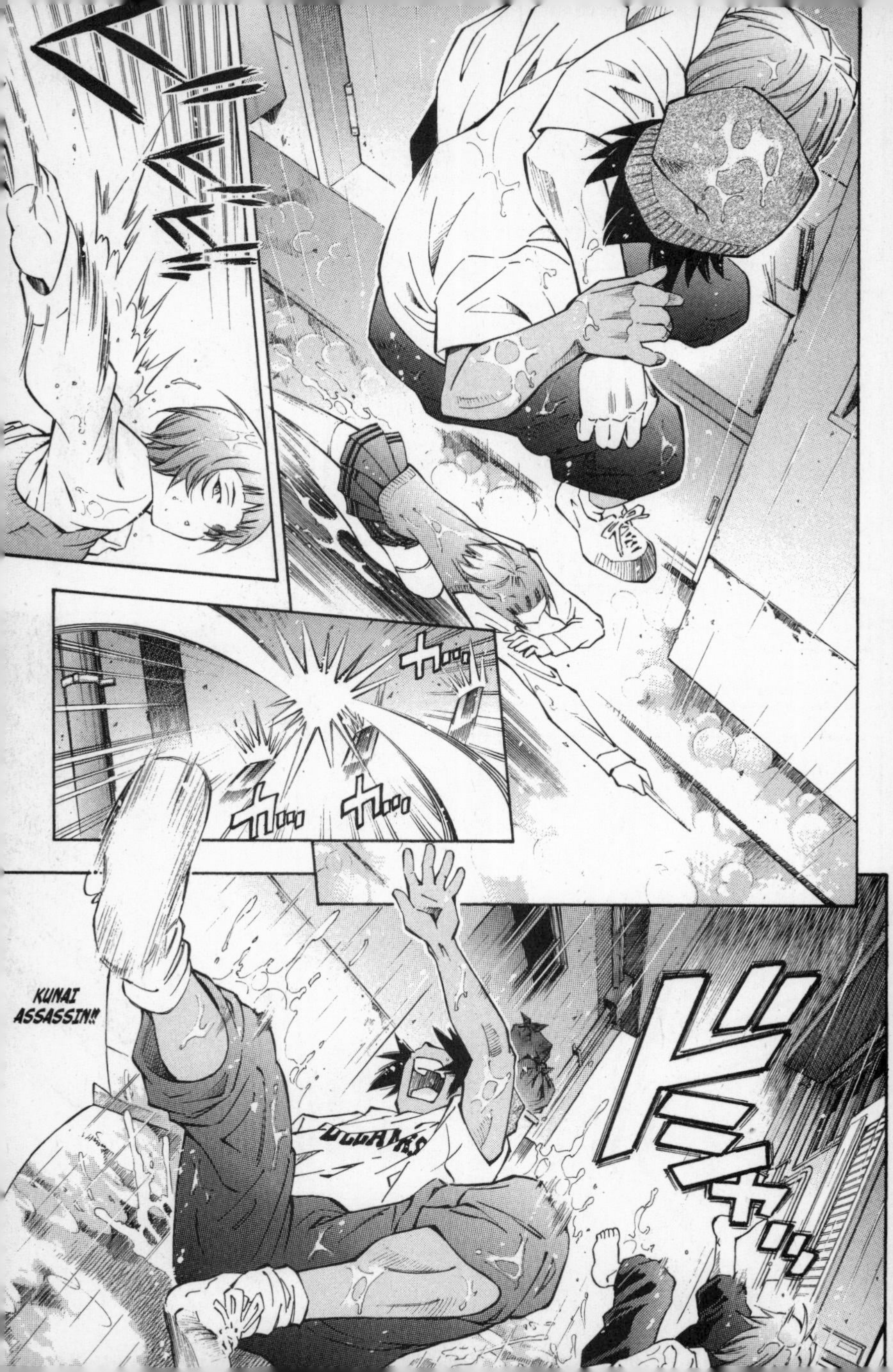
KUNAI ASSASSIN!!

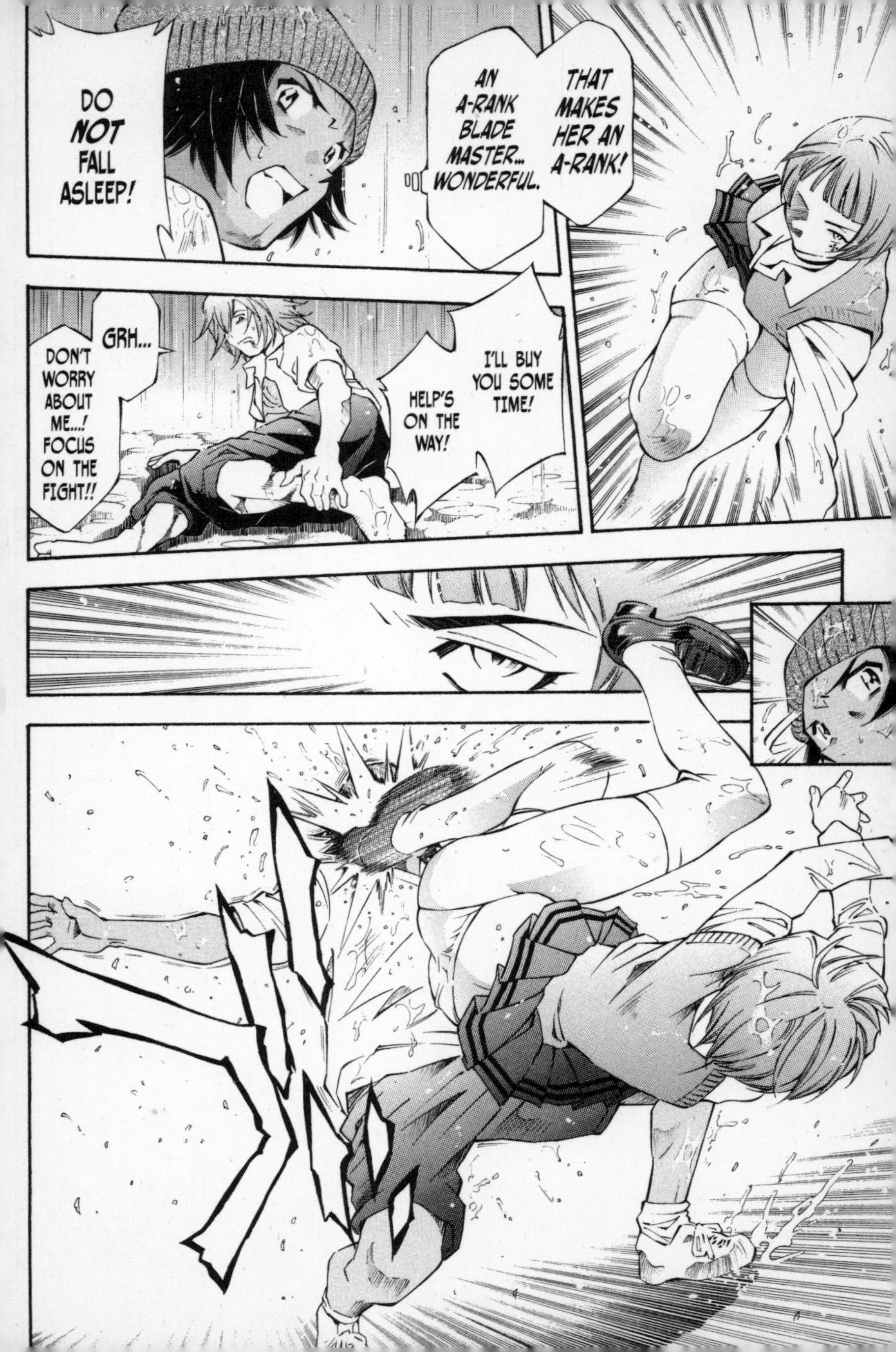
THAT MAKES HER AN A-RANK!
AN A-RANK BLADE MASTER... WONDERFUL.
DO NOT FALL ASLEEP!
I'LL BUY YOU SOME TIME!
HELP'S ON THE WAY!
GRH...
DON'T WORRY ABOUT ME...! FOCUS ON THE FIGHT!!

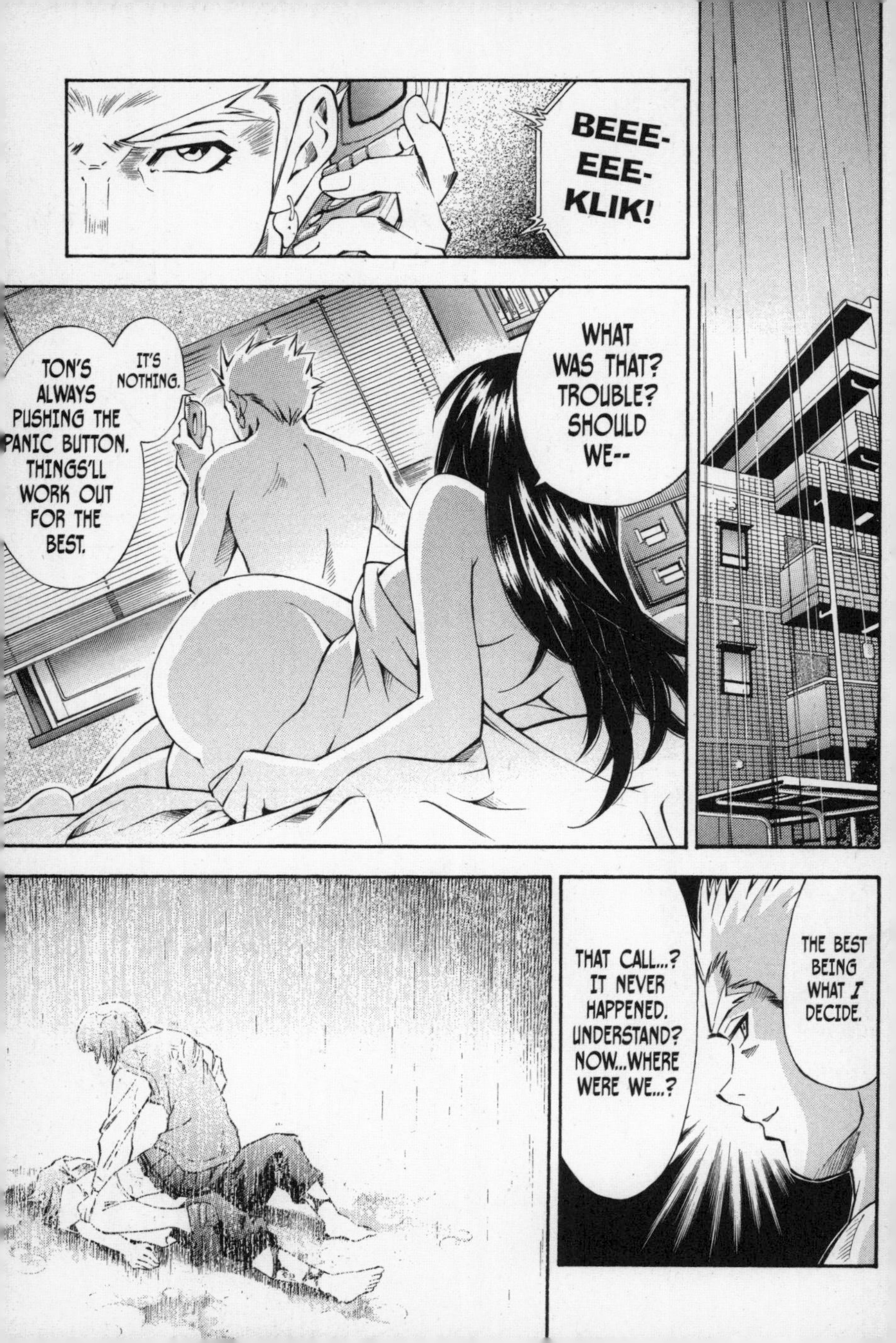
BEEEE-EEE-KLIK!
WHAT WAS THAT? TROUBLE? SHOULD WE--
IT'S NOTHING.
TON'S ALWAYS PUSHING THE PANIC BUTTON. THINGS'LL WORK OUT FOR THE BEST.
THE BEST BEING WHAT *I* DECIDE.
THAT CALL...? IT NEVER HAPPENED. UNDERSTAND? NOW...WHERE WERE WE...?

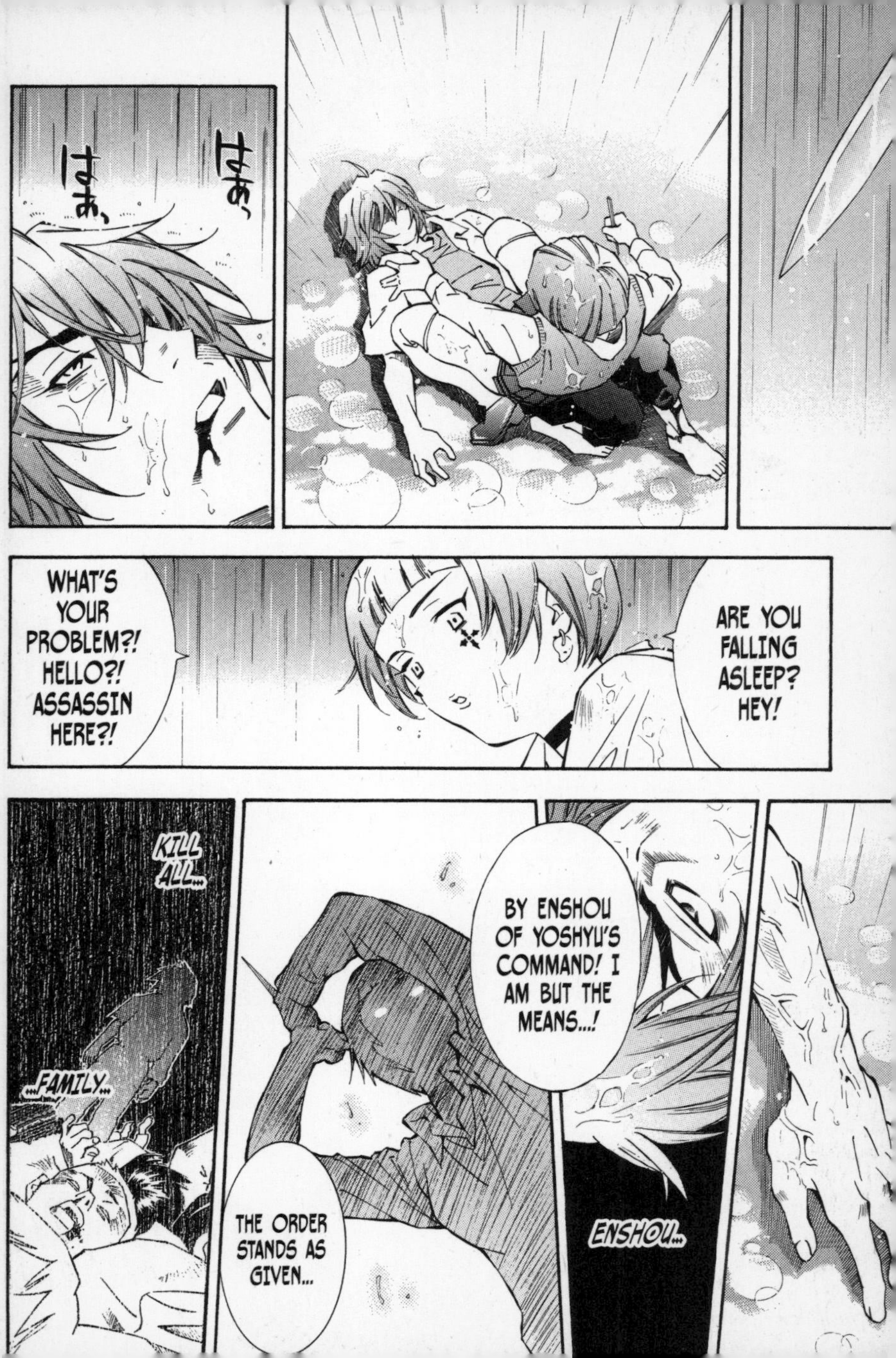
はぁ、
はぁ、
ARE YOU FALLING ASLEEP? HEY!
WHAT'S YOUR PROBLEM?! HELLO?! ASSASSIN HERE?!
BY ENSHOU OF YOSHYU'S COMMAND! I AM BUT THE MEANS...!
ENSHOU...
THE ORDER STANDS AS GIVEN...
KILL ALL...
...FAMILY...

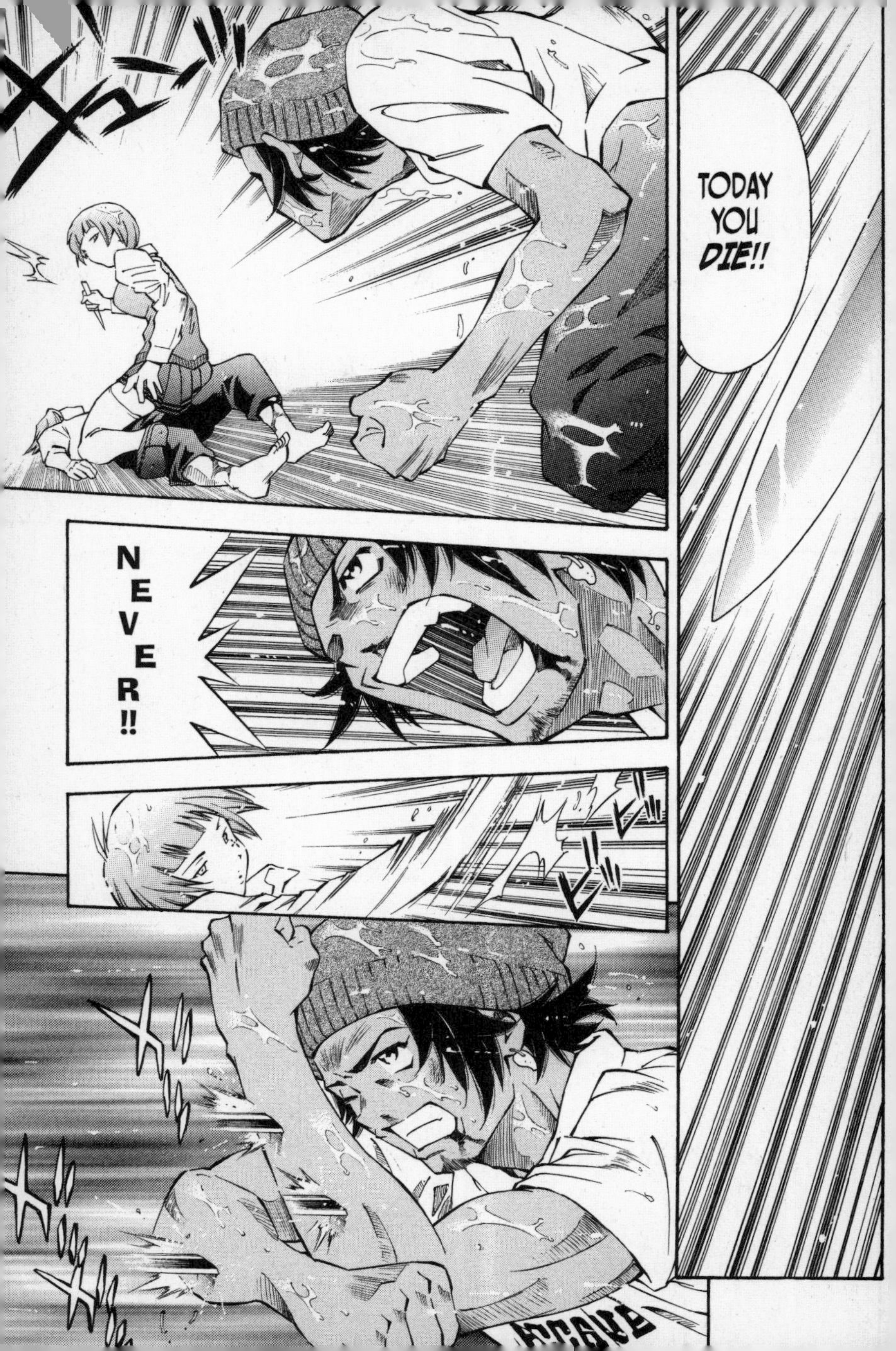
TODAY YOU DIE!!
NEVER!!

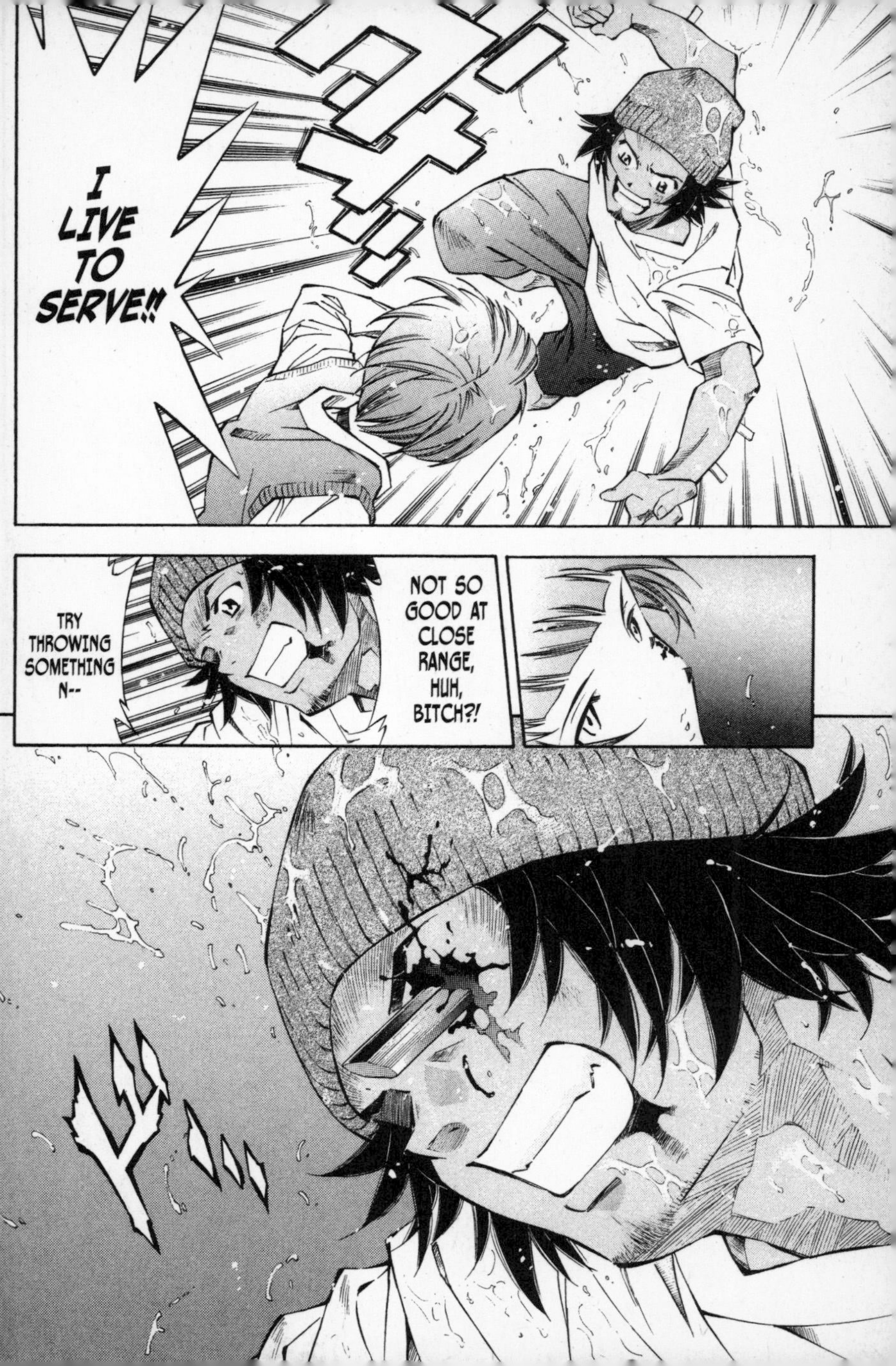
I LIVE TO SERVE!!
NOT SO GOOD AT CLOSE RANGE, HUH, BITCH?!
TRY THROWING SOMETHING N--

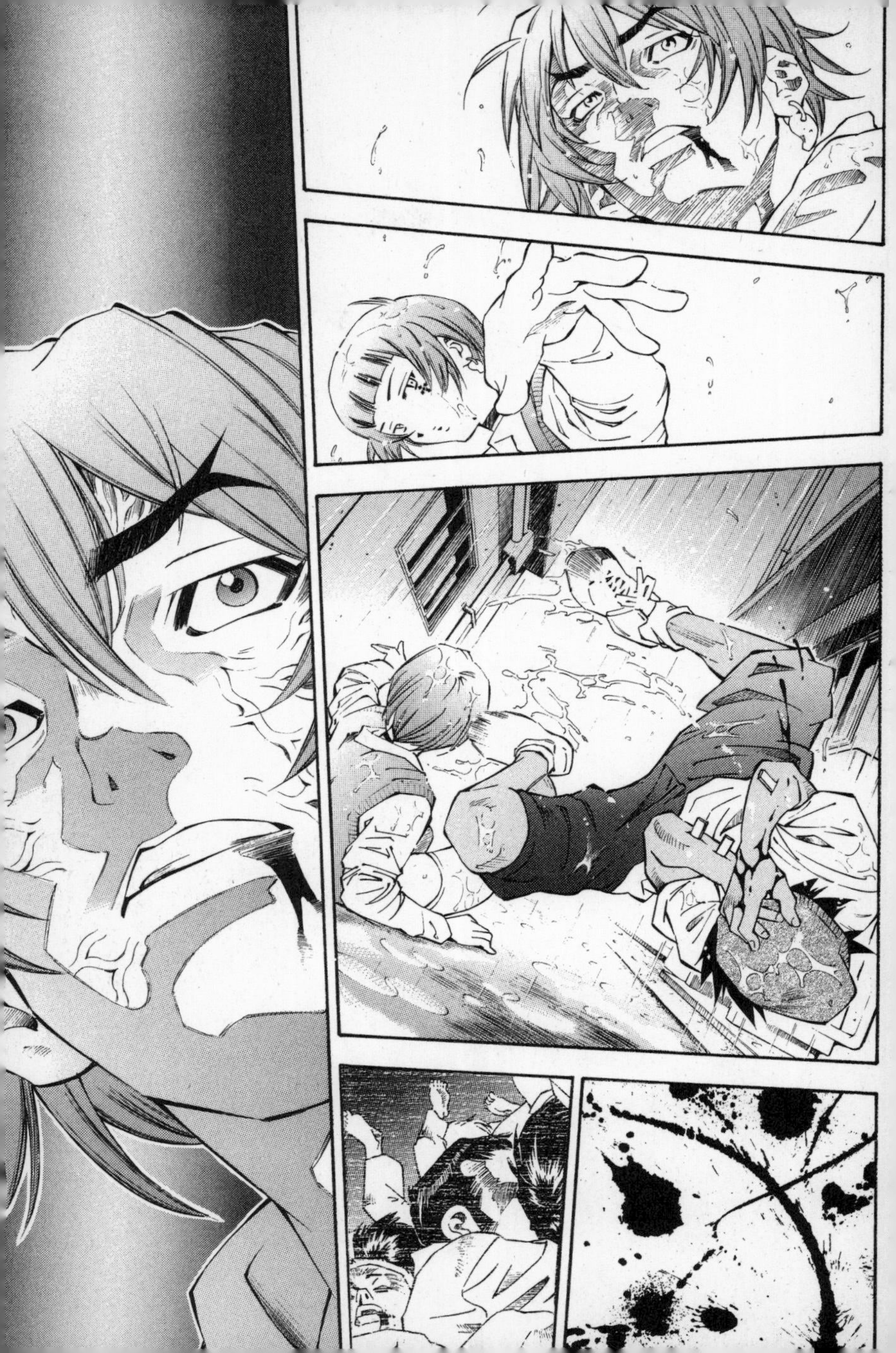

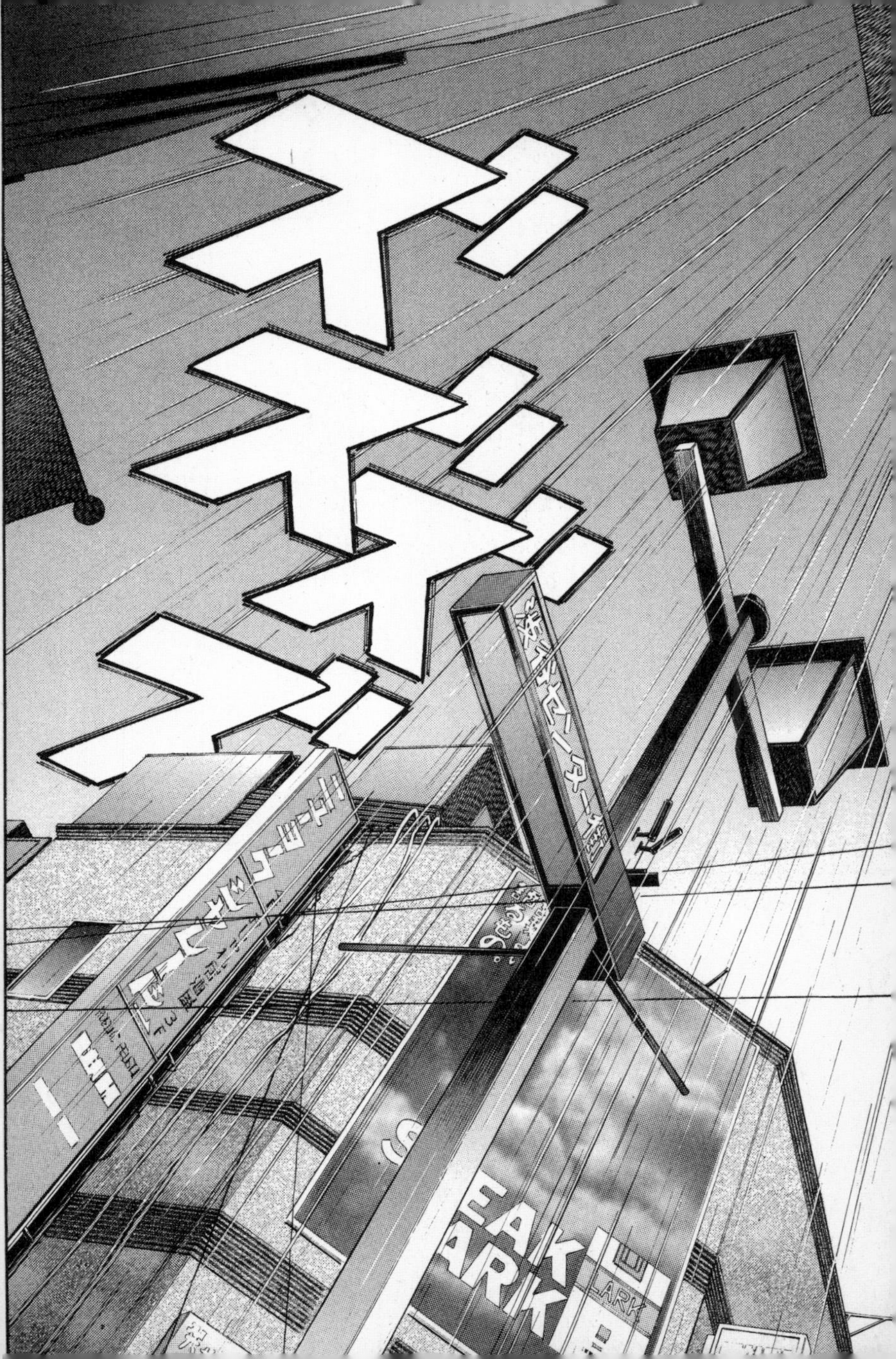
ズズズズ
EAK
ARK
LARK

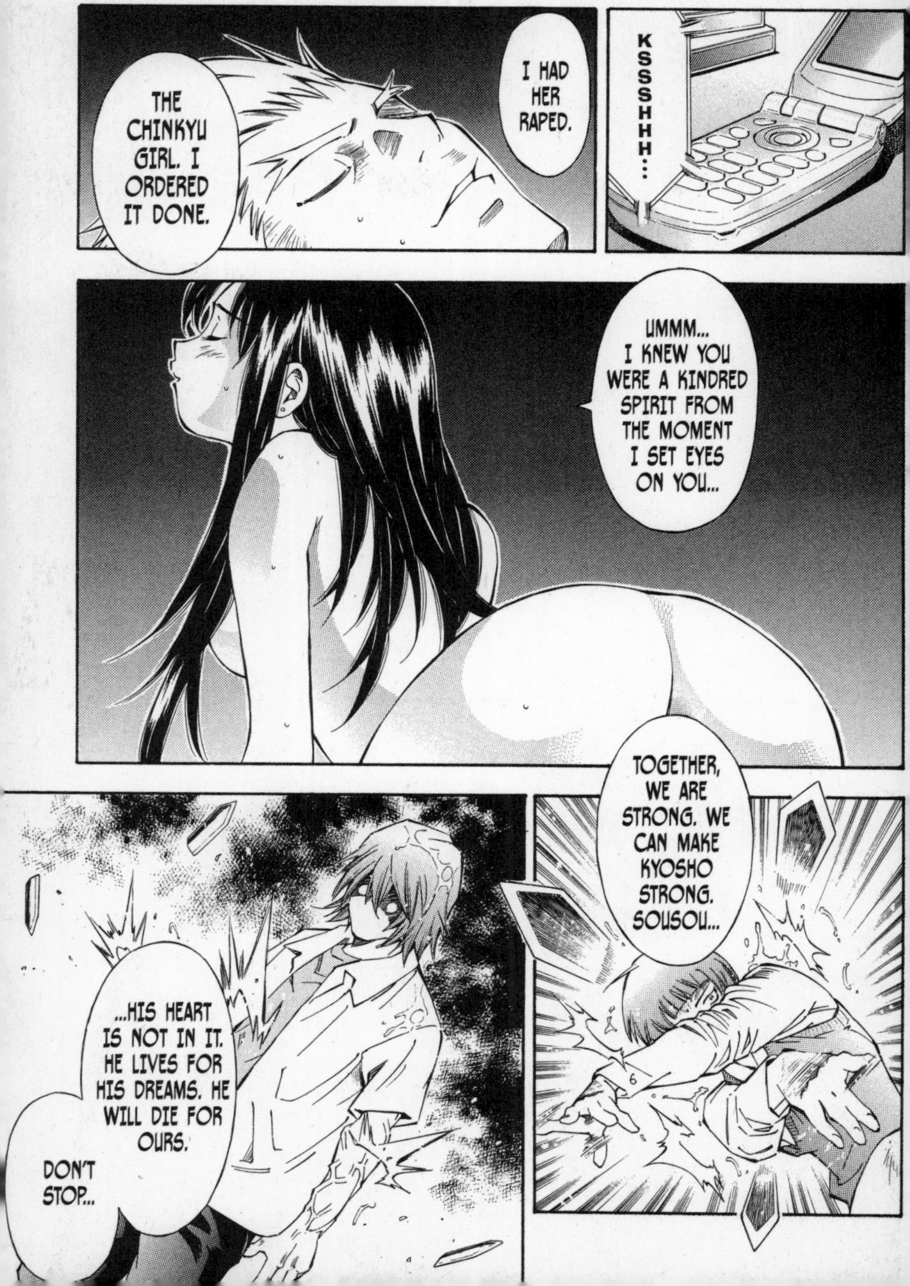
KSSSHHH...
I HAD HER RAPED.
THE CHINKYU GIRL. I ORDERED IT DONE.
UMMM... I KNEW YOU WERE A KINDRED SPIRIT FROM THE MOMENT I SET EYES ON YOU...
TOGETHER, WE ARE STRONG. WE CAN MAKE KYOSHO STRONG. SOUSOU...
...HIS HEART IS NOT IN IT. HE LIVES FOR HIS DREAMS. HE WILL DIE FOR OURS.
DON'T STOP...

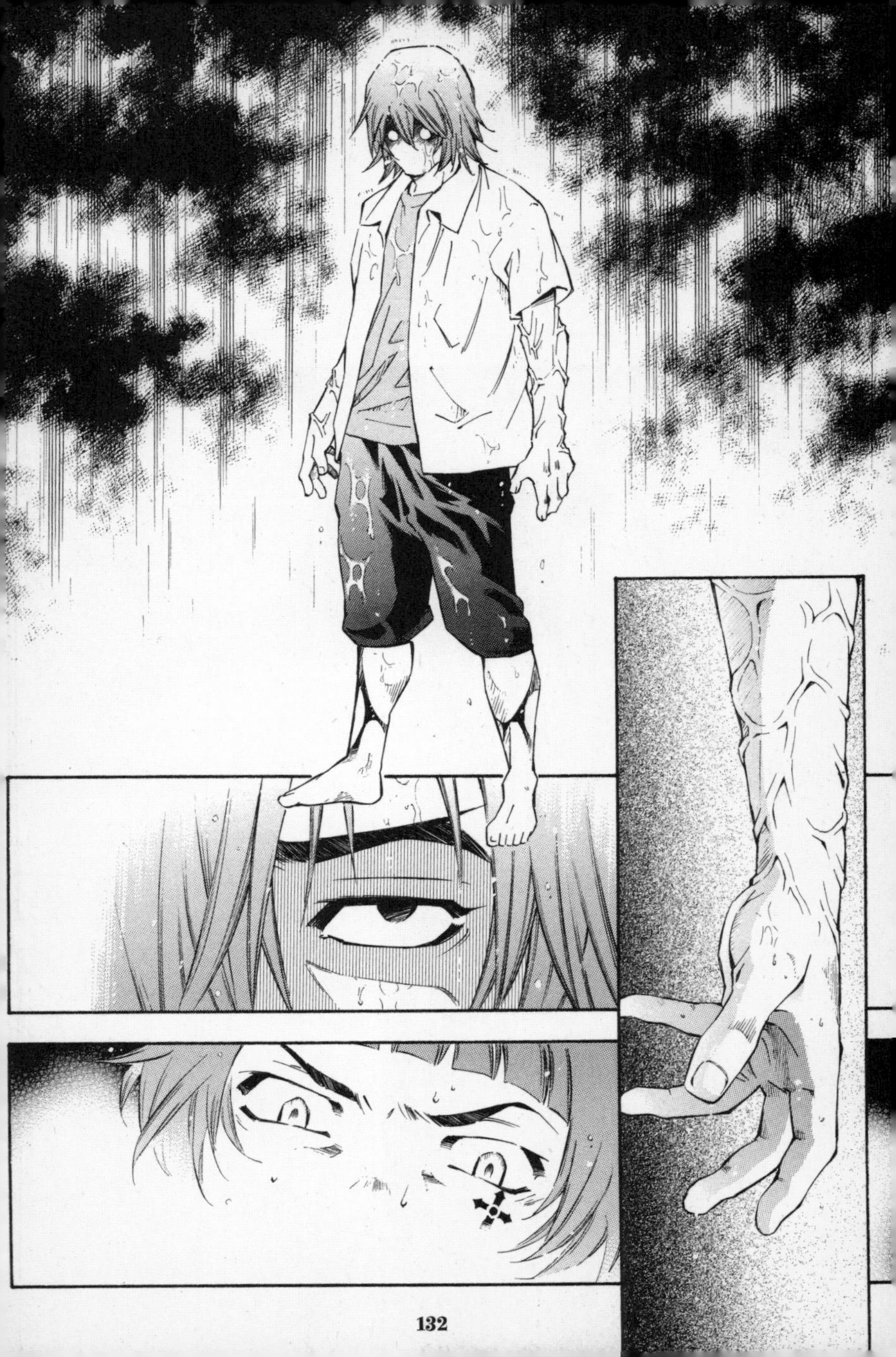

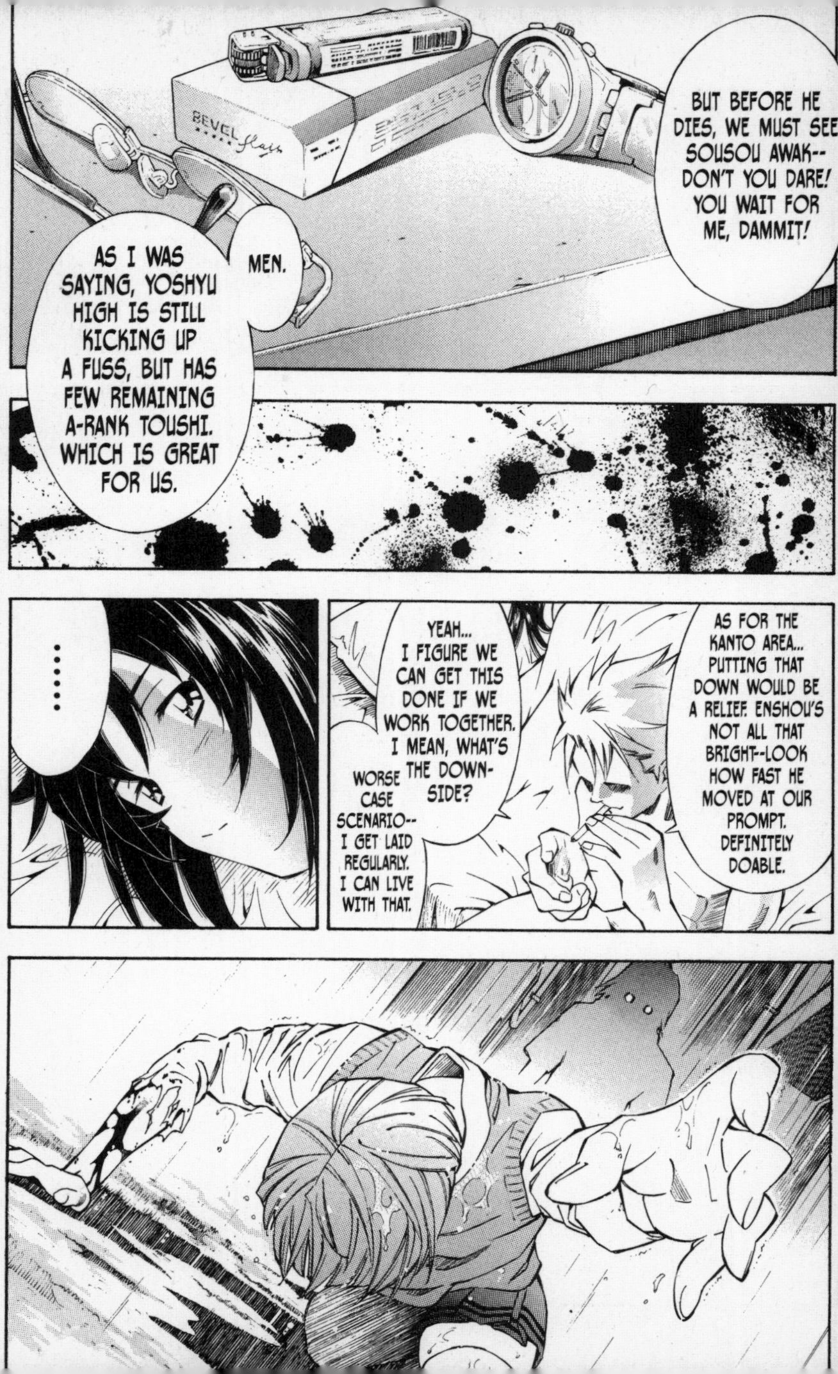
BUT BEFORE HE DIES, WE MUST SEE SOUSOU AWAK-- DON'T YOU DARE! YOU WAIT FOR ME, DAMMIT!
MEN.
AS I WAS SAYING, YOSHYU HIGH IS STILL KICKING UP A FUSS, BUT HAS FEW REMAINING A-RANK TOUSHI. WHICH IS GREAT FOR US.
AS FOR THE KANTO AREA... PUTTING THAT DOWN WOULD BE A RELIEF. ENSHOU'S NOT ALL THAT BRIGHT--LOOK HOW FAST HE MOVED AT OUR PROMPT. DEFINITELY DOABLE.
YEAH... I FIGURE WE CAN GET THIS DONE IF WE WORK TOGETHER. I MEAN, WHAT'S THE DOWN-SIDE?
WORSE CASE SCENARIO-- I GET LAID REGULARLY. I CAN LIVE WITH THAT.
......

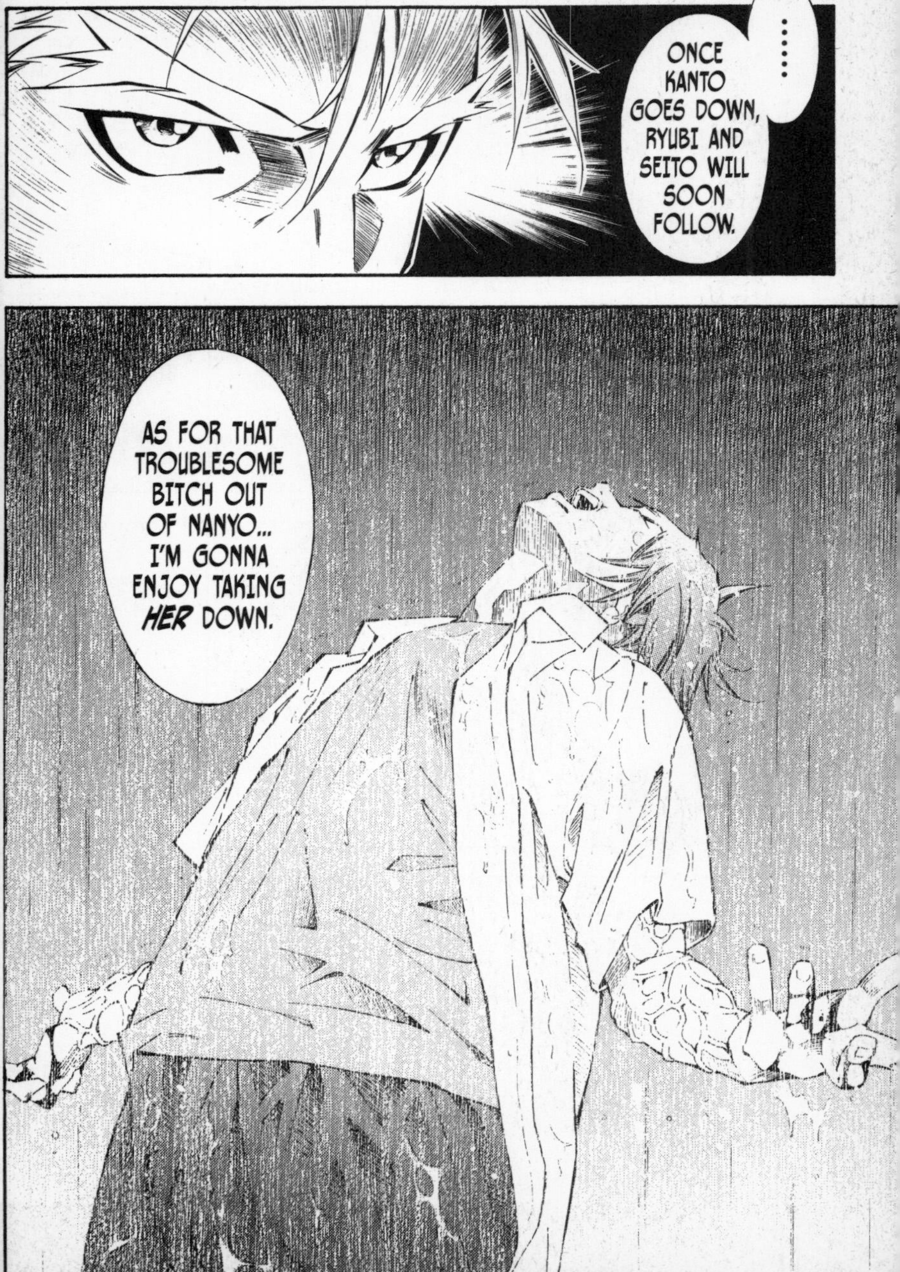
......
ONCE KANTO GOES DOWN, RYUBI AND SEITO WILL SOON FOLLOW.
AS FOR THAT TROUBLESOME BITCH OUT OF NANYO... I'M GONNA ENJOY TAKING *HER* DOWN.

SHISONZUI

A BORN SCHOLAR, SHISONZUI WAS A CO-CONSPIRATOR IN TOUTAKU'S ASSASSINATION, ALONG WITH OUIN AND RYOFU. HE WAS ALSO WELL VERSED IN MILITARY STRATEGY, BOTANY AND BIOLOGY. WHAT--MR. MIYAGI CAN HAVE A BONSAI FETISH AND HE CAN'T?!

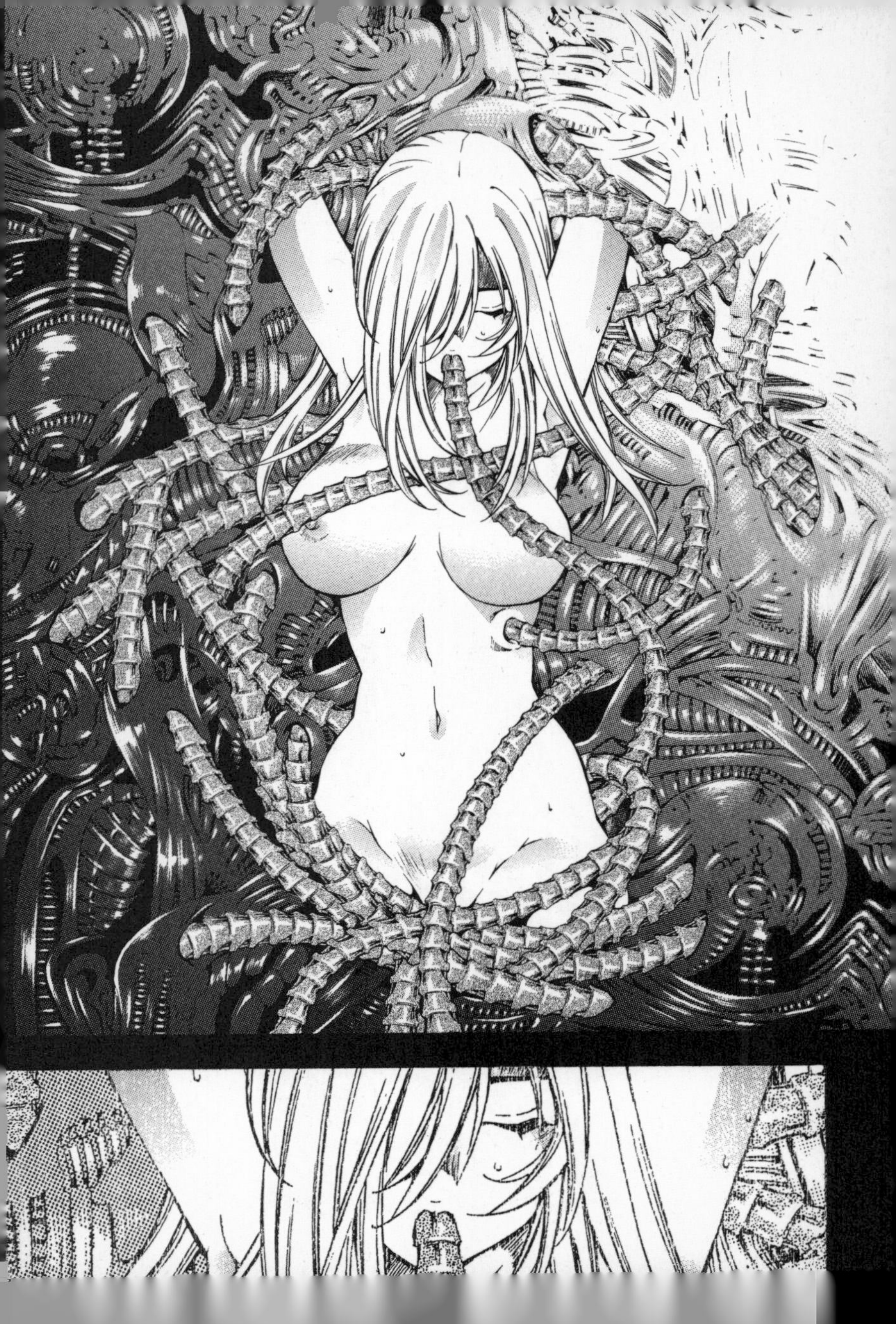

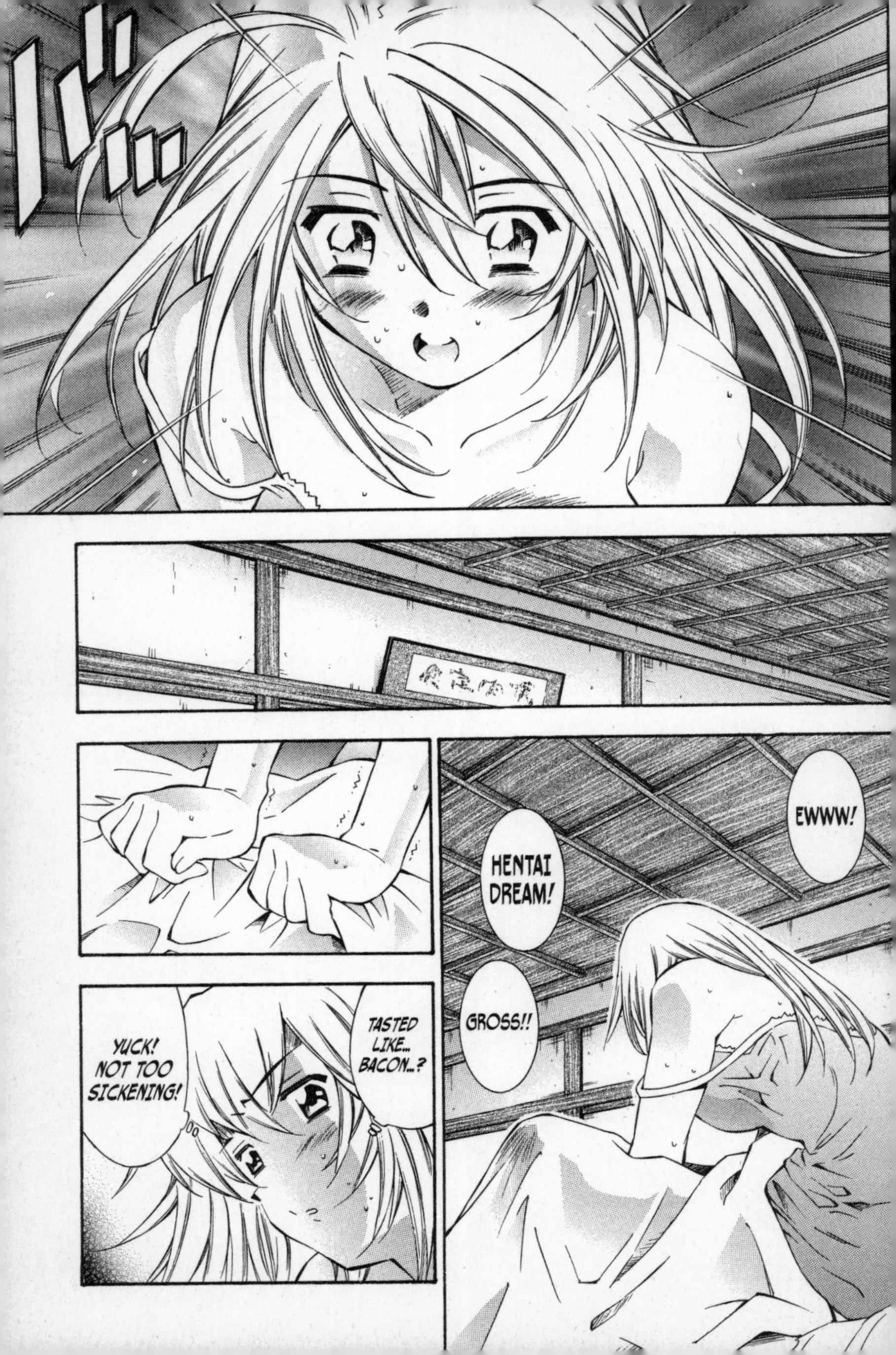
EWWW!
HENTAI DREAM!
GROSS!!
TASTED LIKE... BACON...?
YUCK! NOT TOO SICKENING!

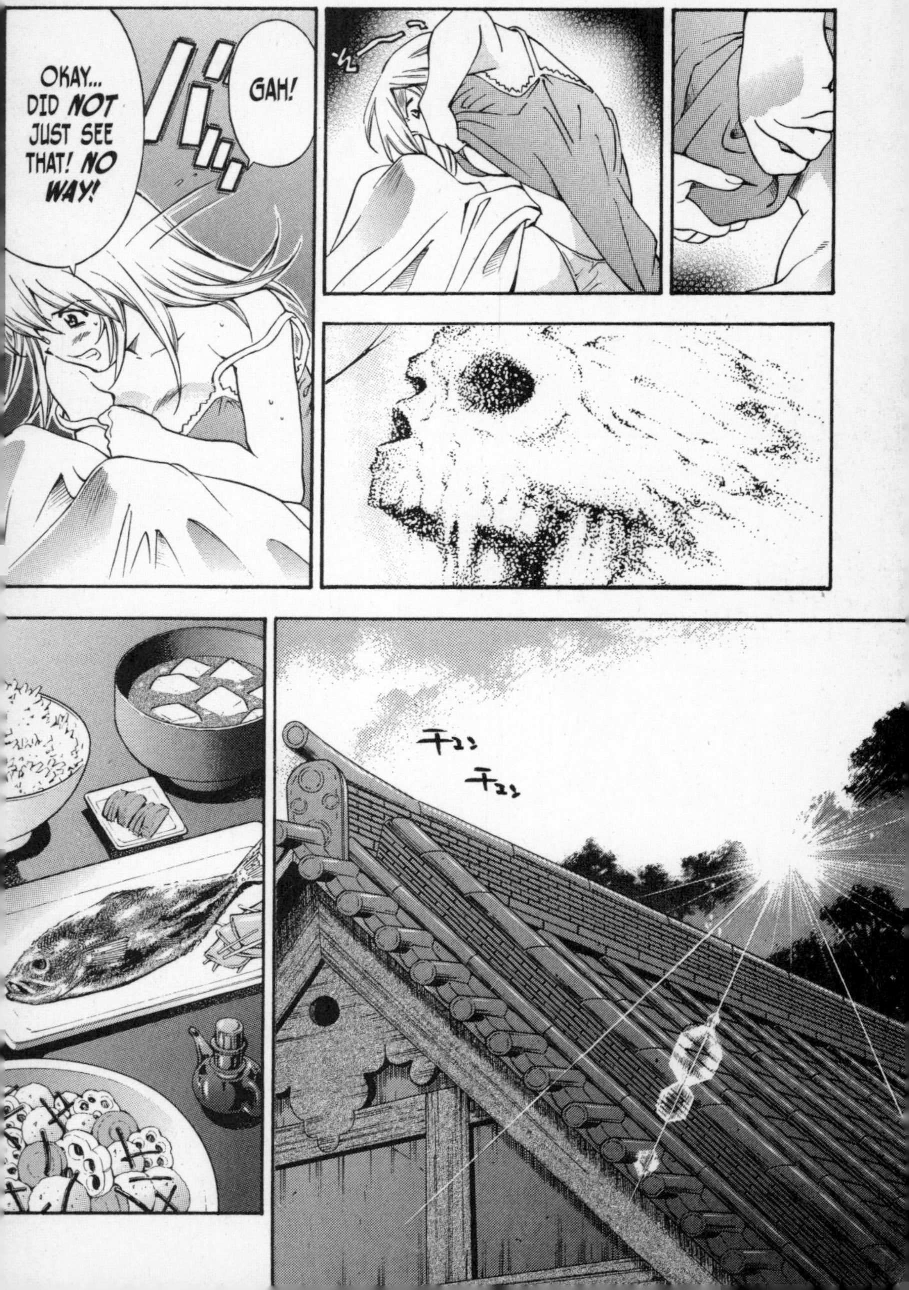
GAH!
OKAY... DID NOT JUST SEE THAT! NO WAY!
チュン
チュン

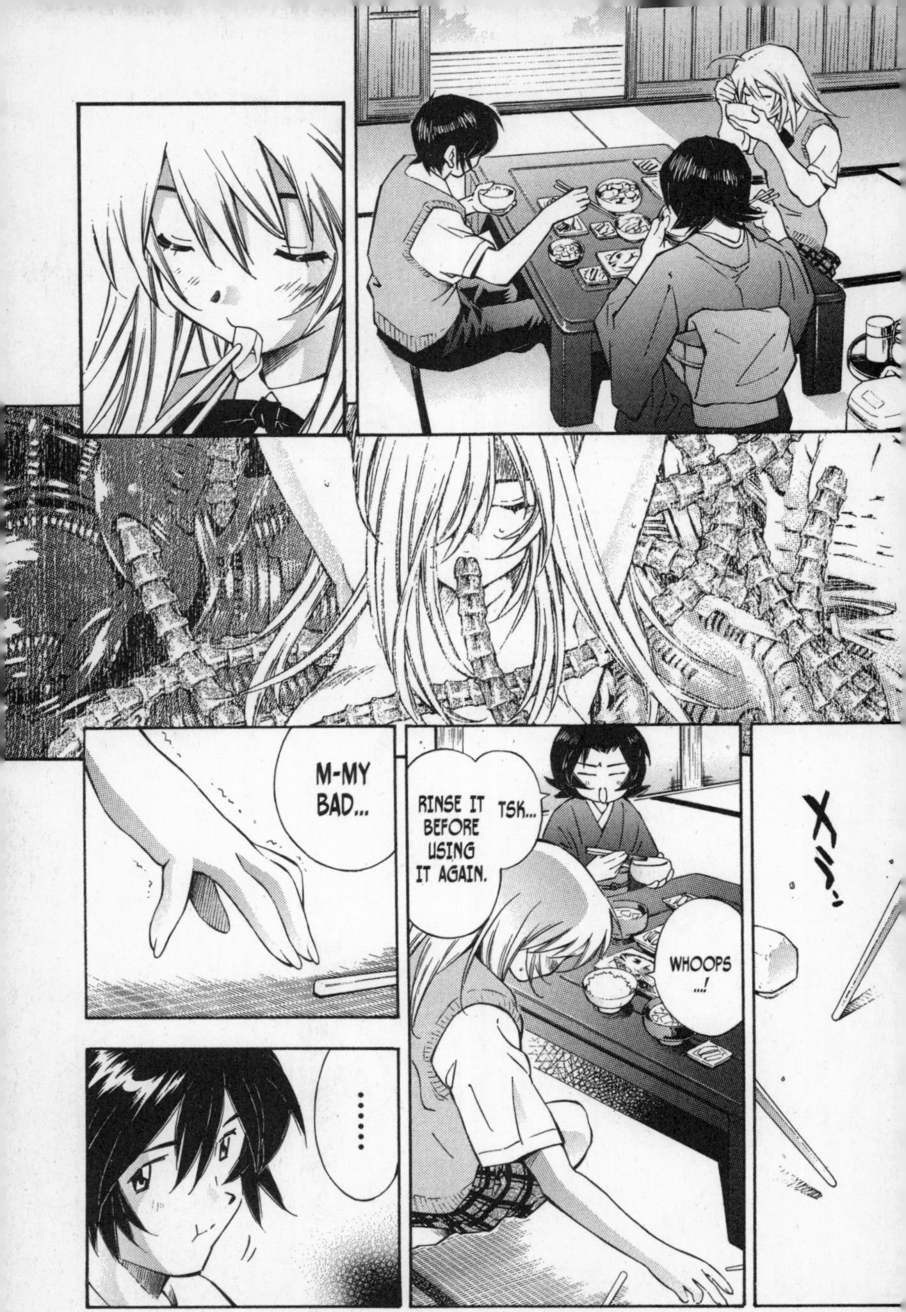
TSK...
RINSE IT BEFORE USING IT AGAIN.
WHOOPS ...!
M-MY BAD...
......

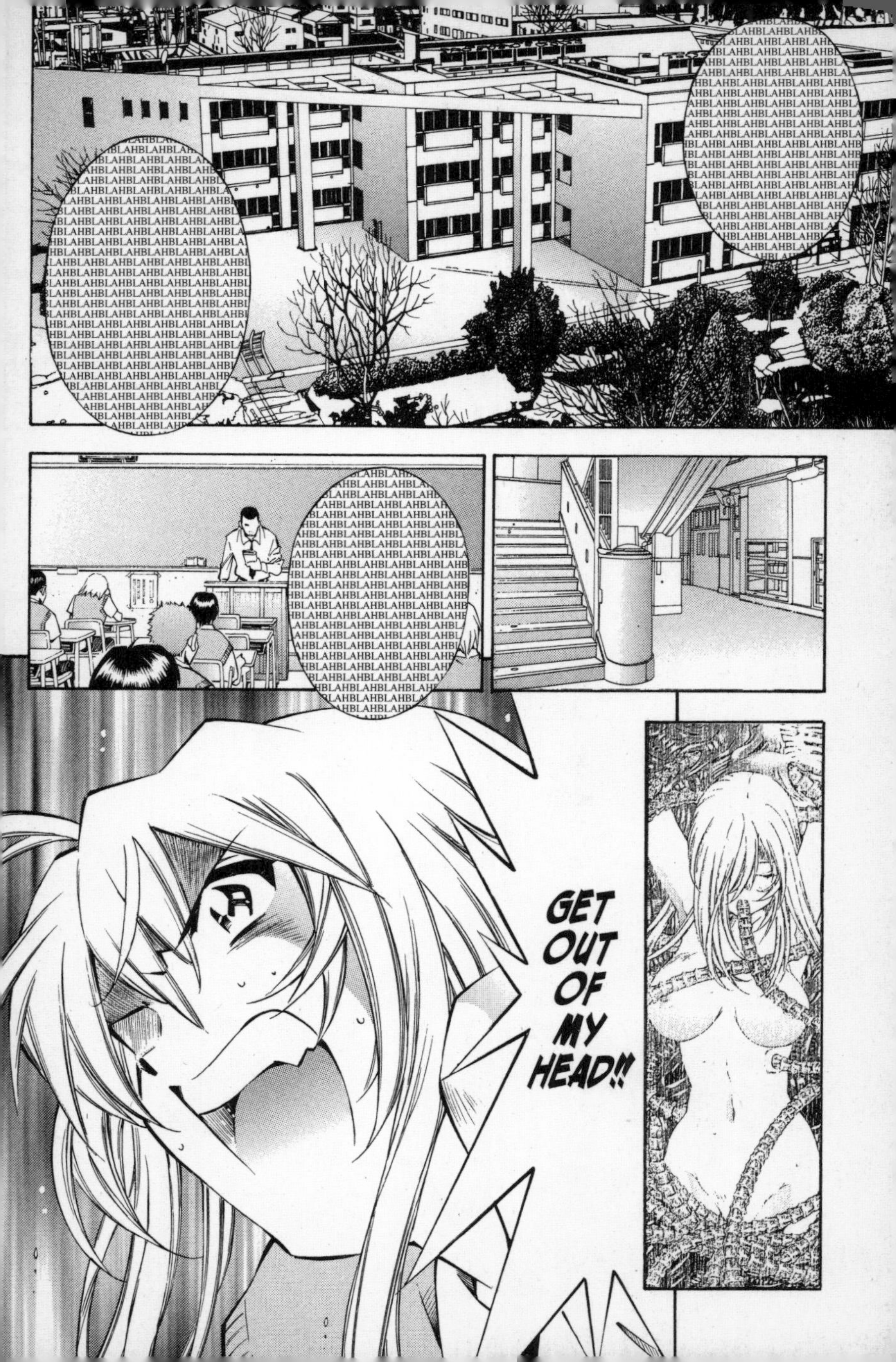
GET OUT OF MY HEAD!!

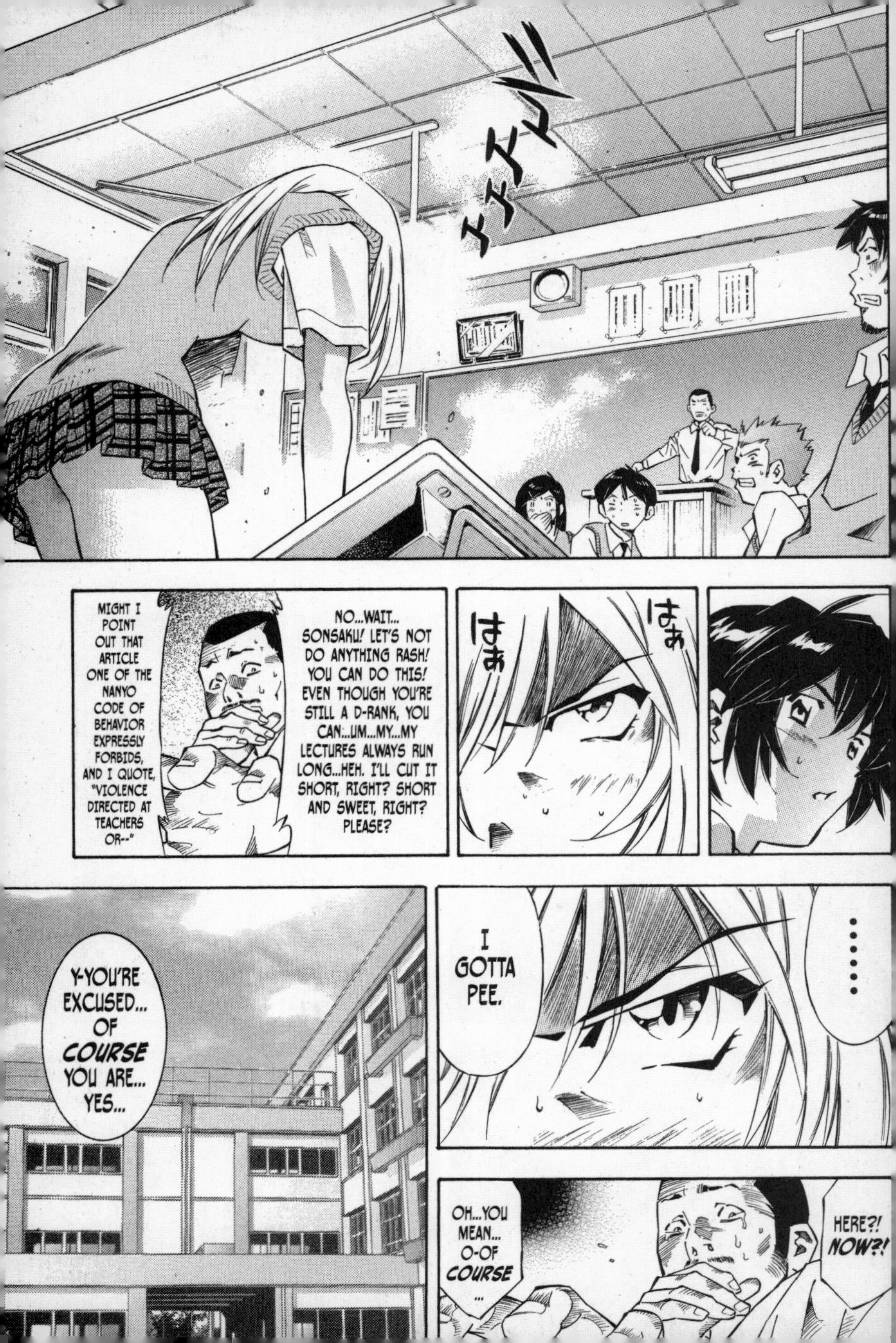
はぁ はぁ
NO...WAIT... SONSAKU! LET'S NOT DO ANYTHING RASH! YOU CAN DO THIS! EVEN THOUGH YOU'RE STILL A D-RANK, YOU CAN...UM...MY...MY LECTURES ALWAYS RUN LONG...HEH. I'LL CUT IT SHORT, RIGHT? SHORT AND SWEET, RIGHT? PLEASE?
MIGHT I POINT OUT THAT ARTICLE ONE OF THE NANYO CODE OF BEHAVIOR EXPRESSLY FORBIDS, AND I QUOTE, "VIOLENCE DIRECTED AT TEACHERS OR--"
......
I GOTTA PEE.
HERE?! NOW?!
OH...YOU MEAN... O-OF COURSE ...
Y-YOU'RE EXCUSED... OF COURSE YOU ARE... YES...

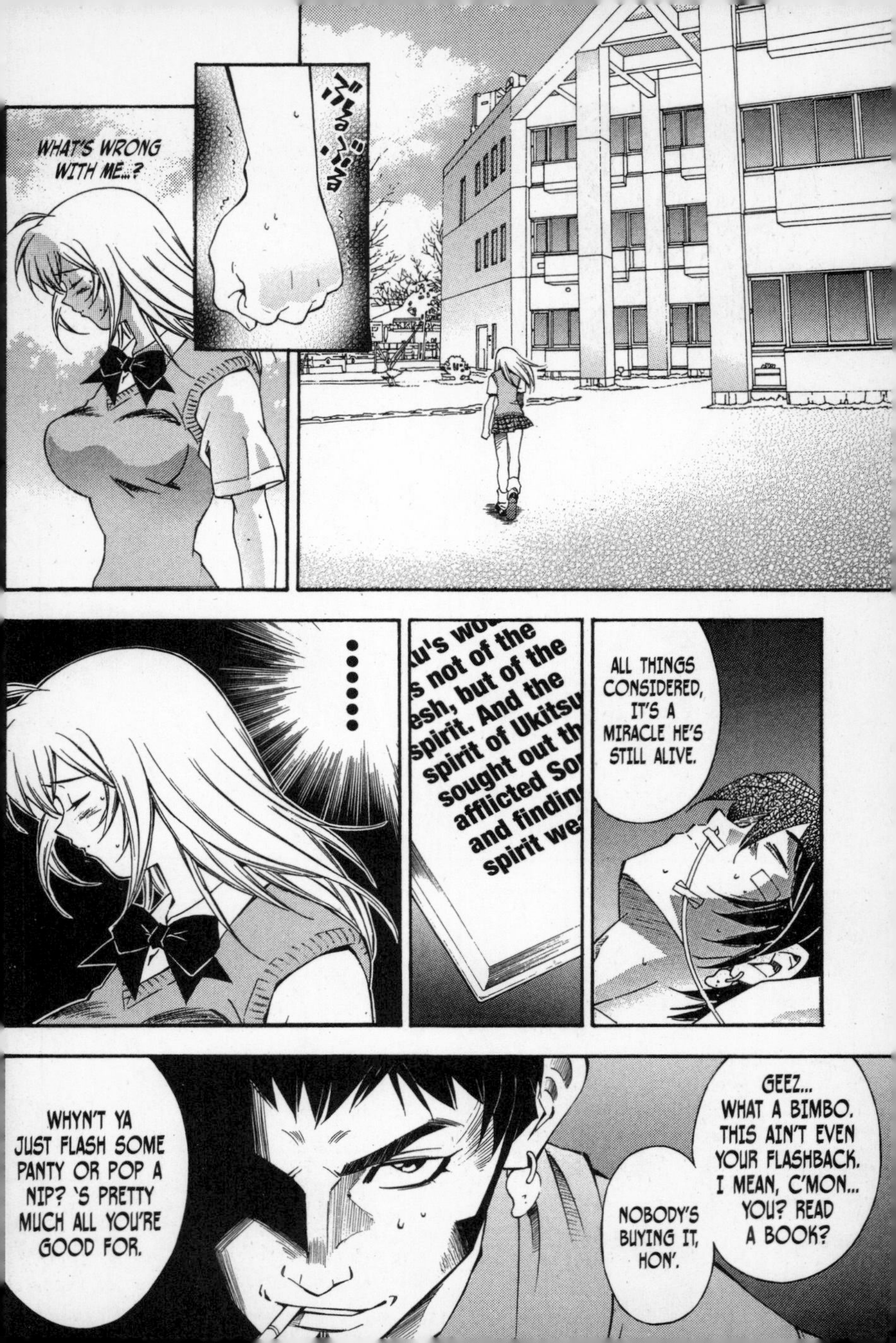
WHAT'S WRONG WITH ME...?
ALL THINGS CONSIDERED, IT'S A MIRACLE HE'S STILL ALIVE.
s not of the
esh, but of the
spirit. And the
spirit of Ukitsu
sought out th
afflicted So
and finding
spirit we
......
GEEZ... WHAT A BIMBO. THIS AIN'T EVEN YOUR FLASHBACK. I MEAN, C'MON... YOU? READ A BOOK?
NOBODY'S BUYING IT, HON'.
WHYN'T YA JUST FLASH SOME PANTY OR POP A NIP? 'S PRETTY MUCH ALL YOU'RE GOOD FOR.

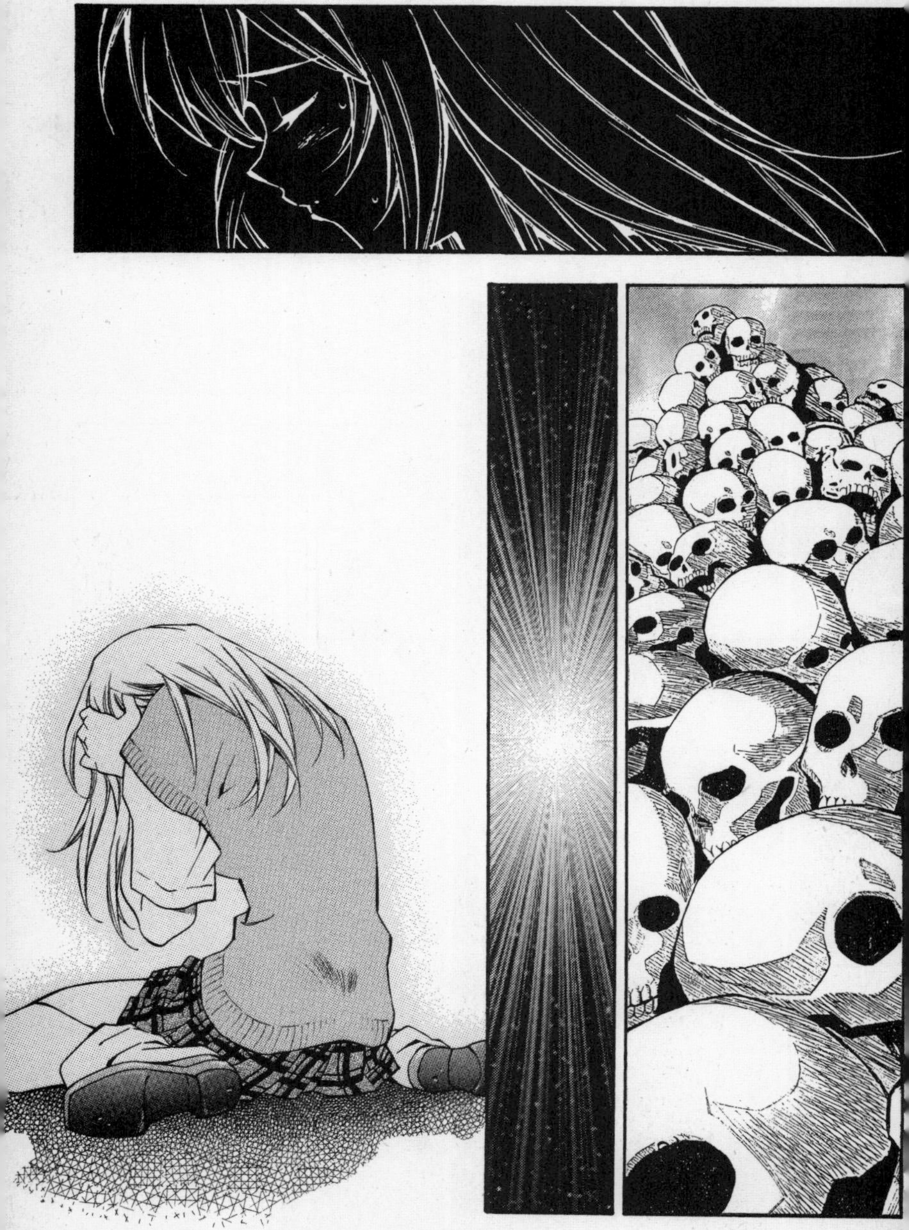

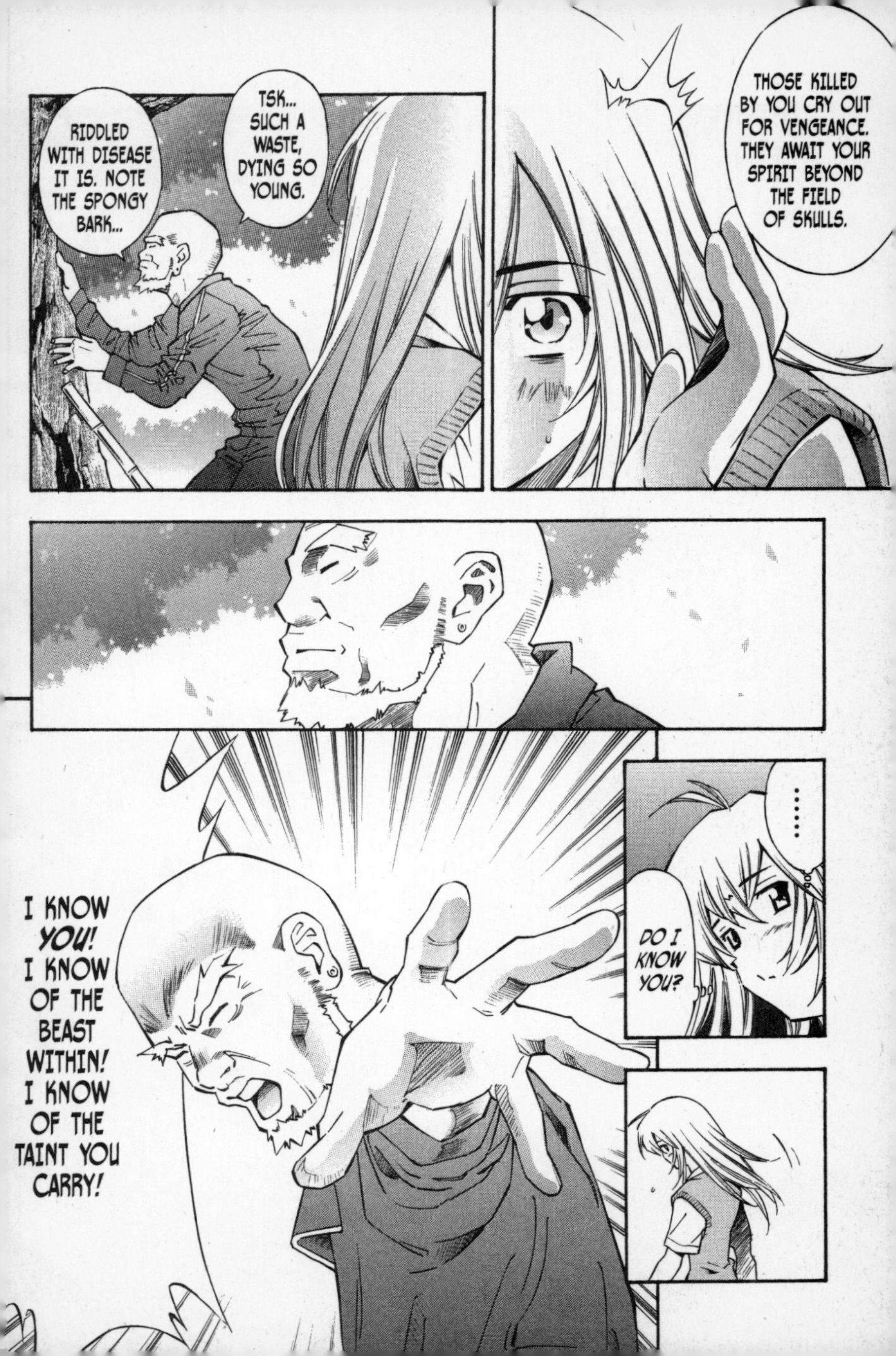
THOSE KILLED BY YOU CRY OUT FOR VENGEANCE. THEY AWAIT YOUR SPIRIT BEYOND THE FIELD OF SKULLS.
TSK... SUCH A WASTE, DYING SO YOUNG.
RIDDLED WITH DISEASE IT IS. NOTE THE SPONGY BARK...
......
DO I KNOW YOU?
I KNOW *YOU!* I KNOW OF THE BEAST WITHIN! I KNOW OF THE TAINT YOU CARRY!

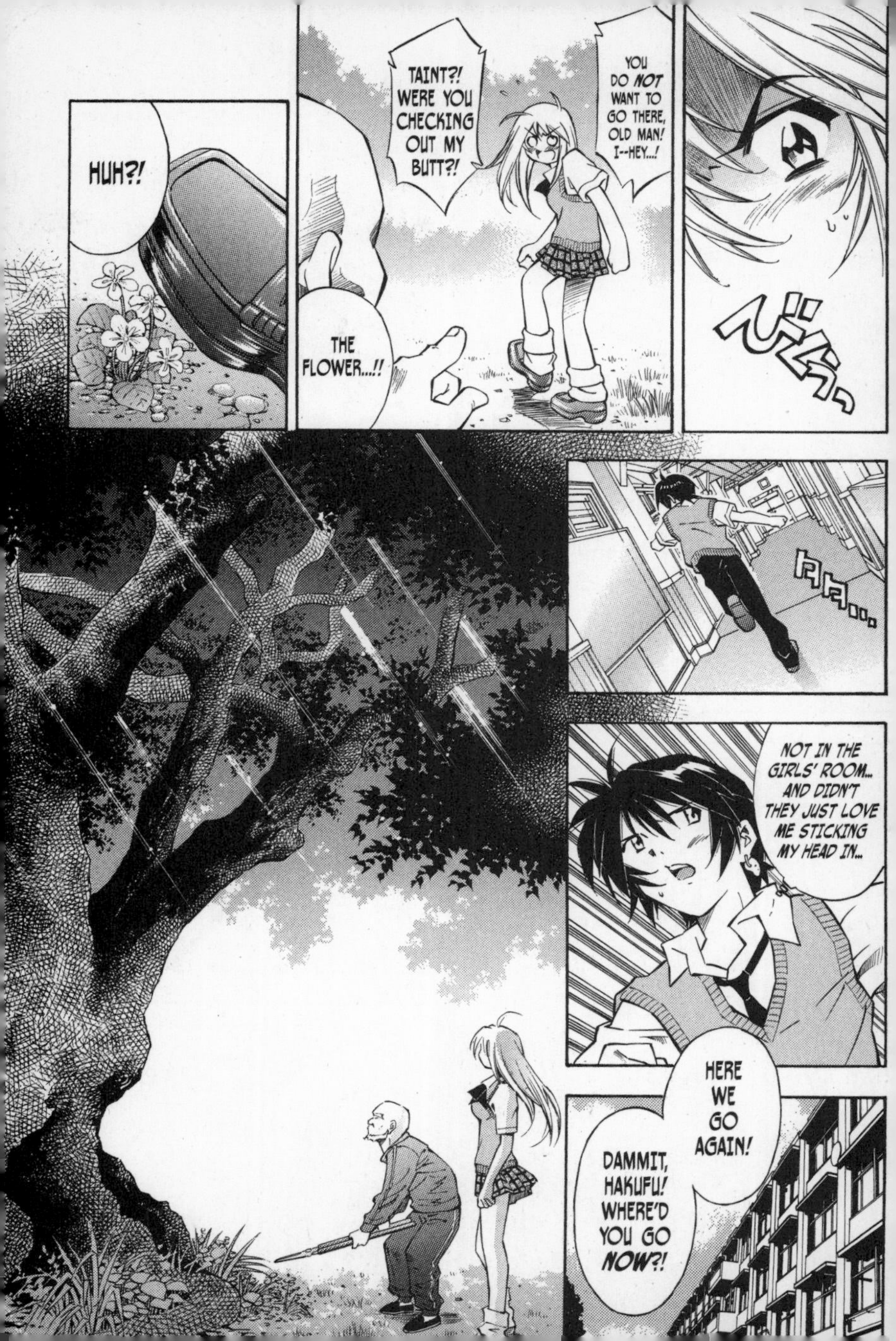
YOU DO NOT WANT TO GO THERE, OLD MAN! I--HEY...!
TAINT?! WERE YOU CHECKING OUT MY BUTT?!
THE FLOWER...!!
HUH?!
NOT IN THE GIRLS' ROOM... AND DIDN'T THEY JUST LOVE ME STICKING MY HEAD IN...
HERE WE GO AGAIN!
DAMMIT, HAKUFU! WHERE'D YOU GO NOW?!

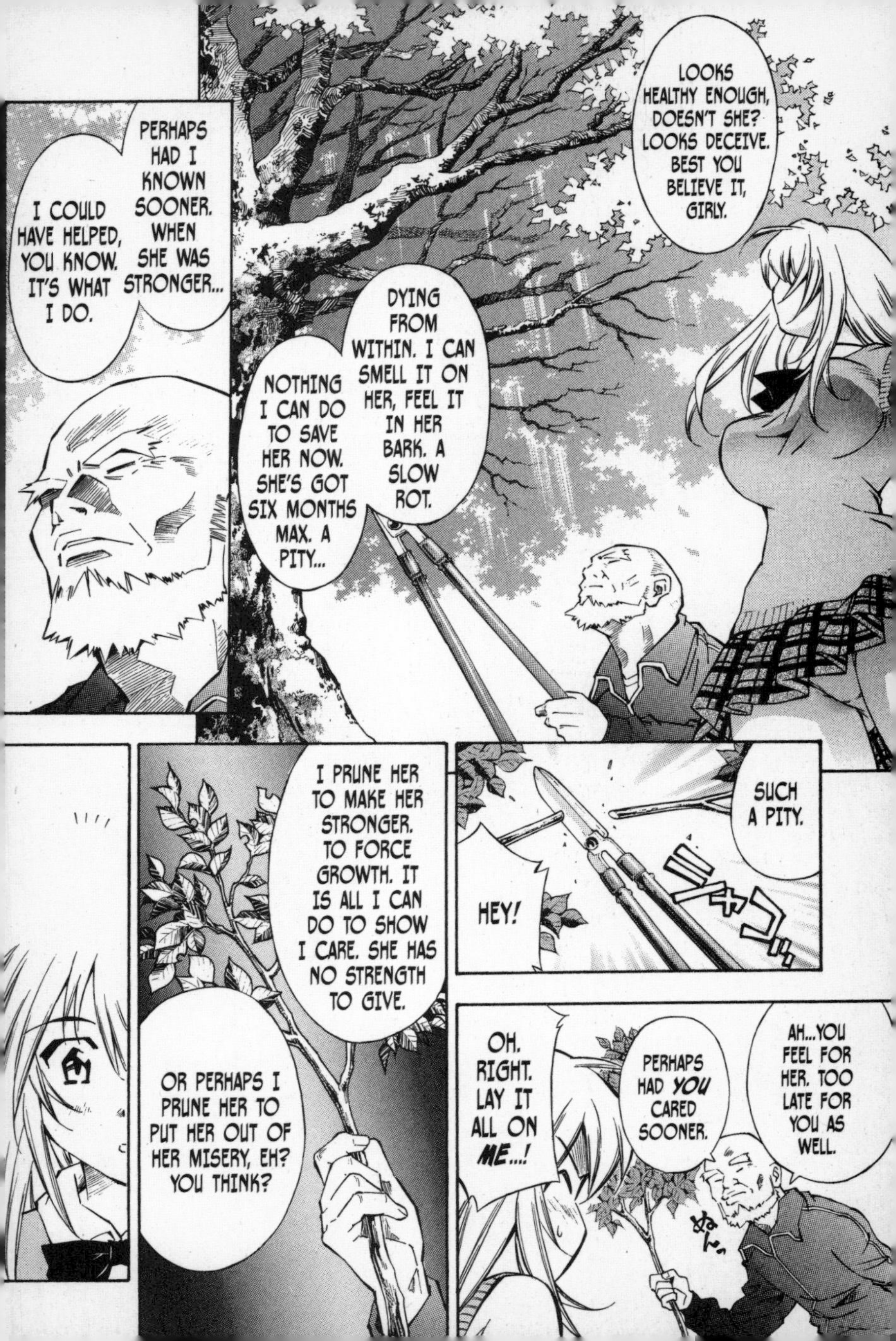
LOOKS HEALTHY ENOUGH, DOESN'T SHE? LOOKS DECEIVE. BEST YOU BELIEVE IT, GIRLY.
DYING FROM WITHIN. I CAN SMELL IT ON HER, FEEL IT IN HER BARK. A SLOW ROT.
NOTHING I CAN DO TO SAVE HER NOW. SHE'S GOT SIX MONTHS MAX. A PITY...
PERHAPS HAD I KNOWN SOONER. WHEN SHE WAS STRONGER...
I COULD HAVE HELPED, YOU KNOW. IT'S WHAT I DO.
SUCH A PITY.
HEY!
AH...YOU FEEL FOR HER. TOO LATE FOR YOU AS WELL.
PERHAPS HAD *YOU* CARED SOONER.
OH. RIGHT. LAY IT ALL ON *ME*...!
I PRUNE HER TO MAKE HER STRONGER. TO FORCE GROWTH. IT IS ALL I CAN DO TO SHOW I CARE. SHE HAS NO STRENGTH TO GIVE.
OR PERHAPS I PRUNE HER TO PUT HER OUT OF HER MISERY, EH? YOU THINK?

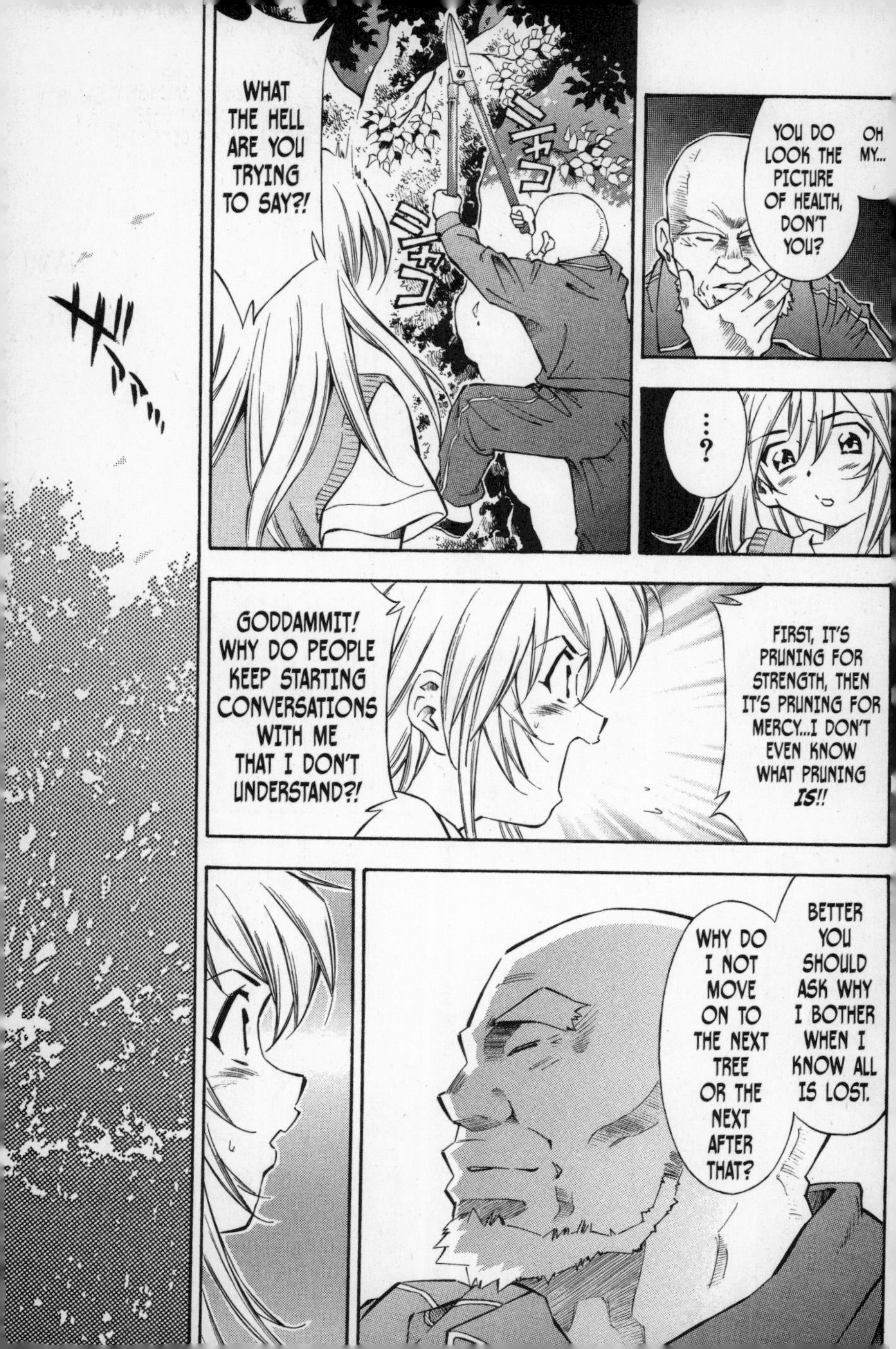
OH MY...
YOU DO LOOK THE PICTURE OF HEALTH, DON'T YOU?
...?
WHAT THE HELL ARE YOU TRYING TO SAY?!
FIRST, IT'S PRUNING FOR STRENGTH, THEN IT'S PRUNING FOR MERCY...I DON'T EVEN KNOW WHAT PRUNING *IS!!*
GODDAMMIT! WHY DO PEOPLE KEEP STARTING CONVERSATIONS WITH ME THAT I DON'T UNDERSTAND?!
BETTER YOU SHOULD ASK WHY I BOTHER WHEN I KNOW ALL IS LOST.
WHY DO I NOT MOVE ON TO THE NEXT TREE OR THE NEXT AFTER THAT?

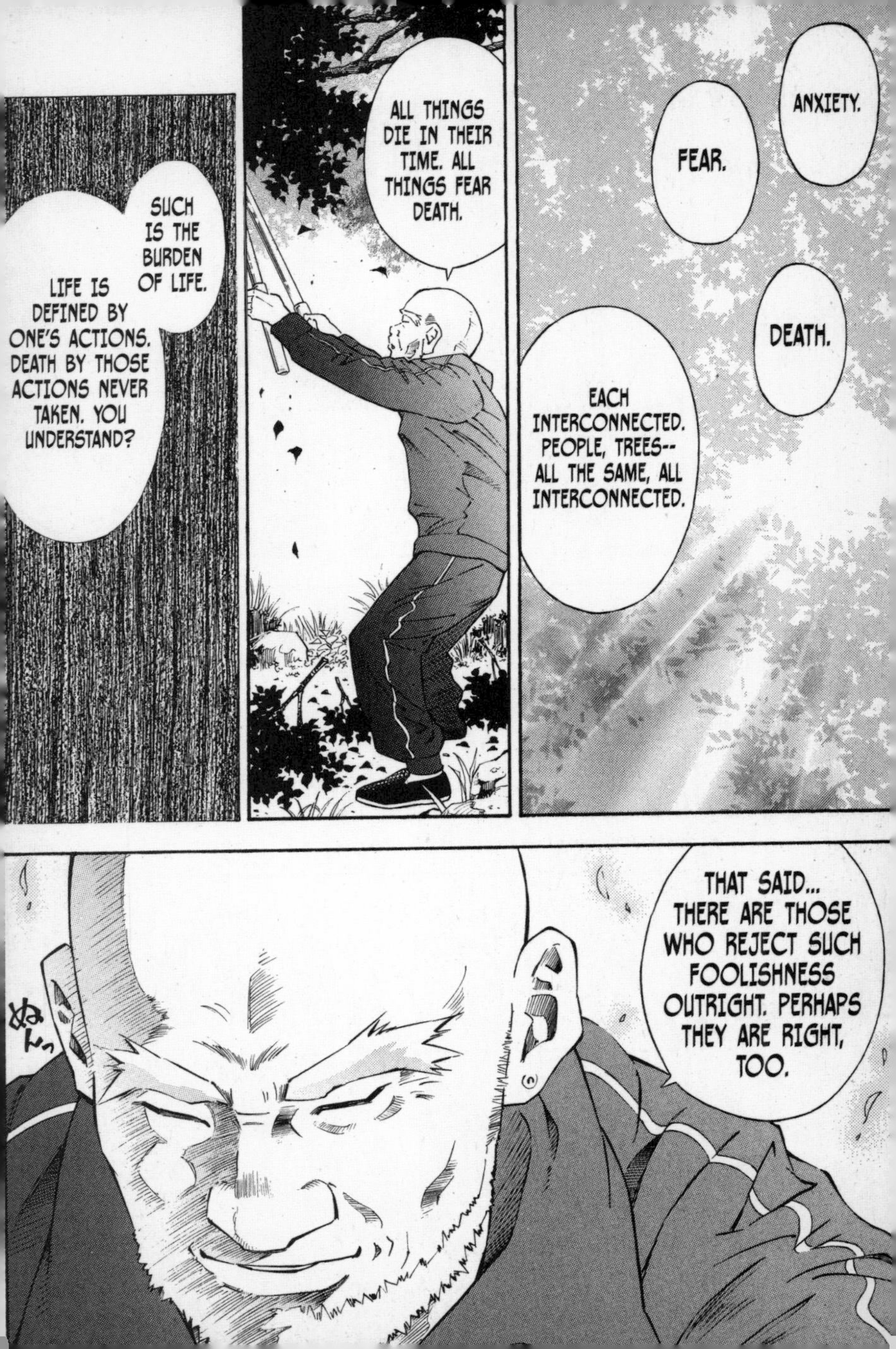
ANXIETY.
FEAR.
DEATH.
EACH INTERCONNECTED. PEOPLE, TREES-- ALL THE SAME, ALL INTERCONNECTED.
ALL THINGS DIE IN THEIR TIME. ALL THINGS FEAR DEATH.
SUCH IS THE BURDEN OF LIFE.
LIFE IS DEFINED BY ONE'S ACTIONS. DEATH BY THOSE ACTIONS NEVER TAKEN. YOU UNDERSTAND?
THAT SAID... THERE ARE THOSE WHO REJECT SUCH FOOLISHNESS OUTRIGHT. PERHAPS THEY ARE RIGHT, TOO.
ぬんっ

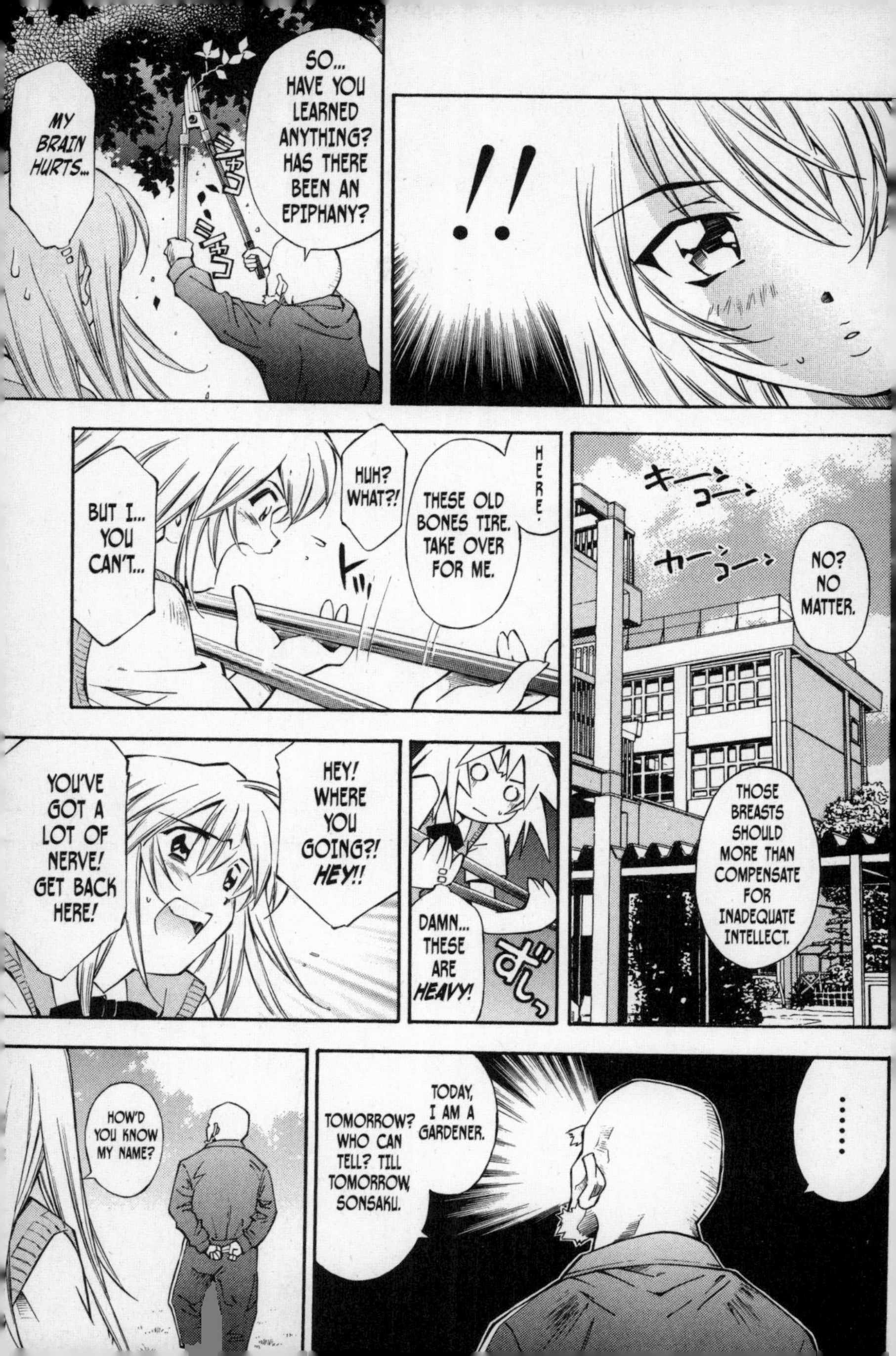
!!
SO... HAVE YOU LEARNED ANYTHING? HAS THERE BEEN AN EPIPHANY?
MY BRAIN HURTS...
NO? NO MATTER.
THOSE BREASTS SHOULD MORE THAN COMPENSATE FOR INADEQUATE INTELLECT.
HERE.
THESE OLD BONES TIRE. TAKE OVER FOR ME.
HUH? WHAT?!
BUT I... YOU CAN'T...
DAMN... THESE ARE HEAVY!
HEY! WHERE YOU GOING?! HEY!!
YOU'VE GOT A LOT OF NERVE! GET BACK HERE!
......
TODAY, I AM A GARDENER.
TOMORROW? WHO CAN TELL? TILL TOMORROW, SONSAKU.
HOW'D YOU KNOW MY NAME?

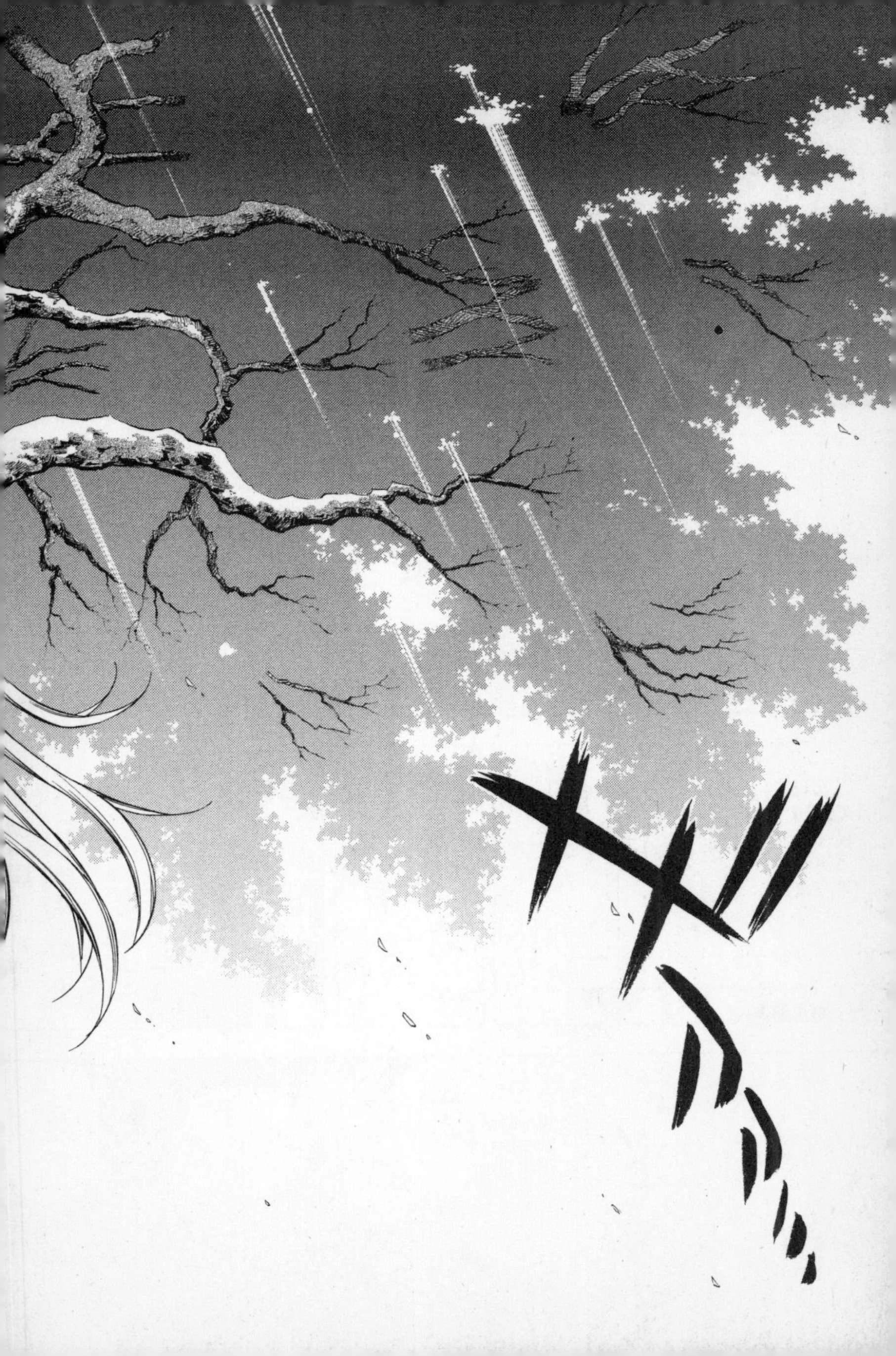
ザ…

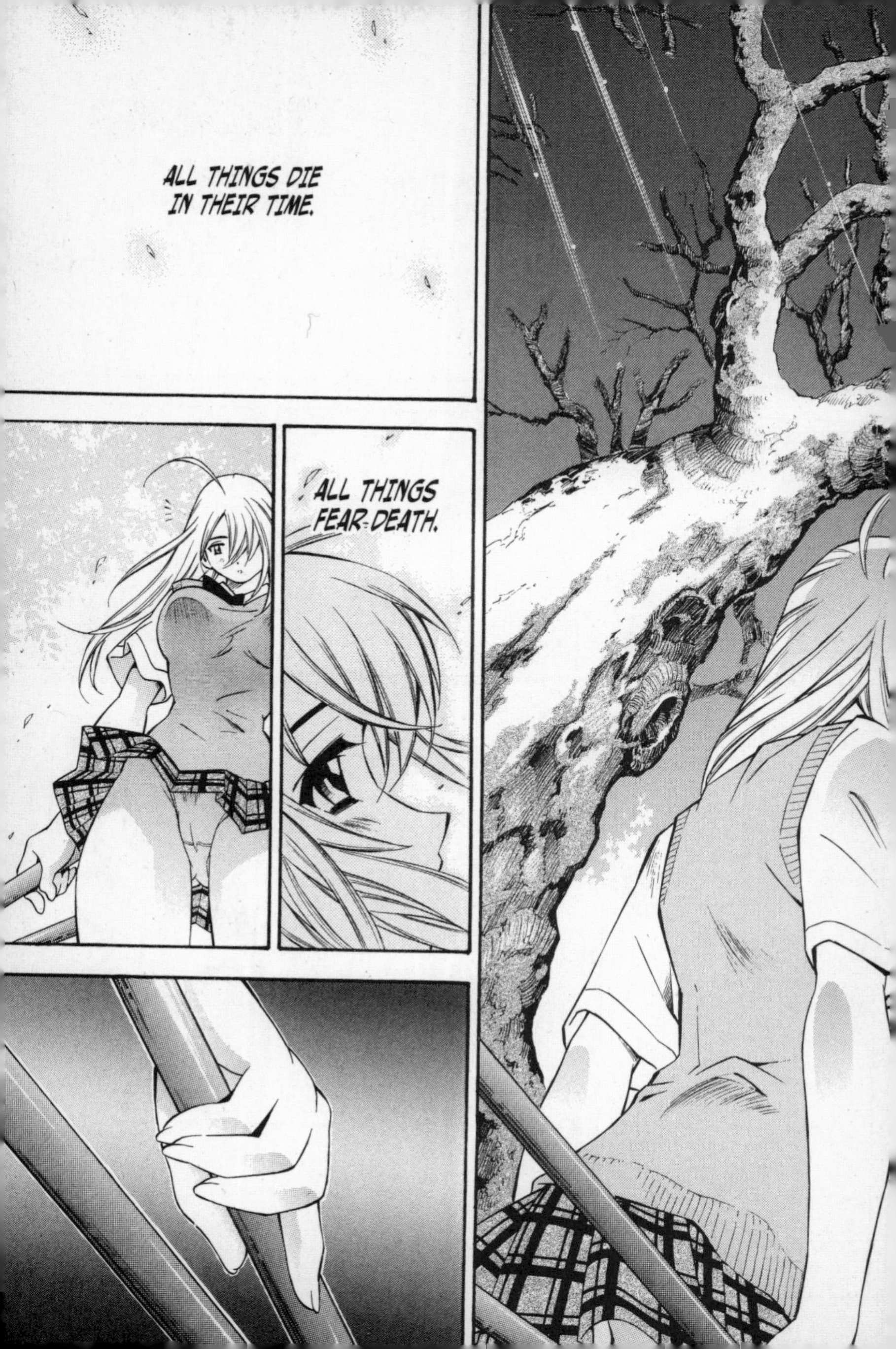
ALL THINGS DIE IN THEIR TIME.
ALL THINGS FEAR DEATH.

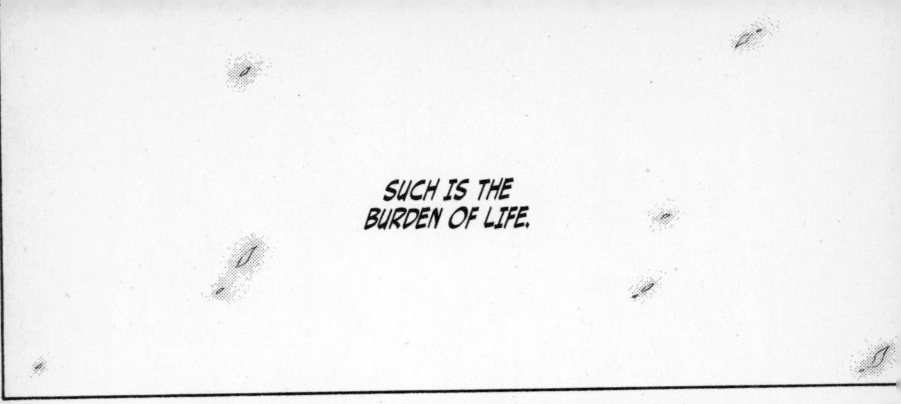
SUCH IS THE BURDEN OF LIFE.

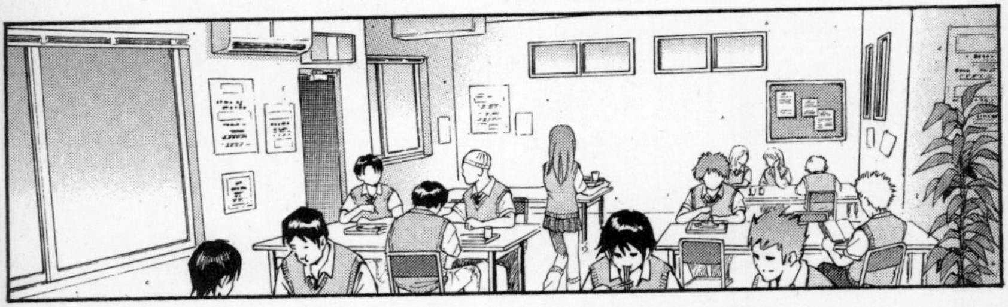

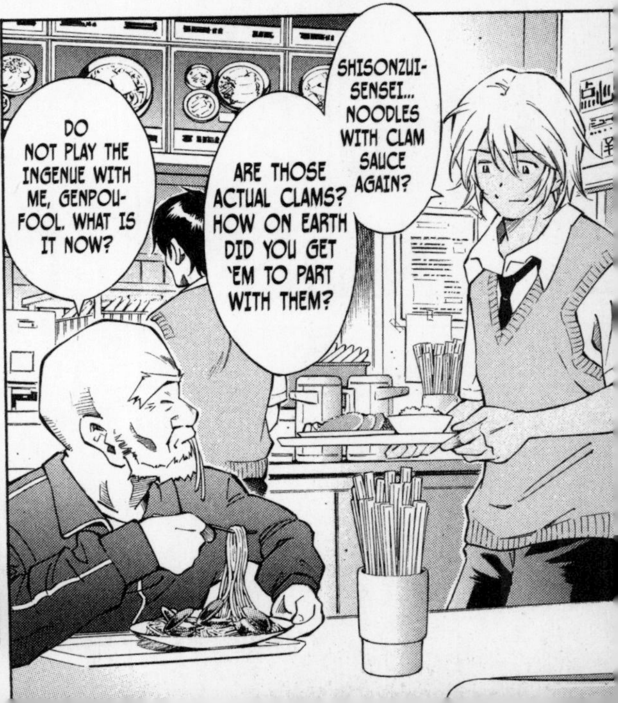
SHISONZUI-SENSEI... NOODLES WITH CLAM SAUCE AGAIN?
ARE THOSE ACTUAL CLAMS? HOW ON EARTH DID YOU GET 'EM TO PART WITH THEM?
DO NOT PLAY THE INGENUE WITH ME, GENPOU-FOOL. WHAT IS IT NOW?

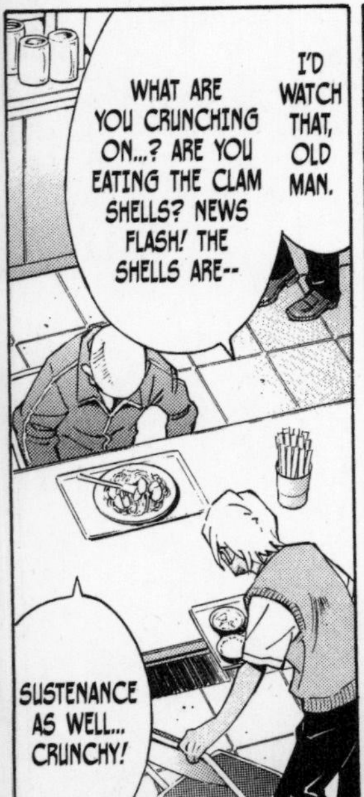
I'D WATCH THAT, OLD MAN.
WHAT ARE YOU CRUNCHING ON...? ARE YOU EATING THE CLAM SHELLS? NEWS FLASH! THE SHELLS ARE--
SUSTENANCE AS WELL... CRUNCHY!

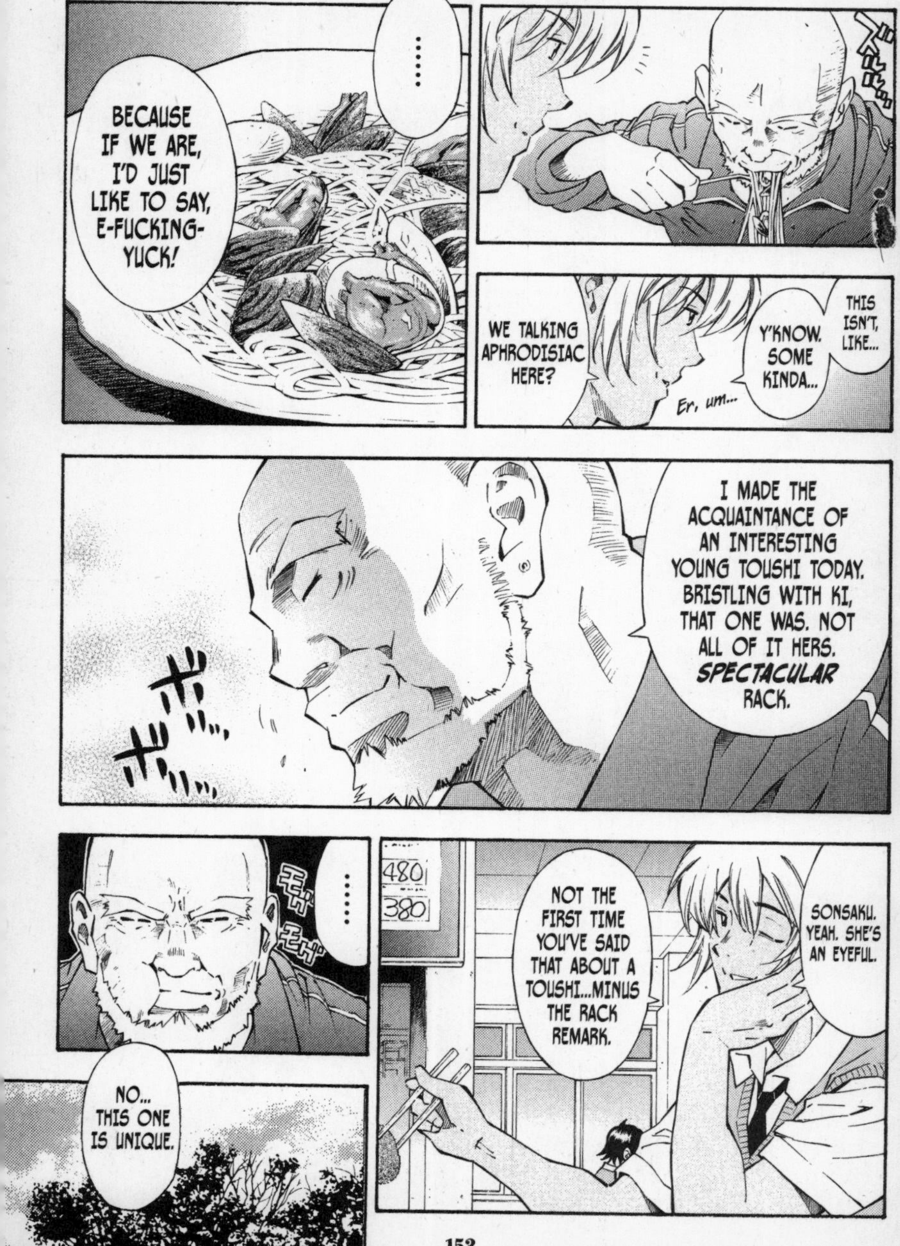

THIS ISN'T, LIKE...
Y'KNOW. SOME KINDA...
Er, um...
WE TALKING APHRODISIAC HERE?
......
BECAUSE IF WE ARE, I'D JUST LIKE TO SAY, E-FUCKING-YUCK!
I MADE THE ACQUAINTANCE OF AN INTERESTING YOUNG TOUSHI TODAY. BRISTLING WITH KI, THAT ONE WAS. NOT ALL OF IT HERS. SPECTACULAR RACK.
SONSAKU. YEAH. SHE'S AN EYEFUL.
NOT THE FIRST TIME YOU'VE SAID THAT ABOUT A TOUSHI...MINUS THE RACK REMARK.
480
380
......
NO... THIS ONE IS UNIQUE.

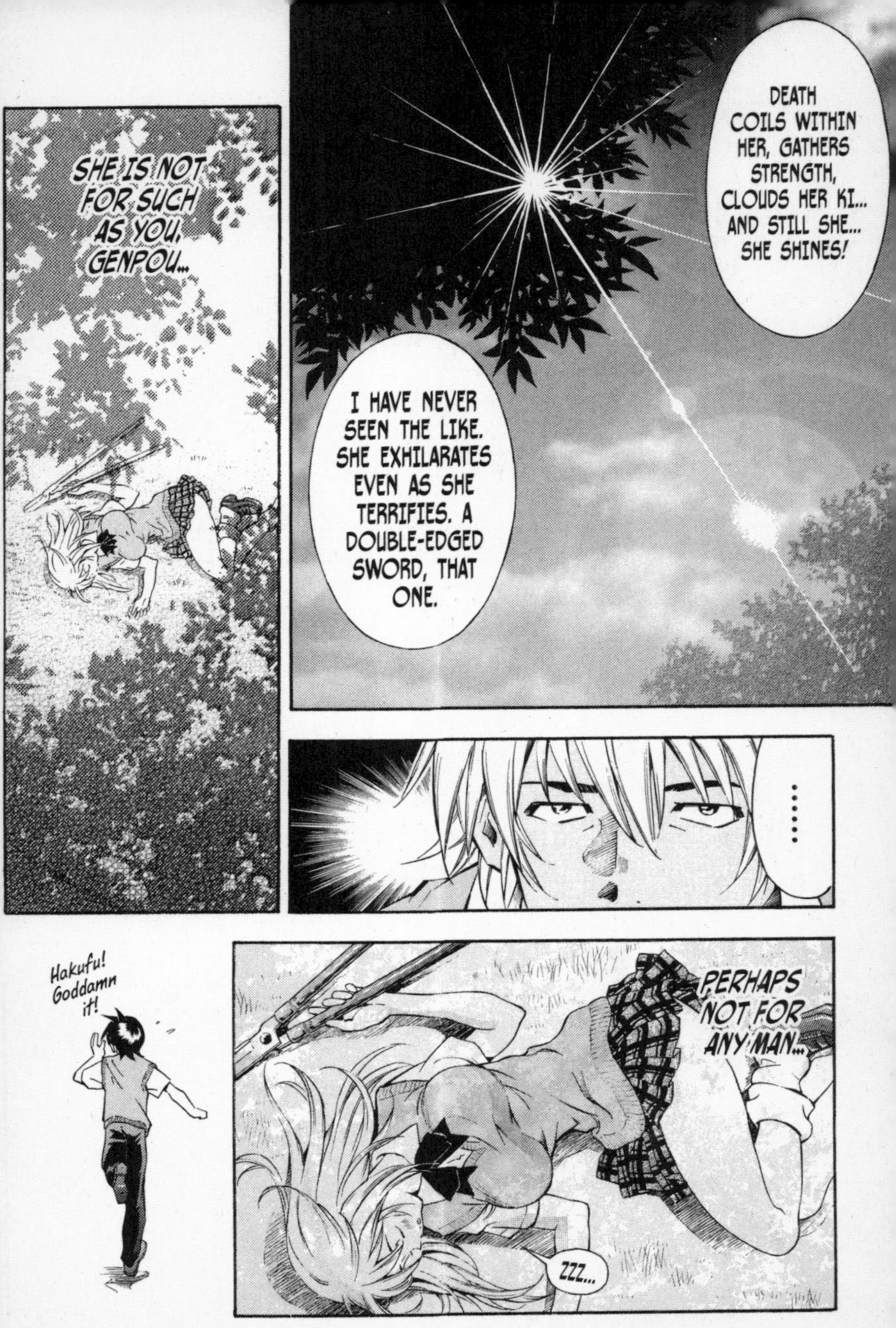
DEATH COILS WITHIN HER, GATHERS STRENGTH, CLOUDS HER KI... AND STILL SHE... SHE SHINES!
I HAVE NEVER SEEN THE LIKE. SHE EXHILARATES EVEN AS SHE TERRIFIES. A DOUBLE-EDGED SWORD, THAT ONE.
......
SHE IS NOT FOR SUCH AS YOU, GENPOU...
PERHAPS NOT FOR ANY MAN...
ZZZ...
Hakufu! Goddamn it!

一騎当千

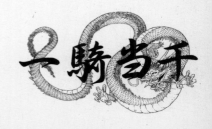

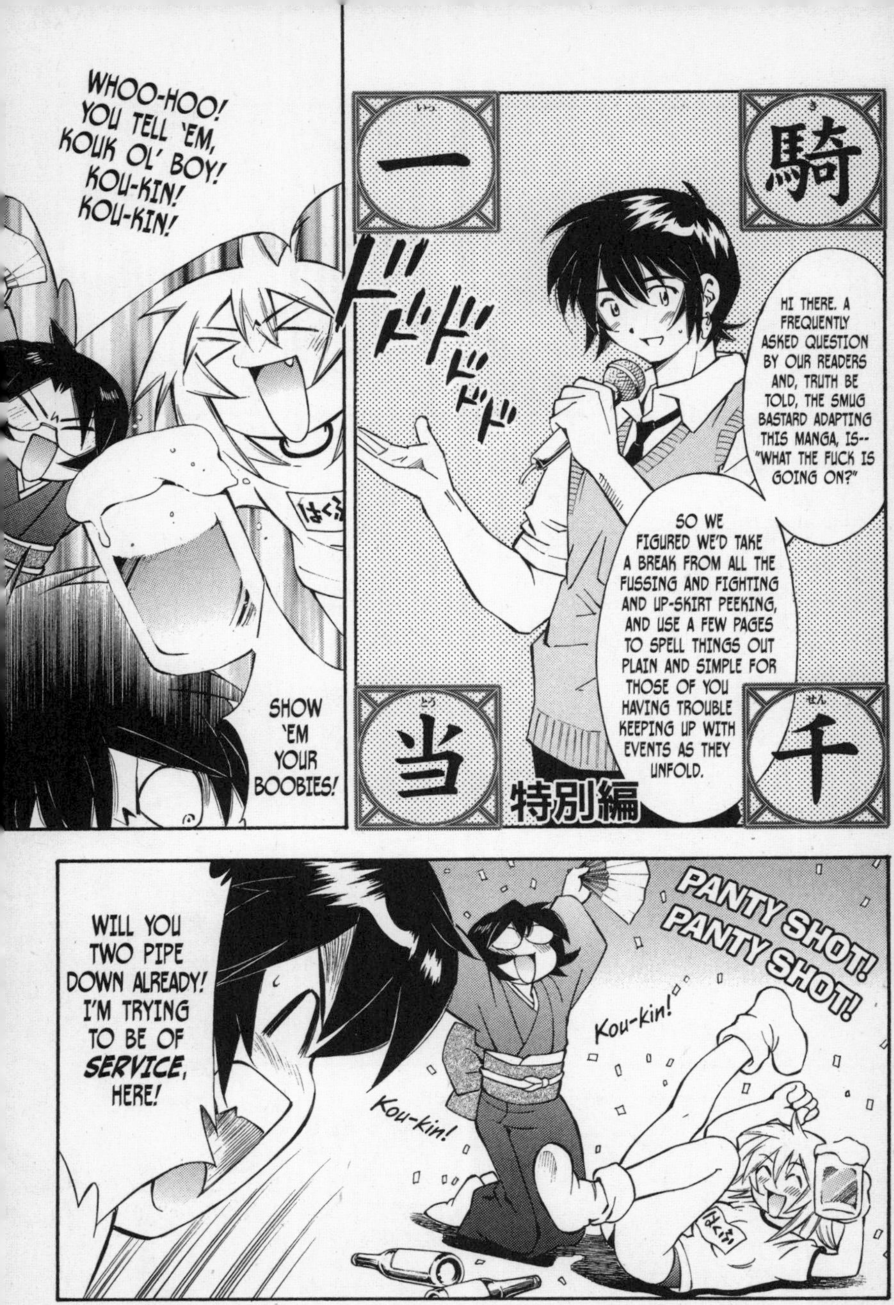
一騎当千
HI THERE. A FREQUENTLY ASKED QUESTION BY OUR READERS AND, TRUTH BE TOLD, THE SMUG BASTARD ADAPTING THIS MANGA, IS-- "WHAT THE FUCK IS GOING ON?"
SO WE FIGURED WE'D TAKE A BREAK FROM ALL THE FUSSING AND FIGHTING AND UP-SKIRT PEEKING, AND USE A FEW PAGES TO SPELL THINGS OUT PLAIN AND SIMPLE FOR THOSE OF YOU HAVING TROUBLE KEEPING UP WITH EVENTS AS THEY UNFOLD.
ドドドドドド
特別編
WHOO-HOO! YOU TELL 'EM, KOUK OL' BOY! KOU-KIN! KOU-KIN!
SHOW 'EM YOUR BOOBIES!
PANTY SHOT! PANTY SHOT!
Kou-kin!
Kou-kin!
WILL YOU TWO PIPE DOWN ALREADY! I'M TRYING TO BE OF SERVICE, HERE!

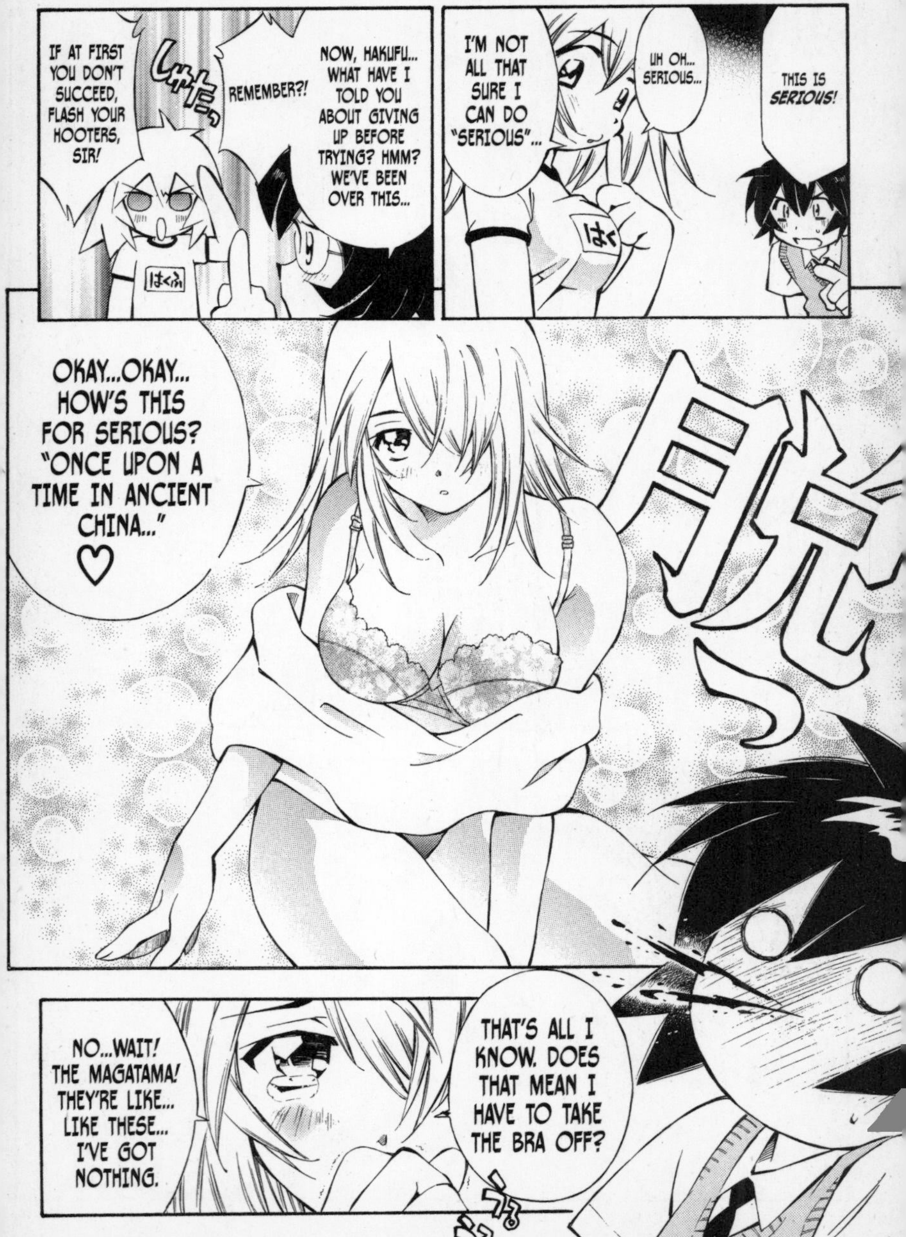
THIS IS *SERIOUS!*
UH OH... SERIOUS...
はく
I'M NOT ALL THAT SURE I CAN DO "SERIOUS"...
NOW, HAKUFU... WHAT HAVE I TOLD YOU ABOUT GIVING UP BEFORE TRYING? HMM? WE'VE BEEN OVER THIS...
REMEMBER?!
しゅたっ
IF AT FIRST YOU DON'T SUCCEED, FLASH YOUR HOOTERS, SIR!
はくふ
脱
OKAY...OKAY... HOW'S THIS FOR SERIOUS? "ONCE UPON A TIME IN ANCIENT CHINA..." ♥
THAT'S ALL I KNOW. DOES THAT MEAN I HAVE TO TAKE THE BRA OFF?
うる うる
NO...WAIT! THE MAGATAMA! THEY'RE LIKE... LIKE THESE... I'VE GOT NOTHING.

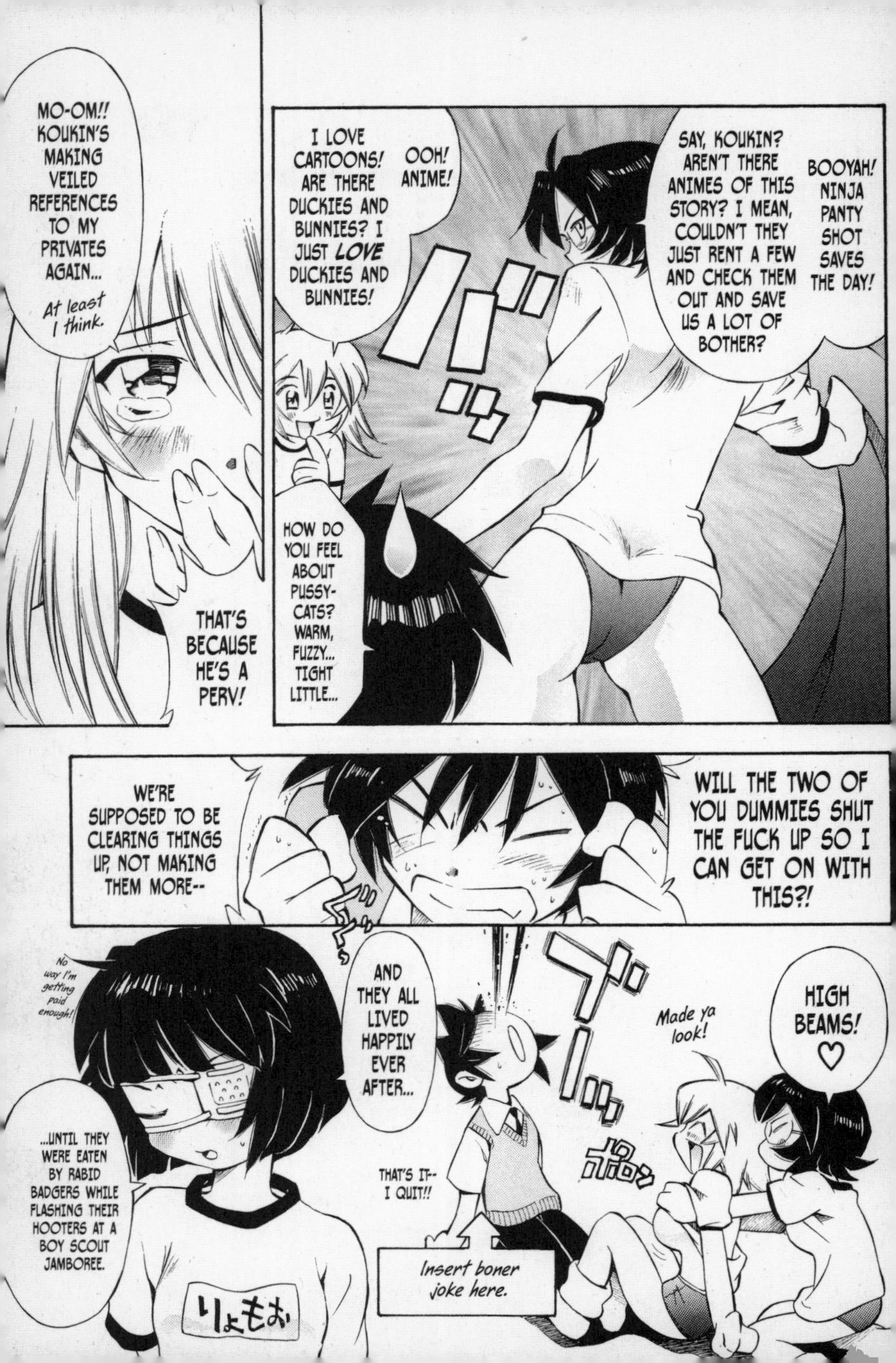
BOOYAH! NINJA PANTY SHOT SAVES THE DAY!
SAY, KOUKIN? AREN'T THERE ANIMES OF THIS STORY? I MEAN, COULDN'T THEY JUST RENT A FEW AND CHECK THEM OUT AND SAVE US A LOT OF BOTHER?
OOH! ANIME!
I LOVE CARTOONS! ARE THERE DUCKIES AND BUNNIES? I JUST *LOVE* DUCKIES AND BUNNIES!
HOW DO YOU FEEL ABOUT PUSSY-CATS? WARM, FUZZY... TIGHT LITTLE...
MO-OM!! KOUKIN'S MAKING VEILED REFERENCES TO MY PRIVATES AGAIN...
At least I think.
THAT'S BECAUSE HE'S A PERV!
WILL THE TWO OF YOU DUMMIES SHUT THE FUCK UP SO I CAN GET ON WITH THIS?!
WE'RE SUPPOSED TO BE CLEARING THINGS UP, NOT MAKING THEM MORE--
HIGH BEAMS! ♡
Made ya look!
AND THEY ALL LIVED HAPPILY EVER AFTER...
No way I'm getting paid enough!
THAT'S IT-- I QUIT!!
...UNTIL THEY WERE EATEN BY RABID BADGERS WHILE FLASHING THEIR HOOTERS AT A BOY SCOUT JAMBOREE.
Insert boner joke here.
りょもお

Ganbare!! Studio T's
Full Throttle

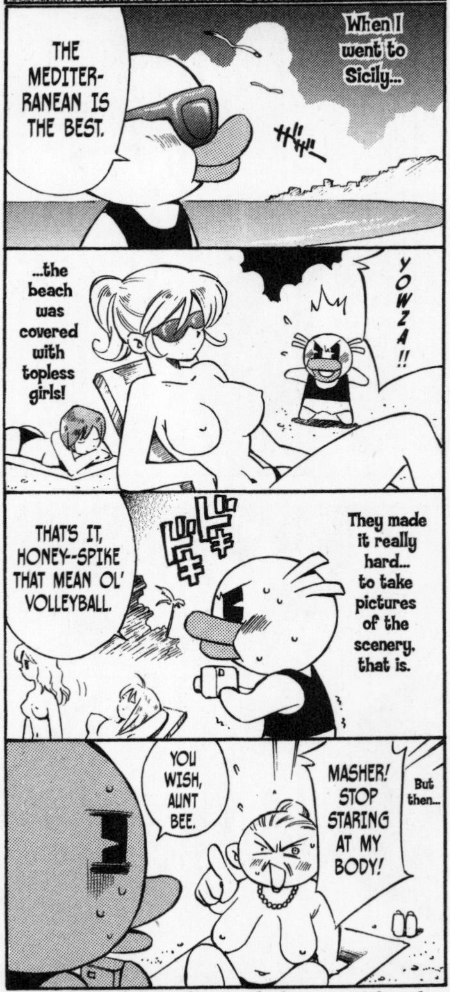

When I went to Sicily...
THE MEDITER-RANEAN IS THE BEST.
YOWZA!!
...the beach was covered with topless girls!
They made it really hard... to take pictures of the scenery, that is.
ドキドキ
THAT'S IT, HONEY--SPIKE THAT MEAN OL' VOLLEYBALL.
But then...
MASHER! STOP STARING AT MY BODY!
YOU WISH, AUNT BEE.

Ugh--like a couple of oranges in tube socks...

IN THE NEXT VOLUME OF

BATTLE VIXENS™

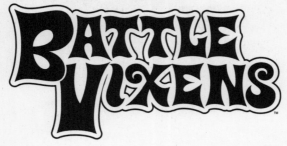

BUSHWHACKED!

Holy shit! Hakufu is targeted for take-down and her attacker puts the "ass" back in "assassin" when our big-chested babe is bushwhacked in her own bathroom, tackled in her own toilet, and laid-out in her lavatory!

Meanwhile, meet Ryubi...insane, dragon-possessed, bloodthirsty she-devil from Hell or klutzy bookworm...or both?

There's also a trip to the hot springs, picking mushrooms, picking fights, and fishing for dragons!

Don't miss *Battle Vixens* volume 7!

WARCRAFT
THE SUNWELL TRILOGY

RICHARD A. KNAAK • KIM JAE-HWAN

From the artist of the
best-selling *King of Hell* series!

It's an epic quest to save the entire High Elven Kingdom from the forces of the Undead Scourge! Set in the mystical world of Azeroth, *Warcraft: The Sunwell Trilogy* chronicles the adventures of Kalec, a blue dragon who has taken human form to escape deadly forces, and Anveena, a beautiful young maiden with a mysterious power.

T
TEEN
AGE 13+

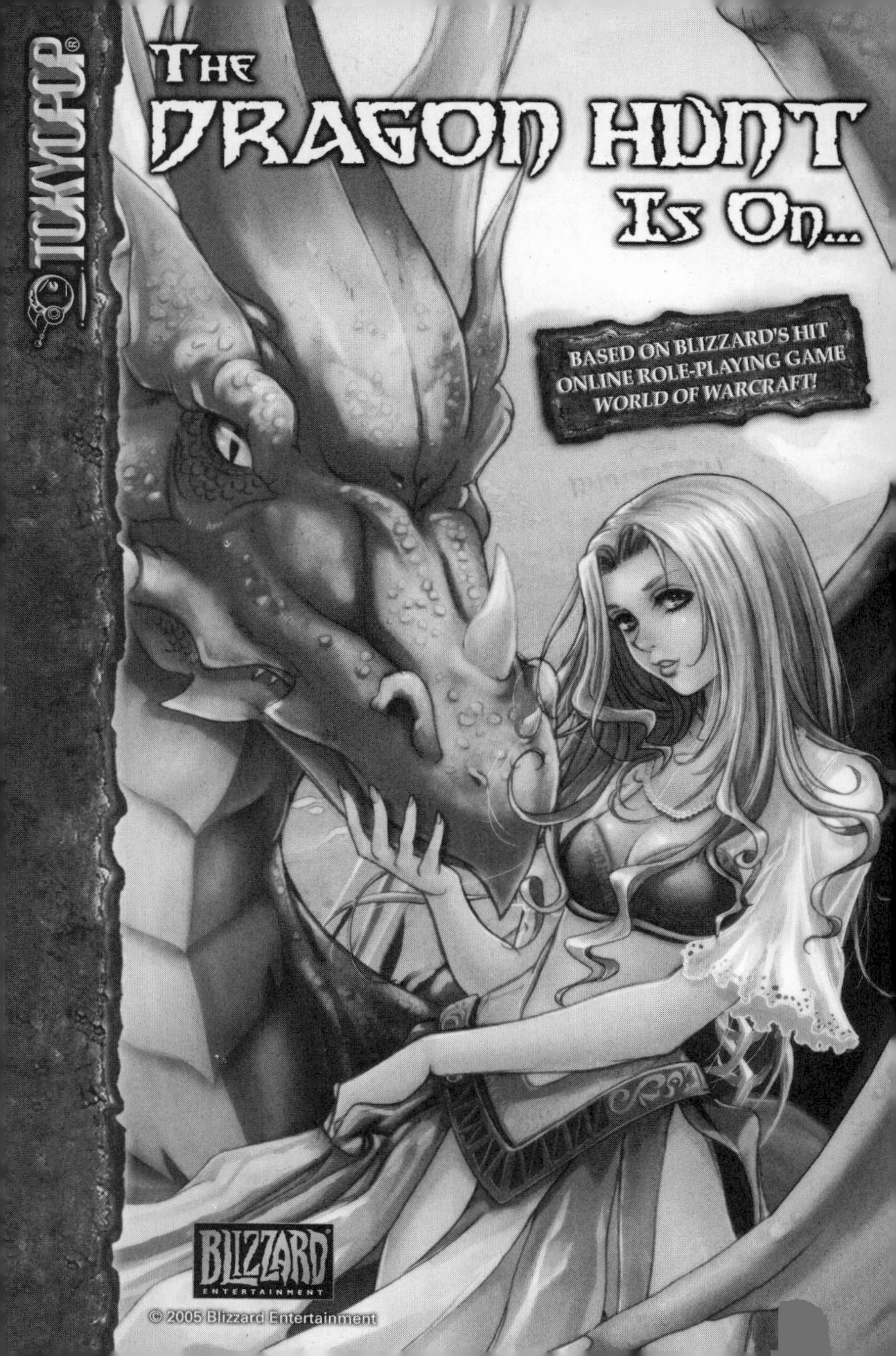
TOKYOPOP
The Dragon Hunt Is On...
BASED ON BLIZZARD'S HIT ONLINE ROLE-PLAYING GAME WORLD OF WARCRAFT!
BLIZZARD ENTERTAINMENT
© 2005 Blizzard Entertainment

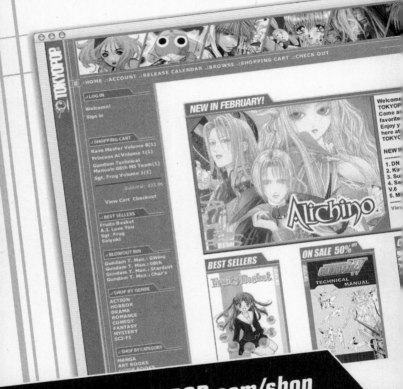

ALSO AVAILABLE FROM 🐸TOKYOPOP®

You want it? We got it!
A full range of TOKYOPOP
products are available **now** at:
www.TOKYOPOP.com/shop

ALSO AVAILABLE FROM 🐾TOKYOPOP®

MANGA

.HACK//LEGEND OF THE TWILIGHT
@LARGE
ABENOBASHI: MAGICAL SHOPPING ARCADE
A.I. LOVE YOU
AI YORI AOSHI
ALICHINO
ANGELIC LAYER
ARM OF KANNON
BABY BIRTH
BATTLE ROYALE
BATTLE VIXENS
BOYS BE...
BRAIN POWERED
BRIGADOON
B'TX
CANDIDATE FOR GODDESS, THE
CARDCAPTOR SAKURA
CARDCAPTOR SAKURA - MASTER OF THE CLOW
CHOBITS
CHRONICLES OF THE CURSED SWORD
CLAMP SCHOOL DETECTIVES
CLOVER
COMIC PARTY
CONFIDENTIAL CONFESSIONS
CORRECTOR YUI
COWBOY BEBOP
COWBOY BEBOP: SHOOTING STAR
CRAZY LOVE STORY
CRESCENT MOON
CROSS
CULDCEPT
CYBORG 009
D•N•ANGEL
DEARS
DEMON DIARY
DEMON ORORON, THE
DEUS VITAE
DIABOLO
DIGIMON
DIGIMON TAMERS
DIGIMON ZERO TWO
DOLL
DRAGON HUNTER
DRAGON KNIGHTS
DRAGON VOICE
DREAM SAGA
DUKLYON: CLAMP SCHOOL DEFENDERS
EERIE QUEERIE!
ERICA SAKURAZAWA: COLLECTED WORKS
ET CETERA
ETERNITY
EVIL'S RETURN
FAERIES' LANDING
FAKE
FLCL
FLOWER OF THE DEEP SLEEP
FORBIDDEN DANCE
FRUITS BASKET

G GUNDAM
GATEKEEPERS
GETBACKERS
GIRL GOT GAME
GRAVITATION
GTO
GUNDAM SEED ASTRAY
GUNDAM WING
GUNDAM WING: BATTLEFIELD OF PACIFISTS
GUNDAM WING: ENDLESS WALTZ
GUNDAM WING: THE LAST OUTPOST (G-UNIT)
HANDS OFF!
HAPPY MANIA
HARLEM BEAT
HYPER RUNE
I.N.V.U.
IMMORTAL RAIN
INITIAL D
INSTANT TEEN: JUST ADD NUTS
ISLAND
JING: KING OF BANDITS
JING: KING OF BANDITS - TWILIGHT TALES
JULINE
KARE KANO
KILL ME, KISS ME
KINDAICHI CASE FILES, THE
KING OF HELL
KODOCHA: SANA'S STAGE
LAMENT OF THE LAMB
LEGAL DRUG
LEGEND OF CHUN HYANG, THE
LES BIJOUX
LOVE HINA
LOVE OR MONEY
LUPIN III
LUPIN III: WORLD'S MOST WANTED
MAGIC KNIGHT RAYEARTH I
MAGIC KNIGHT RAYEARTH II
MAHOROMATIC: AUTOMATIC MAIDEN
MAN OF MANY FACES
MARMALADE BOY
MARS
MARS: HORSE WITH NO NAME
MINK
MIRACLE GIRLS
MIYUKI-CHAN IN WONDERLAND
MODEL
MOURYOU KIDEN: LEGEND OF THE NYMPH
NECK AND NECK
ONE
ONE I LOVE, THE
PARADISE KISS
PARASYTE
PASSION FRUIT
PEACH FUZZ
PEACH GIRL
PEACH GIRL: CHANGE OF HEART
PET SHOP OF HORRORS
PITA-TEN
PLANET LADDER

STOP!

This is the back of the book.
You wouldn't want to spoil a great ending!

This book is printed "manga-style," in the authentic Japanese right-to-left format. Since none of the artwork has been flipped or altered, readers get to experience the story just as the creator intended. You've been asking for it, so TOKYOPOP® delivered: authentic, hot-off-the-press, and far more fun!

DIRECTIONS

If this is your first time reading manga-style, here's a quick guide to help you understand how it works.

It's easy... just start in the top right panel and follow the numbers. Have fun, and look for more 100% authentic manga from TOKYOPOP®!